Electronic Texts in the Human

Electronic Texts in the Humanities
Principles and Practice

Susan Hockey

OXFORD
UNIVERSITY PRESS

OXFORD
UNIVERSITY PRESS

Great Clarendon Street, Oxford OX2 6 DP

Oxford University Press is a department of the University of Oxford.
It furthers the University's objective of excellence in research, scholarship,
and education by publishing worldwide in

Oxford New York.

Athens Auckland Bangkok Bogotá Buenos Aires Calcutta
Cape Town Chennai Dar es Salaam Delhi Florence Hong Kong Istanbul
Karachi Kuala Lumpur Madrid Melbourne Mexico City Mumbai
Nairobi Paris São Paulo Shanghai Singapore Taipei Tokyo Toronto Warsaw
and associated companies in Berlin Ibadan

Oxford is a registered trade mark of Oxford University Press
in the UK and certain other countries

Published in the United States
by Oxford University Press Inc., New York

©Susan Hockey 2000

The moral rights of the author have been asserted
Database right Oxford University Press (marker)

First published 2000

British Library Cataloguing in Publication Data
Data available

Library of Congress Cataloging in Publication Data
Data available

ISBN 0–19–871194–8
ISBN 0–19–871195–6 (pbk.)

1 3 5 7 9 10 8 6 4 2

Typeset by Kolam Information Services Pvt Ltd., India
Printed in Great Britain
on acid-free paper by
Biddles Ltd,
Guildford and King's Lynn

Preface

In recent years there has been a tremendous growth in the use of computing in the humanities, but there are still few places where humanities scholars can find out what computers can and cannot do for them beyond word processing and using the Internet. This book fills that need. It explains how computers can help researchers and teachers in the humanities, particularly those who work with text-based material. The book seeks not only to assess what computers can do, but also to discuss some of the issues: what makes a good electronic text, how scholarship can be improved by judicious use of computers (or endangered by projects which have not been well thought out), what can be accomplished with fairly simple tools, and what needs to be done to make these tools better.

The book is not therefore about using the Internet. It is about tools and techniques which ought to be available via the Internet, but at present are not. The World Wide Web is good for looking at material but it does not provide many tools for analysing and manipulating that material. It is weak for searching and its facilities for identifying the origin of the material are poor. Over the last forty or so years, humanities computing experts have developed a range of tools and techniques for working with electronic texts in the humanities. These tools can be used to assist with analysing literature and language, with compiling dictionaries, publishing scholarly editions, and studying authorship attribution. This book assesses the various approaches to using these tools and demonstrates their value in different application areas. The expectation is that these tools will be available in future versions of the Internet and this book helps to explain why they are needed.

More than anything, the book seeks to explain the intellectual rationale for electronic text technology in the humanities. It focuses on methodological issues and shows how an emphasis on the critical assessment of method can help scholars define and refine their research objectives. The computer can provide an overall picture of material which it would not be possible to obtain in any other way, but it also forces the scholar to address questions of detail and to specify the requirements of a project in small steps. It provides a means for repeated exploration into a collection of texts and a way of assembling concrete evidence to support or refute a hypothesis or intuitive feeling.

The book concentrates on tools and techniques for working with electronic representations of text-based primary source material in the humanities. Its primary audience is therefore humanities scholars and students working in literature and linguistics, with some applications in history. The book is also likely to be used by the growing number of librarians and information scientists who are working with electronic texts. It may also be of interest to computer scientists and computer support staff who are planning to work on humanities projects. It will certainly address the needs of those who are frustrated with the current implementation of the Web for working with humanities texts. Methodologies from corpus and computational linguistics are introduced where they are also appropriate for the humanities. Electronic publication is considered mostly in relation to electronic scholarly editions. The theoretical implications of hypertext and cyberspace have been well treated by many recent publications and are not treated here.

An overview of electronic texts in the humanities is provided in Chapter 1. Chapter 2 discusses methods for creating and acquiring electronic texts and investigates metadata requirements and ways of sampling text. Chapter 3 looks at encoding schemes which are necessary to put intelligence in the text. Some basic text analysis principles are introduced in Chapter 4. Chapter 5 looks at how text analysis tools can be used for literary analysis, and Chapter 6 addresses linguistic analysis, including word class tagging. Various procedures for authorship attribution are examined in Chapter 7. Chapter 8 discusses textual criticism and electronic scholarly editions. Chapter 9 looks at electronic dictionaries and examines how lexical databases can help to refine and improve retrieval and analysis programs. The final chapter speculates on what electronic scholarship of the twenty-first century might look like, and what is needed to make these new modes of scholarship happen.

Many people have directly and indirectly contributed to this book. I would like to thank all the scholars whose projects have provided substance for the arguments I make. Working on the Text Encoding Initiative (TEI) was one of the most intellectually stimulating experiences of my life. I would especially like to thank Michael Sperberg-McQueen, Lou Burnard, David Barnard, Nancy Ide, Antonio Zampolli, and the late Don Walker for their companionship on the TEI Steering Committee, and the many TEI committee members who contributed so much to the intellectual development of the TEI. Thanks are also due to Willard McCarty with whom I co-directed the annual two-week summer seminar of the Center for Electronic Texts in the Humanities (CETH) at Princeton from 1992 to 1996, and also to the many alumni of the seminar who helped to articulate what humanities scholars want to do with computers. Thanks are also due to Perry Willett of the Victorian Women Writers' Project at Indiana University who provided the SGML example in Chapter 3. This book was planned while I was Director of CETH, but I would like to thank the University of Alberta for giving me the opportunity to research and write it in 1997–9. My greatest debt is to my husband Martin, who has been a constant source of support in spite of my many travels away from home, and who read and commented on all the typescript.

S. H.

Contents

List of Figures　　　　　　　　　　　　　　　　　　　　　x

List of Abbreviations　　　　　　　　　　　　　　　　　　xi

　1.　Why Electronic Texts?　　　　　　　　　　　　　　1

　2.　Creating and Acquiring Electronic Texts　　　　11

　3.　Text Encoding　　　　　　　　　　　　　　　　24

　4.　Concordance and Text Retrieval Programs　　　49

　5.　Literary Analysis　　　　　　　　　　　　　　　66

　6.　Linguistic Analysis　　　　　　　　　　　　　　85

　7.　Stylometry and Attribution Studies　　　　　104

　8.　Textual Criticism and Electronic Editions　　124

　9.　Dictionaries and Lexical Databases　　　　　146

　10.　Where Next?　　　　　　　　　　　　　　　165

References　　　　　　　　　　　　　　　　　　　172

Index　　　　　　　　　　　　　　　　　　　　　199

List of Figures

4.1. Part of a word frequency list of *Emma*   50

4.2. Part of a word index of *The Merchant of Venice*   51

4.3. Part of a concordance of *Emma*   52

4.4. Part of a reverse concordance of
The Merchant of Venice   58

4.5. Right-sorted concordance of 'very' from *Emma*   59

4.6. Left-sorted concordance of 'very' from *Emma*   60

4.7. Concordance of 'love' in *The Merchant of Venice*
sorted by character   61

4.8. Part of a concordance of the phrase 'as…as'
in *The Merchant of Venice*   63

4.9. Collocates 'pound' and 'flesh' in *The Merchant
of Venice*   64

List of Abbreviations

ACH	Association for Computers and the Humanities
ACL	Association for Computational Linguistics
ALLC	Association for Literary and Linguistic Computing
ARTFL	American Research on the Treasury of the French Language
ASCII	American Standard Code for Information Interchange
BNC	British National Corpus
CELLAR	Computing Environment for Linguistic, Literary, and Anthropological Research
CETH	Center for Electronic Texts in the Humanities
CHAT	Codes for the Human Analysis of Transcripts
CHILDES	Child Language Data Exchange System
CLAWS	Constituent Likelihood Automatic Word-tagging System
COCOA	Word Count and Concordance Generator for Atlas
DOS	disk operating system
DTD	document type definition
EAGLES	Expert Advisory Group on Language Engineering Standards
ELRA	European Language Resources Association
HTML	Hypertext Markup Language
ICAME	International Computer Archive of Modern English
ICE	International Corpus of English
KWIC	keyword in context
LDOCE	*Longman Dictionary of Contemporary English*
LOB	Lancaster–Oslo/Bergen Corpus
MEC	Middle English Compendium
MECS	Multi-Element Encoding Scheme
MEP	Model Editions Partnership
OCP	Oxford Concordance Program
OCR	optical character recognition
OED	*Oxford English Dictionary*
OHCO	ordered hierarchy of content objects
OTA	Oxford Text Archive
PAUP	Phylogenetic Analysis Using Parsimony
PPCME	Penn–Helsinki Parsed Corpus of Middle English
SGML	Standard Generalized Markup Language
SNOBOL	String Oriented Symbolic Language
SPITBOL	Speedy Implementation of SNOBOL

List of Abbreviations

SUSANNE Surface and Underlying Structural Analysis of Natural English
TACT Textual Analysis Computing Tools
TEI Text Encoding Initiative
TuStep Tübingen System of Text processing Programs
TLG Thesaurus Linguae Graecae
XML Extensible Markup Language
XSL XML stylesheet language

1 | Why Electronic Texts?

With the arrival of word processors, electronic mail, on-line library catalogues, and the Internet, computers have become part and parcel of the daily life of most humanities scholars. It is difficult to imagine writing now without the aid of a word processor. Electronic mail has speeded up communication between scholars and helped to foster collaboration on a scale that was never possible before. Undoubtedly, the Internet has made the biggest impact in the last few years simply because it provides instant access to information anywhere in the world and, moreover, allows many different people to access the same piece of information at the same time. The purpose of this book is not, however, to discuss these basic tools. Indeed, it assumes that the reader is already familiar with them and wishes to explore further what aspects of humanities scholarship can be assisted by the use of computers and electronic texts.

The term 'electronic text' is used specifically to mean a transcription of a text, rather than an electronic or digital image of it. The difference between these two formats is the difference between what happens when a text is word processed and when it is sent by fax. A word processor makes an electronic representation of some textual material, character by character, word by word. This means that the text can be manipulated in various ways, for example by inserting or deleting material, or by searching for words and phrases, although more strictly, the search is for the sequences of letters and characters which constitute words and phrases in the view of the user. A fax machine transmits an electronic picture of a page of text. That text can be read by the recipient, but it cannot be altered or searched electronically. The focus of this book is electronic texts, and the many ways in which they can be manipulated, but digital images will be introduced where they are appropriate for the nature of the project.

The term 'electronic text in the humanities' is used to mean an electronic representation of any textual material which is an object of study for literary, linguistic, historical, or related purposes. Most often these texts are typical primary sources such as poetry, novels, plays, and historical documents, rather than electronic journals, monographs, reference works, and other secondary sources, although these text types can also sometimes be objects of study. I will not attempt to define the term 'text', but will use it to mean any written or spoken material, whether it is a complete work or manifestation of that work, or a sample or other subdivision of that work. The range of material which falls into this definition of primary source texts in the humanities is very broad. It can be anything from clay tablets and inscriptions to different types of present-day literature and non-fiction. It can be in any natural language, or indeed in several languages. The sources used can be printed editions of manuscripts, papyri, and the like, or they can be the original documents in whatever form they were created, from newspapers to audio tapes to handwritten material.

Basic text structures in the humanities include prose, verse, and drama as well as transcriptions of spoken texts (utterances), and dictionary entries. Many texts also have their own canonical referencing systems which scholars regularly use. Humanities texts can include marginalia, variant readings, editorial apparatus, interlineations, and other annotation, as well as non-standard characters and alphabets. Reliable and accurate sources are essential, and where several different editions of a text are available, scholars expect to know the background to the edition which they have chosen to use, to have a sense of its strengths and shortcomings, and to be able to justify their choice.

Most research carried out on humanities texts consists of interpretation of some kind. The research can range from a detailed examination of one or two short texts to a broad study over a wide range of sources. It may be carried out for literary, linguistic, or historical purposes. Research results are normally published as journal articles or monographs, but can now also be disseminated electronically in various formats, perhaps even attached to an electronic representation of the source. In the normal way of humanities research, scholars may disagree with earlier published discussions of a text or texts and publish their own views challenging or supplementing earlier interpretations of the same material.

These general definitions of humanities texts and scholarly research on those texts may seem simplistic. But if any activity is to be carried out on a computer, the processes involved in that activity and the nature of the material on which those processes are carried out must first be thoroughly understood, and then specified in fine detail. If they are not, they cannot be modelled effectively on a computer. Computing imposes a specificity which may at first seem alien to the more 'nuanced' approaches in humanities scholarship, but this specificity is at the core of the intellectual challenges posed by computing in the humanities. It encourages a real clarity of research objectives. It is impossible to avoid the question 'How do I go about doing it?' when embarking on a computer project. To answer the question 'How?' it is necessary first to address 'What am I doing?' and 'Why am I doing it?' and thus to articulate in detail the intellectual rationale for the project.

In later chapters we will look in detail at some important processes and procedures and how they can be harnessed for humanities scholarship, but if we go back to our general definitions now, two things emerge. First, the same text is used by different scholars for different purposes. In an ideal world, the same electronic representation of that text should be able to serve many different purposes, just as the same printed book is used by different scholars for different reasons. Secondly, humanities texts are complex. In an ideal world, these complex features should be adequately represented in the electronic version, so that scholarly debate on the interpretation of these features can continue, and be advanced by the use of the electronic text. It is not therefore surprising that much research has been devoted to establishing what makes a high quality and multipurpose scholarly electronic text.

Because of the Internet, much of the present interest in electronic texts is focused on access. Computer networks can transfer information, or rather copies of information, very rapidly from one place to another. This in itself facilitates many kinds of research by speeding up some processes which, in the case of visits to libraries in other cities or countries, might otherwise take days or weeks, but the access is often to 'electronic print'. That is, it replicates the original form of the material without any of the added value which electronic technology can provide. Because it is such a recent development, many scholars and librarians regard electronic access of this kind as an end in itself. But it is only the beginning. The real power of electronic texts is that they can be searched and otherwise manipulated by computer programs in many different ways. This power will be exploited more and more. Some of the tools and techniques which are discussed in this book in relation to individual scholars' own research can be implemented in a networked environment facilitating new and wide-ranging kinds of research.

The research areas investigated in this book make use of computer programs which are designed to work specifically with humanities electronic texts. These programs are much more powerful than the simple searches provided by word processing programs or the 'Find in Page' function in Web browsers. Computers are good at mechanical processes, such as searching, counting, and sorting into alphabetical or numerical order. They perform these tasks not only much faster than a human being, but also very much more accurately. Later chapters of this book examine and assess how these functions can be used for different research areas in the humanities and how they can supplement other research methods. Writing one's own programs can be rewarding but it can also be time-consuming. Fortunately, programs already exist for many of the tasks which humanities scholars want to carry out on electronic texts, and these programs can be run many times over on the same or different text. This book will show the range of functions which existing programs can perform and thus help in deciding whether it is worth investing the time to learn to write programs and at what stage in a project this might be appropriate. It will also show what the World Wide Web ought to be able to do, but cannot do in its current implementation.

Before any kind of analysis can be carried out, an accurate and unambiguous representation of the text must be created in electronic form. This process, known as encoding, is discussed in detail in Chapter 3, but some general remarks are appropriate here. Since computers only see text as sequences of letters and characters, information which is implicit for the human reader must be made explicit for computer analysis. Otherwise only a crude analysis can be performed on the text. This kind of crude analysis is seen in Web documents where, for example, *I* in *Act I* as the act number within a play is not distinguished from the words *act* and *I* (the personal pronoun). It may be able to make use of the capital *A* in *Act*, but that would not help if *Act* was capitalized for some other reason in the text. An investigation of the use of personal pronouns by characters in the play to indicate, for example, how much they talk about themselves would be cumbersome and inaccurate. In a text containing both French and English, failure to encode what words are in each language will lead to the French word *pain* ('bread') being treated as if it was the same word as English *pain*.

Many early electronic texts were encoded following the typography of a printed edition, but typographic encoding is ambiguous for any kind of computer processing other than printing. Human beings use their cognitive processes to distinguish between, for example, the different functions of italics. A computer program cannot do this and so would not be able to perform an accurate search for foreign words or for book titles. It has gradually become clear that encoding is a very important aspect of working with electronic texts. Computer programs only perform mechanical processes and are unable to apply any intelligence unless that intelligence is defined unambiguously and in small steps within the program. It is now recognized that it is much easier and more sensible to put the intelligence into the text in the form of encoding than it is to build sophisticated intelligence into computer programs. Encoding an electronic text is an act of interpretation, presenting intellectual challenges which themselves bring the researcher closer to the text and thus help to solve other problems as well. The rationale for any particular encoding therefore needs to be recorded in some way.

The first electronic text project in the humanities began in 1949 when Father Roberto Busa started work on his *Index Thomisticus*, a concordance to the works of St Thomas Aquinas and related authors (Busa [1965]). Father Busa understood well the potential of a machine to help alphabetize and organize the entries for the index, but also recognized the limitations of a purely mechanical approach. The *Index Thomisticus* presents every instance of some 11 million words in alphabetical order. It is not difficult to write a computer program that will put 'words' into alphabetical order, if that program has no linguistic knowledge about what constitutes a word, but simply sees it as a sequence of letters separated by spaces and punctuation marks. However, this definition of a word is not very useful. For an inflected language like Latin, each word form would appear as a separate entry in the concordance, in some cases (for example, *tuli*, part of *fero*) a long way apart from the headword under which it would be found in a dictionary. The same problem occurs in English, where, for example, *go, going, goes, gone*, and *went* are all part of the same headword.

Father Busa felt that a lemmatized concordance, that is a concordance organized by dictionary headword, would be much more useful. He carried out this lengthy lemmatization partly by hand and partly with the aid of an electronic dictionary of words in the texts. Lemmatization, like most other kinds of linguistic analysis, is still difficult to carry out without manual intervention, but it is the first step towards more sophisticated analyses of texts. Other linguistic analysis tools are needed to move beyond the simple case of looking at text as sequences of letters towards working with concepts and other semantic interpretations. Although there have been significant advances in technology since Father Busa began to create his electronic text on punched cards using only capital letters, he himself has lamented the lack of intellectual progress in the development of more sophisticated software for manipulating and analysing electronic texts (Busa 1992). But, turned 80 and writing in 1997, he reflects on the potential of the World Wide Web for multimedia delivery of scholarly material accompanied by sophisticated analysis and annotation tools (Busa 1998). The first volume of the *Index Thomisticus* appeared in 1973, some twenty-four years after he began the project. If he were starting this project today, publication would almost certainly be in electronic form, but he would still have to use a mixture of machine and human processing for preparing the material, and it would still take a long time.

However, much can be achieved with judicious use of simple tools. The computer is best viewed as an aid to scholarship, a machine which can help with many repetitive tasks and which can assist with detailed investigations or help to provide an overall picture which would be impossible to obtain by other means. Many humanities electronic text projects which are more than simply putting material on the Web have been based, in one way or another, on word searching, frequency lists, and concordances. These have been used as a basis for further interpretation of textual material, for comparative work, for lexicography, for the preparation of scholarly editions, and for the analysis of different linguistic features.

Until the late 1980s most electronic text projects in the humanities were the work of individual humanities scholars, who were motivated by the need to perform repetitive functions on the same texts. Many of the electronic texts currently available and in use today are the legacy of these individual research projects. Many of these projects began before an adequate methodology for creating and using electronic texts had been established. Researchers therefore prepared their text in a form which suited their own needs, but was not necessarily appropriate for any other application. Anyone starting a project now can benefit from the collective wisdom (and mistakes) of these early projects and create a much better electronic text. But this legacy material remains. It is the reason why so many different formats of electronic text exist today and why many electronic texts that are available do not appear to be part of any coherent publication or collection development policy. One particular text is available because a scholar worked on this text some time ago. That scholar may or may not have been interested in other works by the same author or in the same genre.

Most of the electronic texts in existence today are plain ASCII files, or what are sometimes called DOS text files. Unlike word processor files which are stored in a format peculiar to the specific word processing program, ASCII files can easily be transferred from one computer to another or across the Internet. They can be manipulated by many different programs but are not usable without software. The scholar must acquire software from elsewhere or write it. There is now a trend to distribute electronic texts together with software for manipulating the text, what we will call 'packaged electronic texts'. The package may be delivered on CD-ROM or over the Internet. This approach makes it easier to use the text, but it is important to see exactly what functions that software can perform. Usually it is some kind of retrieval software. The scholar types in a search word and the program retrieves all the instances where the word occurs. The usefulness of this depends to a large extent on how words are defined, how the search is carried out, what is displayed as a result of the search, and whether the results of the search can be manipulated further. The discussion in this book should help readers to assess whether a piece of software is appropriate for a research project and what else could be done with better software.

A computer program can search a text by moving through it sequentially, letter by letter and word by word. For a large text, this can be time-consuming and inefficient, although in the end it can also make the search more flexible, as we will see in Chapter 4. The more usual approach is to process the text first by an ancillary program which indexes the text and stores it in a different format, one that can only be read by the particular text retrieval program. This allows rapid responses to queries, but the kinds of queries which can be answered depend entirely on how the text has been indexed. This is how library catalogues and document retrieval systems normally operate, but they usually respond first with a number indicating how many 'hits' have been found. This is often given, not as the number of occurrences of the hit word, but as the number of documents containing the hit word.

There are two problems with the document retrieval approach for humanities texts. First, it presupposes that the text consists of a collection of 'documents'. Typical academic applications for these programs are journal articles, or case or statute law where what constitutes a document is fairly clear. In the case of most literary texts, it is much less clear. Decisions must be made on defining the basic 'document' unit before the text is indexed. Secondly, humanities scholars are more likely to be interested in the actual occurrences of words and how those words are used. The fact that all the occurrences of the same word are in one document could be of interest, but a document retrieval program will normally only give one 'hit' as the first response, when the scholar is interested in the specific instances within the 'hit'.

Other choices may need to be made when the text is indexed. Information retrieval systems do not normally index common words, making it impossible to search for them. However, research has shown that these words are often the most interesting in a text from a linguistic and stylistic point of view. We will examine this in more detail in later chapters, but looking for words such as *that*, *if*, or *and* is often a good test of a packaged electronic text. Omitted words can often cause problems, for example with words like *will* and *might* which are nouns as well as auxiliary verbs. Another test of packaged electronic texts is the ability to search on the endings of words. This can be useful for verse, or for a language which inflects heavily, or even as a simple way of finding all the present participles in English by looking for words that end in -*ing*, and simply ignoring words like *anything* and *nothing* which are found as well. This facility is simple to program, but it is surprising how rarely it is provided.

As more and more packaged electronic texts become available, with different programs, it becomes more difficult for scholars to keep up with the new interfaces. Each product seems to require learning time, probably several times over, if it is not used very often. The Web provides some movement towards a common user interface, but so much depends on the nature of the text. The current method of delivering large collections of electronic text with search tools over the Web involves a search engine on the host server and an interface consisting of a series of Web forms on the user's client machine. The user fills in boxes on the Web forms and a program running on the server then translates the requests in the boxes to a format which the search engine accepts. The search engine then carries out the search and returns the results to another program on the server, which translates them into the Web language HTML for display in the user's Web browser. This is a cumbersome process and, moreover, the only searches which can be carried out are those which are determined by the pre-defined boxes. They usually offer limited functionality which does not address the needs of many scholars, but with more functionality the learning curve usually becomes steeper. All too often the functionality of these programs is determined by computer programmers who have little understanding of what humanities scholars want to do. It is frustrating to spend a long time learning a particular program only to find that it does not do what is needed. It is equally frustrating to know that what is needed is technically not difficult, but has not been implemented. Software tools are still fairly weak and the range of possibilities discussed in this book should feed into the design of better and more flexible software.

All too many projects which aim to create packaged electronic texts tend to proceed as follows. The researchers announce their intention to 'create a CD-ROM', without really specifying what this means. They then look around for some software and are often induced by a sales-person to select a program which has a 'glitzy' user interface. Images can look particularly impressive, as is the ability to display any non-standard characters which occur in the text. Investigators on these projects do not look hard enough at the functionality of the program, or consider whether they might want to use the same electronic text for another purpose. They then spend much time creating an electronic text in what is probably a proprietary format which is useless for any other program. By the time they have finished creating the text, the software company has either gone out of business or has introduced new versions of its software with added features which require the electronic text to be upgraded as well. The 'create a CD-ROM syndrome' happens all too often, leaving a project with a lot of unusable data and much wasted time. Even if the CD-ROM does get out into the market, there will be a need for technical support and maintenance for several years, all of which is costly in human terms. With a few exceptions, sales of electronic text CD-ROMs have usually been poor. Prices and marketing efforts have generally been directed towards libraries, which have the added problem of needing to support many different user interfaces. The arguments in favour of a common and flexible user interface and creating data which can be used for many different purposes are very strong, but more research needs to be done before this becomes a practical reality.

The picture at the beginning of the new millennium is thus scattered. There are individual projects doing useful and frequently complex work but often in their own idiosyncratic way. There are also some large collections of text available for searching in simple ways over the World Wide Web. The Internet and the World Wide Web are now at the centre of most computing, but this technology is now seen by many people more as a means of distribution or publication of information rather than as a means of manipulation and analysis. The hypertextual interface of the World Wide Web can serve as a means of publishing information which is not intended to be read in a sequential fashion as well as transmitting information which is intended to be read in the same way as more traditional forms. Scholars have begun to use the Web as a new publication medium, concentrating on the use of technology as a way of providing access to information rather than analysing that information. The current implementation of the Web is good at showing things, but it is poor at the other things which computers are good at, that is at providing analysis tools which facilitate interpretation of the material. The analysis tools which will be examined in this book could be embedded in a much more flexible and sophisticated Web environment which would provide a real basis for serious scholarly research rather than as a means of only looking at but not working with electronic resources.

As we shall see, research carried out in humanities computing is contributing to new developments for the Web. Humanities material is an excellent testbed because of its complexity and because it can be expected to have a fairly long useful life. Electronic representations of humanities material need to last for a long time and they need to be capable of assisting scholars to address many different types of research questions. Humanities scholars are beginning to ask many challenging questions of their electronic material. They want to publish it in new ways and carry out many different delivery and analysis functions on it. Computing research which helps to answer these questions is feeding into broader developments on the Web and elsewhere, and opening up new ideas for further research.

2 | Creating and Acquiring Electronic Texts

Many electronic texts now exist, but finding out whether a particular text is available, and whether the text is suitable for the particular research problem, can take some time. There is no single catalogue of electronic texts and indeed as yet no agreement on what information should be contained in that catalogue beyond the author and title of the work. The Internet is usually the starting point to look for an electronic text, normally with a general Internet search rather than with a library catalogue search. It thus does not have any of the precision provided by the structure of the library catalogue and the use of authority files for standard spellings.

A general Internet search for a well-known author or text can yield many results. Internet search engines usually display the beginning of the page which has been found, which is little help for a researcher. With Internet searches it is often not clear until the page is inspected whether it is the actual text, a description of the text or author, or another search engine operating on the text. The Internet site Voice of the Shuttle is one starting point for humanities (Liu 1999). It consists of pointers to many humanities sites. These are organized into categories devised by the editor which work reasonably well. The lists of pointers have some additional information, usually the name of the compiler of the site or its location. However, the Voice of the Shuttle includes many different types of sites, not only texts, and so it is necessary to hunt through the lists to look for texts and then to go to each site to see whether the text can be downloaded.

If the actual text is reached, it should be possible to save it as a plain text file or as an HTML file, but neither of these forms is very suitable for further processing. It will almost certainly be necessary to insert some encoding into a plain text file or to translate the HTML encoding into something more useful (see further Chapter 3). Depending on the format of the plain text file or the nature of the HTML being used, it might be possible to reformat the text using Find and Replace commands in a word processor. But word processors are weak tools for reformatting material and it may be necessary to make several passes through the text to complete all the changes which are needed. These kinds of changes are better made with a programmable editor, for example TextPad or Emacs, but the researcher must weigh the time required to learn a new tool against the benefits of using a more powerful editor.

One of the many problems with texts which are freely available on the Internet is that it is very difficult to ascertain where they came from and what transcription policies were used. Some contain a usage or copyright statement, but this is usually at the beginning or end of the file and, unless it is deleted or encoded in some way, it will be indexed and searched as if it was part of the main text. Many of the Internet texts have been prepared by volunteers and may not have been proof-read well, perhaps only with a spell-checking program which will find some errors but none that are real words. Without reading the text and comparing it to a print source it is very difficult to ensure that none of it is missing, or that no parts of it are duplicated. Often Internet texts do not indicate which edition they have been taken from, or who has compiled the texts and what stages of revision and checking they have been through. In general, the purpose of some of the Internet electronic texts does not seem clear. There seems to be some assumption that they are intended only to be read, but the formatting of the Web browser does not particularly help with this. The advantages of Internet access make more sense for material which is difficult to find in any other way, but this material needs to be prepared for Internet access in a way which makes it suitable for scholarly research.

Another possible approach to finding electronic texts is to use the library catalogue. Some catalogues now include Internet electronic text collections with a pointer directly to the collection site from the Web-based catalogue. More often than not these lead to search engines. Other catalogue entries describe CD-ROM products. The library catalogue model is well developed for bibliographic information, but it is much weaker on specifications of features which are peculiar to electronic representations of objects. It tends to treat computer files as if they are an alternative to books, audio, or maps etc., when in fact computer files can represent all of these types of information in a much more powerful and dynamic format than is possible with their static forms. The catalogue can include detailed specifications of the physical characteristics of CD-ROMs, but it cannot easily include encoding principles and software requirements which scholars need to know before they decide to use an electronic text. Put more simply, it is obvious what a scholar will do with a book. It is much less obvious what scholars may want to do with electronic texts. The catalogue needs to give some indication to help scholars determine whether what they want to do is actually possible with this version of the text. It seems likely that the catalogue will continue to be used as an access point to some large collections of texts, but this model is not really appropriate to compile a general catalogue of all electronic texts. See further Hoogcarspel (1994a, 1994b) and Horowitz (1994).

All this ancillary information is more usually called metadata (data about the data). There needs to be a commonly accepted format to express metadata, a specification for what metadata is included, and a syntax or encoding system for holding it. In order to be useful for research purposes, metadata for electronic texts needs to include information about the source from which the text was transcribed, details of the transcription and encoding policy, and a history of revisions made to the text. The TEI header, discussed in Chapter 3, is one serious attempt to define a specification for metadata for electronic texts, and covers these topics, but many texts do not yet have TEI headers and are not in fact encoded in the SGML language which TEI headers require. Scholars who have created electronic texts for their own purposes have generally not found it necessary to record metadata because they knew most of this information, or else they have recorded it on paper, which tends to get lost. Other groups compiling large collections of electronic texts have tended to record basic metadata in a different electronic format from the texts. It makes sense for the metadata to be in the same format as the text so that the same programs can process it.

The HTML metadata facilities in the HTML header are very general and very weak, and few HTML editors make it easy to insert metadata. But there is a pressing need for better metadata on the Internet. One approach is the Dublin Core (Weibel 1995; Miller 1996). This is a small set of fifteen metadata elements designed 'to facilitate discovery of electronic resources', especially Web pages. It has been developed collaboratively in a series of invitational workshops and made widely available for public comment. Each element represents one aspect of metadata, and the set of elements is designed to be simple, extensible, and international in scope. The Dublin Core is intended to handle many types of information, and the idea is that specific applications can build on this framework to develop their own metadata systems. The Dublin Core is being used by the UK Arts and Humanities Data Service (Miller and Greenstein 1997). Heery (1996) is a useful introduction to metadata systems.

The Oxford Text Archive (OTA) is a repository of electronic text for humanities research (Oxford Text Archive n.d.). It was founded in 1976 to offer scholars a means of depositing their electronic texts once they have completed their research using the texts. See Burnard (1986) for the early history of the archive and Proud (1989) for an assessment of its state in 1989. The OTA contains over 2,500 texts (literary, linguistic, or reference works) in twenty-six different languages, but predominantly in English. A variety of formats is used for the texts, but with the emphasis on SGML (see Chapter 3). The majority of the texts can be downloaded, some immediately, others only with the permission of the depositor. The OTA became part of the UK Arts and Humanities Data Service in 1995 with additional support to work on the task of creating better metadata for the texts, which in some cases was almost non-existent, and preparing a better delivery system. The short record format of the Web catalogue of the OTA contains useful information, for example, what markup scheme is used in the text, whether it is freely available, and the size of the file.

Some collections of text have been prepared for scholarly research in a manner which makes them usable for many different applications. Classicists are particularly well provided for. The Thesaurus Linguae Graecae (TLG) project began at the University of California at Irvine in 1971 with the aim of creating an electronic 'bank of text' of all non-documentary material in ancient Greek from the time of Homer to until AD 600. The first stage of a project like this is to identify the texts and define the canon. Brunner (1993) traces the history of the TLG project, and Berkowitz (1993) discusses the nature of the canon and many of the decisions made encoding the texts. By 1997 there were some 70 million words in all, providing an unparalleled resource for scholars working in Classical Greek. The TLG devised its own encoding system called 'beta code' (Thesaurus Linguae Graecae n.d.). The texts are distributed on CD-ROM in this format, and several third party software tools can search and manipulate the texts in various ways. A similar collection of Classical Latin texts has been created by the Packard Humanities Institute (Lancashire 1991: 215).

Scholars working in Old English also have the advantage of a complete corpus in electronic form. This corpus was created at the University of Toronto and was originally planned as a source for the editors of the new *Dictionary of Old English* (Frank and Cameron 1973). The preparation followed a similar pattern to the TLG in that, following a planning meeting in March 1969, the first stage was the compilation of a complete catalogue of texts and sources. These were classified into genres and each text was assigned an identification code, by which it is now commonly known (Cameron, Frank, and Leyerle 1970). Work then began on entering the texts, which have since been reformatted to new encoding standards and are now in SGML encoding. Healey (1997) traces the history of the corpus, noting that it is not static as updates and amendments continue to be added.

In 1986, a group of scholars at Brown University founded a project to create a textbase of British women's writing up to 1830 (Women Writers Project n.d.). The Women Writers Project was able to take advantage of the knowledge gained over forty years and employ a much more up-to-date methodology for the format of the electronic texts. This group has also been involved in research in electronic text technology for the humanities and has made a significant contribution to our understanding of electronic text creation, encoding, and use. All the texts are transcribed and encoded to a high standard and can be accessed via online searching or by request for specific texts. The Victorian Women Writers Project is also creating and making available transcriptions of mostly lesser-known material from the Victorian period (Willett 1999).

Some publishers, notably Chadwyck-Healey, are creating large electronic textbases of literary material. The Chadwyck-Healey texts were originally published on CD-ROM with a search engine, but now most users, or rather their institutions, subscribe to Chadwyck-Healey's Internet service Literature Online (Literature Online n.d.). At the time of writing, this provides only a search engine enabling the user to scroll through the texts examining occurrences of the search words. It does not provide any other analysis tools and so these texts at present can only be used as a kind of reference tool, albeit a very useful one, especially for the less well known authors. For the English poetry database it is possible to search by keyword, first line, poet, period, and gender of author, and to choose whether or not to include the notes in the search. The Literature Online software does not provide the basic concordance and frequency functions which are discussed in Chapter 4. This is much to be regretted because Literature Online and similar systems are often a scholar's first encounter with electronic texts; thus the scholar tends to be conditioned by what can be done in these systems and to believe that this is all that can be done with computers.

At present it is still rare for several different electronic versions of a work to exist. The Bible and Shakespeare are the obvious ones. Comparative reviews of these can not only help scholars to decide which version of the text to use, but also with the more general question of establishing design principles for better electronic texts. Bolton (1990) reviews three electronic versions of Shakespeare and tools to access them and gives a detailed evaluation from the perspective of a scholar in English studies. This essay highlights the relevance of complex tools for what are complex texts and the need to provide good documentation for them. Most of the current electronic versions of the Bible seem to be intended more for the popular market, and only one or two would be really suitable for scholars and students in religious studies. As yet there are few other comparative reviews such as Bolton's, but soon there will be more versions of electronic texts to choose from and more evaluations are sorely needed. See also Hockey (1994) for more discussion of the evaluation of electronic texts.

Many electronic texts have been created for the purposes of linguistic research. Some of these may also be suitable for literary research or may act as comparative material for a literary project. What is called corpus linguistics began with the compilation of the Brown Corpus at Brown University in the early 1960s, but as Francis, one of the compilers of the Brown Corpus, points out, there were many corpora BC (before computers) (W. N. Francis 1992). It is just that computers provide much better access tools. Research in corpus linguistics on the design of corpora which consist of samples of text is also relevant for literary and other humanities applications. The design of the Brown Corpus was mapped out by a group of scholars who convened at Brown University to discuss what a representative corpus should look like. The model they established is important because it was followed by a number of other corpus compilers. The corpus is described in detail in Francis and Kucera (1964). Briefly, it consists of 1,014,312 words of running text of edited English prose printed in the United States during the calendar year 1961. An attempt was made to ensure that the writers were all native speakers of American English and that all the material first appeared in 1961. The corpus is divided into 500 samples of 2,000+ words each. Each sample begins at the beginning of a sentence and ends at the first sentence ending after 2,000 words. The samples are grouped into a range of genres broadly divided into informative and imaginative prose. Informative prose includes press reportage, press editorials and reviews, religion, skills and hobbies, popular lore, *belles-lettres*, miscellaneous (mostly government reports), and learned (academic papers). Imaginative prose includes various kinds of fiction: general, detective, science, western, romance, and humour. Dialogue was avoided wherever possible in the fiction samples. The Brown Corpus is still much used for research, even though it represents only a portion of the kinds of language in daily use. Specifically it does not include verse, drama, or spoken texts.

The Lancaster–Oslo/Bergen (LOB) Corpus follows a similar pattern for British English; its composition is described in Johansson (1978).

The manuals for both these corpora also describe the markup scheme, which predates SGML and is easy to work with. The encoding scheme for the LOB Corpus is a little more comprehensive than that for the Brown Corpus. Versions of these corpora with embedded word class tagging are now available (see Chapter 6.) The tagging consists of a code attached to the end of each word and it is possible to search this tagging, for example to find all instances where *lead* occurs as a verb, but not as a noun.

The Kolhapur Corpus consists of Indian English, and its design was also modelled on the Brown and LOB corpora with the same sets of genre categories (Shastri 1986), although the use of this design has been criticized by Leitner (1991: 215) in his discussion of varieties of English 'imposed on the British Empire'. The Brown and LOB corpora presuppose Anglo-American society and use material written by native speakers, whereas English may not be the first language of many English speakers elsewhere. Other genre categories may be more appropriate, but the argument in favour of corpora modelled on the same design is that they can be used for comparative purposes. The Australian Corpus of English and the Wellington Corpus of Written New Zealand English follow a similar but not identical pattern to Brown and LOB for exactly this reason (Bauer 1993; Peters n.d.).

These and several other corpora are distributed by ICAME (International Computer Archive of Medieval and Modern English) which is located in Bergen (International Computer Archive of Modern English n.d.).Under the influence of its founder Stig Johansson this group has fostered the use of corpora for English language research. It distributes corpora, organizes an annual conference, publishes a journal, and maintains a discussion list and a very comprehensive bibliography on its Web site. The major corpora are available on CD-ROM as plain text files with some markup.

The International Corpus of English (ICE) is planned to include almost twenty corpora of English from countries where English is the first language or is used as a second official language (Greenbaum 1996a). Each corpus contains 1 million words, made up of 2,000-word samples, mostly dating from 1990 to 1994. The size of each corpus and the samples within it are thus modelled on the Brown Corpus, but the composition differs considerably. Each ICE corpus is planned to contain 300 samples or 600,000 words of spoken text, and 200 samples or 400,000 words of written text. Spoken texts are divided into dialogues (private and public) and monologues (scripted and unscripted). Approximately 25 per cent of the written texts are taken from 'non-printed' works, for example personal letters and student essays (Nelson 1996).

Other projects have been developed elsewhere in Europe, but especially in Germany, France, and Italy, for the purposes of both linguistic and literary research (Ejerhed and Church 1997; Lamel and Cole 1997). The European Language Resources Association (ELRA) maintains corpus resources mostly intended for research in natural language processing (European Language Resources Association 1999). The Linguistic Data Consortium is a similar organization based in the United States (Linguistic Data Consortium n.d.).

Interest has also grown in diachronic corpora which make it possible to compare linguistic change over time. The Helsinki Corpus is the best-known diachronic corpus. It contains texts from Old, Middle, and Early Modern English (Kytö 1996). The Old English texts (some 413,000 words) are based on material taken from the *Dictionary of Old English* project. The Middle English component totals just over 600,000 words, and the Early Modern (up to 1710) consists of 550,000 words. The corpus is encoded in the COCOA, (Word Count and Concordance Generator for Atlas) format for ease of use with the Oxford Concordance Program. Texts are identified by specific text types, not all of which are applicable to all three periods. Rissanen (1992) discusses the problems of compiling diachronic corpora with reference to the Helsinki Corpus. Sociolinguistic parameters are difficult to define for the early period and the definition of text types also changes over time. More general questions associated with diachronic corpora are addressed by Kytö and Rissanen (1997) who also list some other diachronic corpora. In the same volume, Schmied and Claridge (1997) discuss the problem of genre in historical corpora.

When the early corpora were compiled, 1 million words was a large amount of text, but as computers became more powerful and corpora became more widely used, researchers began to want to work with much larger corpora. The British National Corpus (BNC) is a much larger undertaking. It was built as a collaborative project between several British publishers (Oxford University Press, Longman, and Chambers), the British Library, and the universities of Lancaster and Oxford (British National Corpus 1999). It consists of 100 million words of synchronic British English. Approximately 10 per cent of the corpus is spoken material and the remainder written texts. The written sources consist of samples of up to 45,000 words selected according to three criteria: informative or imaginative; medium of publication (books, periodicals, and miscellaneous published and unpublished items such as memoranda, brochures, and written to be spoken); and time (mostly dated after 1975). The texts are all identified by a number of other classification criteria including information about the author, intended audience, level of difficulty, and place (region) of publication. The spoken component consists of a demographic part and a context-governed part. For the demographic part, 124 informants were recruited by a market research bureau. They represented four social groupings (used widely in other British market research surveys) and they lived in thirty-eight different places within the UK. All carried a tape recorder to record their conversations over a period of a few days. Demographic information was added to the transcriptions of the conversations. The context-governed spoken material was built from lectures, meetings, sermons, speeches, radio phone-ins, and the like. The entire corpus is encoded in SGML and includes word class tagging. The texts have comprehensive headers which can be used to select material from different genres or classifications (Dunlop 1995). A sampler CD-ROM of 184 texts, comprising just under 1 million words of spoken text and just over 1 million words of written text, is also available with associated searching software. A description of the searching software can be found in Aston and Burnard (1998).

Spoken material can be very time-consuming and costly to collect, and much less was known about collection methods when the BNC began its work. An earlier collection of spoken material, the London–Lund Corpus, consists of 500,000 words of spoken material taken from the Survey of English Usage (SEU) (Svartvik and Quirk 1980). The electronic version differs slightly from the SEU material and does not include all the features that are transcribed, but it does include some paratextual information in a fixed format at the beginning of each line. The design of the BNC's spoken component is described in Crowdy (1993). A pilot study was conducted for the demographic samples where a group of people, selected by region, age, social class, and sex, recorded some of their conversations and information about other participants in the conversation. The aim of the pilot was to estimate how much recording would be needed to meet the target number of words, and to identify problems with the instructions, type of recorder, etc. From this pilot the BNC was able to estimate that one hour of recording would yield about 7,000 words.

So the design of a corpus is not easy. Some corpora are designed for one specific purpose, and their contents and description reflect this purpose. Others, like the Brown, LOB, and BNC, are intended to be general-purpose and try to address many requirements. Some researchers have argued that the benefits of using a principled and well-documented corpus do not outweigh the time and care needed to compile the corpus. Much depends on the particular application. For detailed linguistic analysis and for comparative work, the nature of the corpus will affect the results. For other broader applications such as natural-language processing, the nature of the material can be less important, although it may still influence the result. A corpus of material from the *Wall Street Journal* is more likely to yield instances of *bank* as a financial term than of *bank* denoting the side of a river. McNaught (1993), in a paper assessing the corpus needs of researchers in natural language processing, thinks that the most successful applications are those for specific domains or sublanguages. This seems to be exactly the situation for most literary or historical projects. Although they would perhaps not use the same terminology, these projects are usually working with subsets of material in a specific area or genre. The size and nature of the samples in a general-purpose corpus are both problematic. The bigger the corpus, the more likely it is that words and phrases will be found in it, but very large corpora are difficult to handle on desktop computers. They also contain very many occurrences of common words which are difficult to sift through.

Atkins, Clear, and Ostler (1992) discuss a range of criteria for the design of written and spoken corpora. First, they note that it is difficult to define the total population. There is no obvious unit of language. This might be considered as words, sentences, or texts. A further question is whether to sample the language that people hear and read, or the language that people speak and write. They attempt to provide a typology of texts viewed from many different dimensions but entirely on a theoretical basis. Practical experiments in corpus design have been carried out by Biber. In Biber (1993), he discusses a range of issues in corpus design where representativeness is the goal. He proposes starting with some theoretical research then moving to empirical work. The work then proceeds in cycles with the evidence from the empirical work leading to more theoretical work and improvement in the design. Both the range of text types and the range of linguistic distributions need to be considered. For spoken texts in particular it is difficult to define the population from which the samples are taken. Stratified samples are the best way of ensuring coverage, but the corpus compiler is then faced with deciding on the strata, which can be viewed from many different perspectives.

Atkins, Clear, and Ostler (1992) also hint at the kind of corpus favoured by Sinclair. His work at Cobuild has centred on a core corpus and what he calls a 'monitor corpus'. The core corpus of somewhere between 10 and 20 million words is deemed to be adequate for the study of frequent patterns and linguistic features (Sinclair 1991: 24–6). The monitor corpus is much larger. It is updated continually with 'automatic' feeds from newspapers and other typesetting sources. It thus benefits from the constant addition of new material. Sinclair notes also that it will be more difficult to achieve a balanced flow of text with this kind of input, and he makes clear the distinction between what he calls a sample corpus, and a monitor corpus which is now called 'The Bank of English'. McEnery and Wilson (1996: 22) also note that the monitor corpus is more suitable for lexicographic work, as is carried out at Cobuild, rather than for quantitative studies which are assumed to be based on representative samples.

Newspaper material has been used as a source for several modern corpora. Newspapers represent the modern day-to-day language and also include many different types of material, including short items. They are difficult to encode, not only because of their complex structure, but also because they contain many names of people and places, and many dates and other numbers. Burr (1996) discusses her choice of newspapers for her corpus of modern non-literary Italian where she is interested in obtaining empirical data for socio-cultural and situational variation. She argues that newspapers create a specific type of language from a fusion of literary language and some spoken and special purpose language (1996: 220). They represent the modern language as it is, and can be viewed as both homogeneous and heterogeneous. Newspapers were the source for Allén's comprehensive study of Swedish vocabulary (Allén 1970) and for Jones's investigation of loan words in modern Turkish (Jones 1971). Of the 500 samples in the Brown and LOB corpora, eighty-eight, or just under 20 per cent, are taken from newspapers. The BNC description groups together newspapers, journals, and magazines under 'periodicals'. These constitute just over 25 per cent of the corpus, but it is not clear how much of this is newspaper material.

If the text is not already available in electronic form, it will either have to be keyboarded or converted into electronic form by optical character recognition (OCR). OCR became feasible for some kinds of material in the early 1980s, but in general it is only suitable for modern printed material. OCR systems work by making an image representation of a page of text on a scanner and then attempting to convert the image or picture of the page into text characters by recognizing each character. Most OCR systems begin with a training phase where the user feeds some text to the machine, which makes guesses for the character shapes and thus 'learns' the characters in the text. It can then apply what it has learned to attempt to recognize more text in the same format. OCR has been thought to be the solution to the bottleneck of text entry in the humanities, but, even if the OCR system is able to recognize most of the characters in the text, it may not be the best method for large-scale text entry. So much depends on the nature of the material and the institutional support for the process. Desktop scanners are now relatively cheap to buy, but there are a number of practical issues to be considered. First of all many desktop scanners are designed for pieces of paper, not for books. It is either difficult to place the book on the scanner at all, or the image will be skewed, especially near the binding, as happens when a book is put on a photocopier. The OCR software will normally rely on a straight and level baseline of type as it scans along each line of text.

OCR systems see everything on the page, including running heads, footnotes, line numbering, and other marginalia, but it does not make sense to scan all of these. Footnotes need to be treated separately from the main text rather than appearing at the end of the page, as will happen when the complete page is scanned. Often the documentation for OCR programs recommends using the mouse to outline the area of text to be scanned if not all the page is required, but this is very cumbersome if the area to be scanned is different on each page, which is normally the case with footnotes. A better procedure is to cover them with white paper so that the scanner does not see them at all. A bigger problem with OCR is that it delivers a typographic representation of the text, which, as we have seen, is ambiguous for computer processing. Some means must be found to map the typography on to another markup scheme, and this usually involves some computer programming. OCR systems can generate text in various word processor formats for further editing, but care needs to be taken with verse text to ensure that the word processor format does not automatically format the text as prose and thus lose the line divisions.

Any material prepared via OCR needs to be proof-read carefully. Claims of 99.9 per cent accuracy mean one error per thousand characters, or about every ten to fifteen lines. Common errors are confusion between *e* and *c*, between *h* and *b*, and between the letter *l* and the number *1*. Some of these can be found with a spell checking program, but by no means all. OCR systems tend to have more difficulty with material printed before the end of the nineteenth century, with newspapers, or anything else where the paper causes the ink to bleed, with footnotes and marginalia, non-standard characters, and with words in italic, or small capitals. Any extraneous marks on the page tend to be interpreted as apostrophes. The more complex the layout and the older the text, the less suitable it is for OCR. Handwriting is impossible because of the joined letters and the inconsistency in the letter shapes. Even if there is some considerable success with OCR, the scanning is only a small part of the process of creating an electronic text. Proof-reading, error correction, and encoding take up most of the time.

The Kurzweil Data Entry Machine, which was one of the most successful OCR systems used in the humanities, is described in Hockey (1986). See also the collection of papers from a workshop on OCR in the historical disciplines for the humanities (Netherlands Data Archive and Nijmegen Institute for Cognition and Information 1993), especially the paper by Olsen, which gives some costs for large-scale data entry (Olsen 1993). Olsen bases his figures on his experience at ARTFL (American Research on the Treasury of the French Language). He is very strongly in favour of not using OCR, but of getting a first version of the text keyboarded by a keyboarding company, and then using various short programs to carry out some verification and to insert markup. The TLG texts were also entered by this means. Several other large-scale projects also get their data entry done in this way, finding that it is much more accurate and therefore cheaper than the full cost of scanning then verifying and correcting OCR text. Much simple structural markup can be created automatically from the keyboarded text if the keyboarding follows some pre-defined rules.

Typesetting tapes are another possible option for acquiring electronic text, but these are often in an idiosyncratic typesetting format which needs some programming effort to convert into a usable form. This might only be worthwhile if a good deal of text is coming from the same source in the same format. Some corpus projects, notably the Bank of English, get material in this form from newspapers and other sources, but typesetting material is less likely to be a suitable source for humanities electronic texts.

Keyboarding the text is the best solution in most cases. It enables the researcher to get closer to the text and it also makes it possible to insert interpretative encoding at the same time. The creation and encoding of an electronic text then become part of the same process. Verification can be speeded up by the use of some programming tools to check for inconsistencies and perhaps to expand the encoding from a simple scheme devised for the purposes of entry of the text. Whatever the method of acquisition of the electronic text, there will be a need to visit and revisit it to make sure that it is accurate and that the encoding is consistent. Some of the tools discussed in later chapters are basically pattern-matching functions and they can also be used with some success to help find errors and inconsistencies.

3 | Text Encoding

The purpose of encoding within a text is to provide information which will assist a computer program to perform functions on that text. On their own, computer programs are not able to carry out 'intelligent' analysis of electronic text, for example to recognize the difference between the personal pronoun *I* and the roman numeral *I*. This will remain the case until further advances in artificial intelligence and natural language processing have been made. If the program is unable to incorporate the level of intelligence needed, that intelligence must be embedded in the text in such a way that the program can derive information from it. The information embedded in the text is variously called encoding, markup, or tagging, although the term 'tagging' is also used somewhat more narrowly in corpus linguistics to denote encoding for grammatical categories and possibly other linguistic features (see Chapter 6).

Without markup, only very simple searches can be carried out on a text. Those who have used the word processor 'Find' function or the Web browser 'Find in Page' function on a humanities text which does not have any markup will be aware of the problems. These functions find sequences of letters, but they cannot distinguish between ambiguous forms. Neither can they provide citation references indicating where a form occurs in a text. When large quantities of text are being searched, markup becomes more crucial. It is the only way to indicate the location of words that have been retrieved or to restrict the search to portions of the textbase, for example works by a particular author or within a specific period of time. Attempting to search a text without markup is rather like searching a library catalogue which is a continuous sequence of text, where the records and fields (author, title, subject, etc.) are not distinguished at all.

The use of markup goes back to the beginnings of electronic text technology. See for example the discussions by Fogel (1962), Parrish (1962), Markman (1964), and Clayton ([1965]). Almost all early markup schemes followed one of two types which served different purposes. The first of these is typographic markup; the second is structural encoding, which denotes features such as chapters, page numbers, line numbers, acts, scenes, etc. Typographic markup provides information to a word processing or typesetting program which is to display or print a text. In a move from old technology to new, it is natural to imitate the old technology, and typographic markup is a good example of this. It is intended to generate print from an electronic document, that is, to create something which will be read by people, but will not be processed in any other way by them or by computers. Typographic markup incorporates features which are found in print materials, such as italics, bold, centred text, text in different point sizes, footnotes, and running heads. These features reinforce the text, making it easier to read it. Anyone who has worked with old computer systems that use only one typeface in one size will know how much easier it is to read text which has typeset features with better-designed fonts and sizes of type.

The problem with typographic markup is that it is ambiguous or difficult to interpret for any other kind of computer processing. Something in italic might be a foreign word, an emphasized word, a title, or a stage direction, all of which humans can recognize because of their ability to process natural language. With only typographic markup, it would be impossible for a computer program to make a list of titles in a work, or to index foreign words. Running heads are very difficult to identify automatically, and are not required in an electronic text, but as we have seen in the discussion on optical character recognition (Chapter 2), they will be incorporated in the text unless the OCR program can delete them.

Typographic markup is used to the full to aid the reader of two types of material commonly found in the humanities: a dictionary entry and a critical apparatus. In a dictionary entry, the headword might be in bold, the etymology in italic, and the definition in roman, but also followed by one or more quotations. The text of each quotation might be in roman, but with its title and author in italic. Using this kind of markup to search for all the quotations from a particular author would be almost impossible. In a critical apparatus, the lemma is typically followed by a list of variants, each with witness lists and possibly some accompanying notes, where italic is often used to indicate conjectured readings, or the names of manuscripts, or possibly abbreviations in the editor's comments. A computer program would need more information to identify the components of a variant if these were to be included in an index, or to generate different versions of the text.

An appreciation of typographic markup is important because much electronic text is still created by word processors in typographic form today. Word processors are easy to use and are not going to go away. A word processor can be used to create an electronic text which can be transformed by program into another markup scheme which is more suitable for computer analysis. With an appreciation of the issues raised here, it is possible to use a word processor to create a text. Specific features within the text can be represented unambiguously and thus be transformed automatically to another markup scheme later. Researchers need to be aware of possible problems if an attempt is made to use typesetting tapes as a source of electronic text (see Chapter 2). This has been done in some projects but it usually requires some programming skills to attempt to recognize the different features in the text based on the typography of the surrounding material.

In contrast, early text retrieval programs used simple markup schemes to help users identify the 'hits' which were retrieved. These schemes used simple data for author, title, keywords, and date rather like the fields in a simple bibliographic record, and placed them at the beginning of each document or text. The program (and user) 'knew' the format of the information at the beginning of each text and that this information was to apply to the whole text. The text may also have markup embedded in it to identify the beginning of a new section of the text, or a page number if the electronic text was derived from something that was already printed. The embedded markup would be recognized, perhaps because it was on a separate line and began with a full stop or tilde, for example

.chapter 1
~part 3

Most of these programs were developed for information retrieval applications where the user is interested in finding all the documents that contain certain terms. The programs return a set of documents as the number of hits, and the markup is designed for this purpose. It is less helpful for the more common kind of literary or linguistic search where the user is more interested in specific occurrences of words than in the documents which contain those words, but for many humanities texts it is not easy to decide what constitutes a document. Is it a whole novel or a chapter? Or is it a play, or an act, or a scene within the play? Two separate implementations of the *Divine Comedy* in document retrieval programs chose different structures. In the Oxford Text Searching System each canto is a document (Hockey, Freedman, and Cooper 1991: 120); in the Dartmouth Dante Project, each terzina is a document, resulting in rather different responses to queries (Hollander n.d.).

Specialized markup schemes for citations or locations within texts were developed for programs designed specifically for literary and linguistic computing. These schemes were able to handle the many different types of text and text structure which exist in the humanities. The simplest way of encoding citations is to include an abbreviated form of a citation reference at the beginning of every line, as in

VirAen01001arma virumque cano, Troiae qui primus ab oris

where the first three letters (Vir) are an abbreviation of the author's name Virgil, the next three represent the work (*Aeneid*), the next two the book number (Book 01 or 1), and the last three the line number, in this case line 1, written as 001 to allow for line numbers up to 999. The actual text begins in the twelfth character position on the line. The *Dictionary of Old English* project adopted this method when they first compiled their corpus, mostly because it allowed them to break the text up into units suitable for dictionary citations (Frank and Cameron 1973: 322). Other early corpora, including the first versions of the Brown and LOB corpora, also used this format (Francis and Kucera 1964; Johansson 1978).

The best-known of these early schemes is COCOA, used by the Oxford Concordance Program (Oxford University Computing Service 1988) and, in an extended form, by TACT (Textual Analysis Computing Tools) (Lancashire *et al.* 1996). COCOA was first used in the 1960s by the original COCOA program (Russell 1967) and also by projects in Edinburgh (Hamilton-Smith 1971). Most recently it has been implemented in Rob Watt's Concordance program (Watt 1999). In this format, what are called references are enclosed within angle brackets and embedded in the text. Other characters can be used instead of the angle brackets provided that they are consistent. For example,

<W Shakespeare>
<T Merchant of Venice>

where the single letter W (called a letter category) represents writer (author) and T represents title. The user can define letter categories for structural units within the text, for example A for act, S for scene, C for speaker. Note the choice of W for author and C for speaker to avoid ambiguity. Each precedes the beginning of a new instance of that structural unit and holds true until the beginning of the next instance. Expanding our previous example, we have

<W Shakespeare>
<T Merchant of Venice>
<A 2>
<S 6>

```
<C Graziano>
This is the penthouse under which Lorenzo
Desired us to make stand
<C Salerio>
His hour is almost past
<C Graziano>
And it is marvel he outdwells his hour
For lovers ever run before the clock.
    ...

<S 7>
<C Portia>
Go, draw aside the curtains, and discover
```

Line numbers are not given in the text, on the assumption that a computer program can count them automatically provided that the text is given line for line and that the program does not count lines consisting only of references. The COCOA scheme reserves the letter category L for line numbers and specific L references can be inserted into the text to account for non-sequential numbering. An index of *desired* could, if the user chooses, indicate that the word is on line 2 and is spoken by Graziano in Act 2, Scene 6 of Shakespeare's *The Merchant of Venice*. In fact this line is broken into two speeches and the insertion of a + as a continuation character at the end of the first line ensures that the line numbering remains accurate. In

```
<C Graziano>
This is the penthouse under which Lorenzo
Desired us to make stand +
<C Salerio>
His hour is almost past
```

the word *hour* would also be on line 2.

The COCOA scheme allows for multiple overlapping referencing schemes in the same text. If we wanted to include page numbers from a printed edition in our text of the *Merchant of Venice*, a P reference could mark a new page anywhere in the text, as in

```
<W Shakespeare>
<T Merchant of Venice>
<A 2>
<S 6>
<C Graziano>
This is the penthouse under which Lorenzo
Desired us to make stand
<C Salerio>
His hour is almost past
```

```
<P 98>
<C Graziano>
And it is marvel he outdwells his hour
For lovers ever run before the clock.
    . . .
```

Except for the start of the text on page 1, there is no relationship between a new page and any of the other referencing codes. A new act, scene, or speech does not coincide with the start of a new page, unless of course the previous instance happens to finish at the bottom of a page. Another example of overlap is when a printed edition of a manuscript records the folio and line numbering of the original manuscript, but also has page and line numbering for the printed version. We have already seen a third kind of overlap where the line is divided between two speakers. In this case, speeches do not contain complete lines, but lines overlap between speeches.

The COCOA scheme does have one significant drawback, which can be illustrated by different examples. In it, there is no way to mark the end of an instance of a reference other than the beginning of a new instance, or making a null instance such as

```
<C >
```

This makes it rather more difficult to encode, for example, the stage directions in *The Merchant of Venice* in the same format since they are scattered throughout the text. One way might be to make them a special kind of speech as in

```
<C stage direction>
```

but this would become clumsy, especially if many other similar features were to be encoded. The electronic version of the complete works of Shakespeare (Wells and Taylor 1991), which uses the COCOA encoding scheme except for line numbers, circumvents this problem in a somewhat clumsy but effective way. It uses a letter category T for text type with possible values of prose, verse, song, stage direction, etc. Although this method might also be appropriate for the cast list, it does not work very well for any kind of editorial notes or apparatus, which are themselves composed of other sub-features. To put it in more general terms, the COCOA syntax is not very suitable for features such as foreign words, quotations, abbreviations, names, front and back matter, additions, deletions, and other interpretative markup, all of which are small amounts of text which need to be encoded individually. It would be very clumsy to use a COCOA reference for each of these and to mark the end of them with a null instance. In reality, most COCOA users have preferred to encode these features either by surrounding them with extra brackets, as in

> Lean, rent, and beggared by the strumpet wind!
> ((Enter Lorenzo, [with a torch]))
> <C Salerio>
> Here comes Lorenzo. More of this hereafter.

or by inserting extra characters at the beginning of each word, as in

> Wretyn at ^Paston in hast @e Wednesday next after %Deus %qui %errantibus, for defaute of a good secretarye, &c.

where a per cent sign introduces all Latin words. A retrieval or concordance program can then find all stage directions by searching for text within double brackets. Or it can find Latin words by retrieving words which begin with a per cent sign and, in this case, possibly also not display the per cent sign in the results.

TACT extends the COCOA scheme by allowing categories, which it calls tags, to consist of more than one letter, for example

> <title The Merchant of Venice>
> <act 1>
> <scene 1>

This makes a more readable text and encourages encoding for a wider variety of features. Appendix 1 of Lancashire *et al.* (1996) includes a set of exemplary texts showing, and explaining, the TACT tagging within the texts. The accompanying CD-ROM has many more texts. Like COCOA, TACT has no way of encoding the end of something other than by beginning a new instance, but these examples illustrate the tagging of many features using – (a hyphen) as a null end tag, for example

> <modern the>ye<modern ->

for modernized spelling (Lancashire *et al.* 1996: 214).

Any text encoding scheme for the humanities must also address the problem of character sets and non-standard characters. These may range from accented characters and the occasional non-standard letter such as the thorn to texts which are written in several languages and writing systems, some of which may be non-alphabetic. At the lowest level, each character is stored in the computer as a pattern of bits, most usually still in 8-bit bytes, giving a maximum of 256 characters. The first or lower 128 of these characters, known as lower ASCII, are the only characters that can safely be transmitted across all networks. At present, all others are best encoded in some form, although this is likely to change in the future.

Several issues need to be considered when choosing an encoding method for non-standard characters. Proprietary systems such as word processors which can handle Greek and other alphabets are easy to use, and they display and print all the characters well, but they may not produce a version of the text which can be processed by other programs for word searching and indexing. It is as well to investigate how these programs store the non-standard characters before starting to use them to create text. In general the ability to display or print a non-standard character does not indicate that a program is able to insert that character into an alphabetical sequence for sorting words, or process it in any other way. Many *ad hoc* methods have been proposed and used for encoding individual characters, for example *s*∧ for š, @ for thorn, or *e*/ for *é*. Provided that they are unambiguous, these can be very effective for text creation and proof-reading, and they can be transformed to another encoding scheme later. In the short example illustrating the Latin words above, the symbol @ is used for a thorn. Instances where two characters represent one symbol, for example *s*∧, require a little more careful programming, but are widely used.

Three issues need to be considered when there are substantial amounts of text in a non-roman alphabet. These are the language, the writing system, and the direction of writing. There is no direct one-to-one mapping between language and writing system. For example, several different languages are written in the Arabic or Cyrillic alphabets. A processing program will need to know the language in order to carry out anything other than very simple processing on the text. Since computer programs normally operate from left to right as they go through a line of text it is advisable to enter text in a right-to-left script in left-to-right order and assume that a display or printing program can reverse the text on output. Mixed left-to-right and right-to-left text is particularly problematic, and in prose texts word wrap can also affect the display.

For practical purposes, texts in non-roman alphabets are usually encoded in a transliterated form, making it possible to work with standard tools for manipulating the text, which can then be mapped on to the original writing system to display the results. The best-known transliteration scheme is beta code, devised for ancient Greek by the TLG (Thesaurus Linguae Graecae n.d.). Beta code has a simple one-for-one representation of the Greek letters, using *a* for alpha, *b* for beta, *g* for gamma. It avoids conventional multiple characters such as *th* for theta, or *ph* for phi, preferring the single characters *q* or *f* which make processing easier. Accents are encoded with a combination of brackets and other symbols. In beta code the first line of the *Iliad* appears as

Mh=nin a)/eide, qea\, Phlhi+a/dew Axilh=os

Gaylord (1995) is a useful starting-point for character set issues for the humanities.

Unicode is a new standard for encoding characters (Unicode Consortium n.d.). Unicode is based on 16-bit, not 8-bit, characters, and so it has the capacity to encode approximately 65,000 different characters. It also incorporates an extension mechanism for encoding many more characters. Unicode has not yet been implemented in the software tools which humanists use most often, but it is an important development and should solve many character set problems once it is more widely available.

The transcription and encoding of spoken material raise many specific questions which are not yet very well understood. Crowdy (1995) discusses the transcription features of the spoken component of the BNC. Ballester and Santamaria (1993) consider transcription issues for a corpus of contemporary spoken Spanish. Johansson (1995) discusses the TEI approach to encoding spoken texts. Leech, Myers, and Thomas (1995) is a very useful collection of papers on various topics concerned with spoken texts. See also Edwards (1992) for a discussion of transcription policies for spoken texts. CHAT (Codes for the Human Analysis of Transcripts) is a comprehensive transcription system for spoken texts devised originally for the CHILDES (Child Language Data Exchange System) Project (MacWhinney 1995). A possible solution is linking transcriptions to digital audio, but decisions must still be made about what paratextual features to encode for searching and how they should be encoded.

In the discussion of markup so far, we have argued that typographic markup is ambiguous and that the most effective way of encoding is to embed within a text encoding tags which provide a meaningful description of the text. The most widely used example of encoding tags embedded in text is HTML, the HyperText Markup Language used by the World Wide Web (World Wide Web Consortium 1999). HTML is a markup language which was designed to be interpreted by Web browsers. In HTML opening and closing tags surround sections or features within a text (a Web page) and provide information to the Web browser causing the browser to display that feature in a certain way. For example the HTML code

```
<h2>Second level heading</h2>
```

where <h2> represents heading level 2, causes Netscape 4.0 and Internet Explorer 4.0 to display the text 'Second level heading' flush left in large size bold.

HTML is an advance on the COCOA/TACT schemes in that it has a mechanism for marking the end of a feature, with a closing or end tag identical to the opening tag except for the addition of a slash (/). This means that it is easy to detect the end of features, or 'elements' as we shall call them. Elements can also nest inside each other, for example an unordered list (<ul>) consists of one or more list items (<li> elements). An entire HTML document is enclosed within an <html> element which contains two major parts, the <head>, which includes the <title> of the Web page, and the <body>, which includes the text and other material of the page itself. HTML editing programs which create Web pages are aware of this structure and can prevent list items appearing outside lists, or pages without a <body>.

HTML-encoded texts are thus easy to create and easy to distribute. The problem with HTML is the set of tags that it uses. HTML is a pre-defined tag set. It has been extended several times but it is still focused very much on how Web browsers will display the text within each tag. In fact HTML is a rather curious mixture of tags. It has developed from a tag set which originally included typographic tags to one that consists mostly of simple structural tags, for example <p> for paragraph, <ul> for unordered list, <body> for body. But the structural tags within HTML are not designed for providing citations in retrieval or indexing. They are too simple for the range of features likely to be of interest to humanities scholars and so are of little use for any kind of analysis of the text.

An encoding scheme to suit many purposes would, then, have a syntax which would include start and end tags, and allow the user to define the encoding tags to suit the nature of the text and the features of interest within it. Such a scheme does exist in the form of the Standard Generalized Markup Language (SGML) (Goldfarb 1990; van Herwijnen 1994). SGML became an international standard in 1986 (International Organization for Standards 1986). Technically, SGML is not an encoding scheme in itself, but a syntax or framework within which encoding tags can be defined. The principle of SGML is 'descriptive', that is, it provides a means of describing or encoding the components or features within a text of a text. This is in contrast to a 'prescriptive' or procedural scheme such as typographic markup which indicates what processes are to be performed on the text. For a further discussion of the rationale for descriptive or generic markup see Coombs, Renear, and DeRose (1987).

The descriptive nature of the encoding means that different programs can carry out different functions, such as indexing, searching, printing, and hypertext linking on the same text without the need for making any changes to the text. Given the time and expense of creating an electronic text, the advantages of this approach are obvious. Typical components of a text may be title, author, paragraph, chapter, act, scene, speech, or features such as quotations, lists, names, addresses, dates, etc., but SGML allows anything within the text and pertaining to the text to be encoded. As in HTML, which is in fact an SGML-based encoding scheme, the encoded features are marked by start and end tags within the text. What is called an 'SGML application' provides the set of tags for one application area. Chapter 2 of Sperberg-McQueen and Burnard (1994) is a very useful 'gentle' introduction to SGML for the humanities. Additional material can also be found in Burnard (1995).

At one level SGML considers a text to be composed of objects of various kinds, which are known as 'elements'. These identify whatever components or features within the text are to be encoded. The following example shows the normal syntax for start and end tags:

. . . the novel <title>Pride and Prejudice</title> is associated with . . .

This would enable, for example, the construction of an index of titles, or the display or printing of titles in a particular font. Attributes may be associated with elements to give further information about the element. For example, for the tag <section>,

<section n='1'> . . . text of section . . . </section>

to give the number of the section, or for the tag <name>

| type | type of name |
| normal | normalized form |

<name type='personal' normal='SmithJ'>John Smyth</name>

This would enable an index of personal names to be made in which John Smyth could be indexed as SmithJ. Attributes can also be used for cross-references, which are resolved into concrete references only when the text is processed.

SGML requires the elements which may appear in a set of documents to be specified in a document type definition (DTD). The DTD gives not only the names of the elements and their possible attributes, but also the relationships between the elements. Each document is assumed to have a hierarchic structure where large structural elements such as novels or chapters enclose smaller ones such as paragraphs, titles, bibliographic references, etc. A simple definition of a play might be that it consists of title, author, cast list, followed by one or more acts, each containing one or more scenes, each containing a number of speeches and stage directions. Within the speeches, line numbers might be encoded, but also elements which can occur anywhere within the text, for example names of persons or places, abbreviations, quotations, emendations, and also notes of various kinds, which may themselves contain abbreviations and the like.

Sperberg-McQueen and Burnard (1994) use the example of a simple anthology to show how a DTD is constructed. The anthology consists of a number of poems, each of which has one title followed by any number of stanzas. A stanza consists only of lines, and lines must be within a stanza. These rules can be used by an SGML-aware editing program to help encode the anthology, for example to ensure that each poem begins with a title and that lines are contained within stanzas. They can also be used to minimize the markup by omitting some end tags. A title need not have an end tag because there can only be one title and it must be followed by at least one stanza. The end tag for stanza can be omitted because a stanza must contain lines, and a line can only be followed by another line or a new stanza. The end of a poem is also implied by the start of the next poem. Sperberg-McQueen and Burnard (1994: 18) give the following example of an anthology

```
<anthology>
<poem><title>The SICK ROSE
  <stanza>
      <line>O Rose thou art sick.
      <line>The invisible worm,
      <line>That flies in the night
      <line>In the howling storm:
  <stanza>
      <line>Has found out thy bed
      <line>Of crimson joy:
      <line>And his dark secret love
      <line>Does thy life destroy.
  <poem>
  <!–more poems go here>
</anthology>
```

More generally, the DTD enables an SGML 'parser' to validate the markup in a text, and it helps other SGML processing programs to know what to expect next as they go through the text. Therefore to say that a text is in SGML provides very little information to the reader since it only indicates that the syntax of the markup tags conforms to SGML. The specific DTD, or a description of the specific tags being used, is needed to describe the markup scheme properly. The DTD may contain very few elements or very detailed tags, several of which may be associated with each word in the text.

SGML also uses what are called 'entities'. An entity is any named bit of text, and an entity definition associates a name with a bit of text. One use for entities is to encode non-standard characters. For example the entity reference β could be used for the Greek letter beta, or &alef; for the Hebrew letter alef, or é for é. Of course inserting and working with characters in this form can be very cumbersome without SGML software, but simpler encoding formats for non-standard characters can be converted to SGML entities for an archival version of the text. Standard sets of entities already exist for many character sets and can be located via the search engine on the SGML/XML Web page (Cover 1994–). But entities have much broader applications. A second use is for expanding abbreviations or for boilerplate text, for example &LLC; for the journal *Literary and Linguistic Computing*. The same entity may be expanded in different ways when the text is processed for different purposes. Entities may also be used as placeholders for material to be inserted later, for example &chapter2; for the entire text of chapter 2. The entity mechanism ensures that SGML consists only of lower ASCII characters and can thus be moved very easily from one computer system to another.

For an SGML application to succeed, the process of defining the set of SGML tags for one application, known as document analysis, can take considerable time, involving sessions with groups of users who examine samples of the documents and clarify what they intend to do with the documents. Fortunately for the humanities scholar, an SGML application already exists which was designed for encoding texts for use in literary, linguistic, and historical research. The application, called the Text Encoding Initiative (TEI), developed as a major collaborative international initiative sponsored by the Association for Computers and the Humanities (ACH), the Association for Computational Linguistics (ACL) and the Association for Literary and Linguistic Computing (ALLC) (Text Encoding Initiative n.d.). It began with a planning meeting convened in November 1987, where leading humanities computing practitioners and representatives of existing text archives, who were tired of the incompatibilities and deficiencies in existing encoding schemes, agreed on a set of principles (the 'Poughkeepsie Principles') to govern the definition of a new encoding scheme for the encoding and interchange of electronic text (Burnard 1988).

The TEI formed an organizational structure which enabled a number of work groups to examine texts in their areas of interest and propose sets of SGML elements (Hockey 1991). Two editors then put together the resulting tags into a set of DTDs which are documented in two large volumes (Sperberg-McQueen and Burnard 1994). These volumes are guidelines in that they give recommendations on what features are to be encoded and how those features are to be encoded. The guidelines are intended for text in any kind of written or spoken language. They can be used by scholars and researchers who work with electronic textual resources in many disciplines and by the librarians who maintain and document these resources. The features discussed in the guidelines include both those which are explicitly marked and those which are the result of analysing and interpreting the text. Because of diversity of the texts, no simple set of absolute requirements can be applicable to all texts and purposes, but the encoding of a certain minimum number of features is highly recommended. In many types of textual analysis, the textual features studied vary widely depending upon the theoretical orientation of the researcher. The TEI approach to dealing with a wide variety of text types was to attempt to define a comparatively small number of basic textual features, and to allow for these to be used in combination with user-definable sets of more specialized features. This approach also has the advantage of being extensible, allowing for additional tags and tag sets to be incorporated later.

The TEI guidelines are built on the assumption that virtually all texts share a common core of features, to which can be added tags for a specific discipline, text type, or application. The encoding process is seen as incremental, so that additional tags may be inserted in a text as new researchers work on it. The guidelines provide for multiple views of a text and multiple encodings for individual phenomena within a text. They also provide a means of documenting any interpretation so that a new user of the text can know why that interpretation is there. The encoder can choose whether to encode in a way which makes it possible to recover the source completely, or whether to use a more interpretative form of encoding where the source is not directly recoverable.

A TEI DTD is built up from a number of tag sets in a manner that has been likened to the preparation of a pizza with a base, essential ingredients (tomato and cheese), and one or more toppings (Sperberg-McQueen and Burnard 1995: 27). The base is one tag set chosen from the following: prose, drama, verse, dictionaries, spoken texts, and terminological data. The essential ingredients are the core tags—a set of tags common to all text types and including features such as abbreviations, simple forms of names, quotations, and bibliographic citations—and another set of tags called the header which provide metadata for documenting the text. Optional additional tag sets (the 'toppings') include critical apparatus, names and dates, transcription of primary sources, hypertext linking across documents, and simple forms of linguistic analysis. Mechanisms are provided for modifying existing tags or adding new ones. Although the TEI has defined over 400 tags, the user can choose what is appropriate. In fact very few tags are required and these are mostly in the header which provides the metadata.

This model for building the DTD is not very easy for beginners, especially when they are working with complex texts. A simplified 'starter set' of TEI elements has been defined in a single DTD called TEILite (Burnard and Sperberg-McQueen 1995). This includes most of the core tags, basic structural components, and an adequate set of header elements. TEILite is a good starting point for simple analyses, but it is more appropriate for large collections of text which are being made available as part of a digital library project than for a detailed analysis of a small number of texts. New approaches to the DTD using a technique called architectural forms are now being proposed (Simons, Sperberg-McQueen, and Durand 1999).

A TEI text consists of a header followed by the body of the text. The TEI header is believed to be the first systematic attempt to provide in-file metadata for an electronic text. Including the metadata in the text file not only ensures that it does not get detached from the file or lost, but also enables it to be processed by the same software (Giordano 1994, 1995). The header consists of four sections. Of these the file description is the most important. It contains a full bibliographic description of the electronic file, which can be used for creating catalogue entries or bibliographic citations. Three elements are mandatory within the file description. A title statement gives the title of work and those responsible for its intellectual content. A publication statement identifies the publication or distribution of an electronic text. A source description gives a bibliographic description of the source or copy text from which the electronic text was derived. Additional optional elements provide a means of documenting who was responsible for making the intellectual decisions necessary for creating the electronic text and their role in doing so.

The second section, the encoding description, documents the methods and editorial principles which governed the transcription of the text. It describes the aim or purpose for which an electronic text was compiled, the rationale and methods used in sampling texts, and details of the editorial principles and practices applied during the encoding of the text. The third section, the profile description, collects together more information about the creation of a text, if this cannot be inferred from the bibliographic description. It includes details of the languages used in a text which might be helpful for processing it, and also, for spoken texts, further details of the situation in which the text was produced and a description of the participants in the conversation. The revision history is the final major section provided in the header. It provides a log of every change made to the text including what the change was, who made it, and when it was made.

The TEI has a special mechanism for handling the metadata for a corpus or other composite text. In this case some of the information which goes in the header is relevant for all the corpus, whereas other elements change for each unit or individual text within the composite collection. A corpus header provides information common to the entire composite text and individual headers identify distinctive elements for each component within the composite text. Mechanisms are also supplied for dealing with multiple occurrences of certain elements in the corpus and text headers. Dunlop (1995) describes the implementation of headers in the BNC.

The following example shows the beginning of Catherine Mumford Booth's *The Iniquity of State Regulated Vice* as encoded in TEI SGML by the Victorian Women Writers Project at Indiana University (Willett 1999). This text uses many tags in the header, but the encoding is much lighter once the text itself begins. Other texts in the collection have very similar material in the header and so it is possible to work with a template header for each new text, changing only those tags which are different.

```
<!DOCTYPE TEI.2 PUBLIC "-//TEI//DTD TEI Lite 1.6//EN" "../teilite.dtd" [
<!ENTITY amp SDATA "[amp ]">
<!ENTITY copy SDATA "[copy ]">
<!ENTITY eacute SDATA "[eacute]">
<!ENTITY gt SDATA "[gt ]">
<!ENTITY ldquo SDATA "[ldquo ]">
<!ENTITY lsquo SDATA "[lsquo ]">
<!ENTITY lt SDATA "[lt ]">
<!ENTITY mdash SDATA "[mdash ]">
<!ENTITY rdquo SDATA "[rdquo ]">
<!ENTITY rsquo SDATA "[rsquo ]">
]>
<TEI.2>
<TEIHEADER>
<FILEDESC>
<TITLESTMT>
<TITLE>The Iniquity of State Regulated Vice
<DATE>(1884)</DATE>:</TITLE>
<TITLE TYPE="gmd">a machine-readable transcription</TITLE>
<AUTHOR><NAME KEY="ECP1708">Booth,
Catherine Mumford</NAME> (1829–1890)</AUTHOR>
<RESPSTMT>
<RESP>Transcribed and encoded by</RESP>
<NAME>Margaret E. Parks</NAME>
</RESPSTMT>
<RESPSTMT>
```

```
<RESP>Edited by </RESP>
<NAME>Perry Willett</NAME>
</RESPSTMT>
</TITLESTMT>
<EXTENT>TEI formatted filesize uncompressed: approx. 22 kbytes
   </EXTENT>
<PUBLICATIONSTMT>
<PUBLISHER>Library Electronic Text Resource Service (LETRS), Indiana
University</PUBLISHER>
<PUBPLACE>Bloomington, IN</PUBPLACE>
<DATE>1996-Aug-30</DATE>
<AVAILABILITY>
<P> &copy; 1996, The Trustees of Indiana University. Indiana University
makes a claim of copyright only to original contributions made by the
Victorian Women Writers Project participants and other members of the
university community. Indiana University makes no claim of copyright to
the original text. Permission is granted to download, transmit or otherwise
reproduce, distribute or display the contributions to this work claimed by
Indiana University for non-profit educational purposes, provided that this
header is included in its entirety. For inquiries about commercial uses, please
contact:
<ADDRESS>
<ADDRLINE>Library Electronic Text Resource Service</ADDRLINE>
<ADDRLINE>Main Library</ADDRLINE>
<ADDRLINE>Indiana University</ADDRLINE>
<ADDRLINE>Bloomington, IN 47405</ADDRLINE>
<ADDRLINE>United States of America</ADDRLINE>
<ADDRLINE>EMail: LETRS@indiana.edu</ADDRLINE>
</ADDRESS></P>
</AVAILABILITY>
</PUBLICATIONSTMT>
<SERIESSTMT>
<TITLE>Victorian Women Writers Project: an Electronic Collection</TITLE>
<RESPSTMT>
<NAME>Perry Willett, </NAME>
<RESP>General Editor.</RESP>
</RESPSTMT>
</SERIESSTMT>
<SOURCEDESC>
<BIBLFULL>
<TITLESTMT>
<TITLE>The Iniquity of State Regulated Vice. A Speech Delivered at Exeter
   Hall, London, on February 6th, 1884.</TITLE>
<RESPSTMT>
<RESP>by </RESP>
<NAME>Catherine Mumford Booth.</NAME>
```

```
</RESPSTMT>
</TITLESTMT>
<EXTENT>14 p.</EXTENT>
<PUBLICATIONSTMT>
<PUBLISHER>Dyer Brothers </PUBLISHER>
<PUBPLACE>London: </PUBPLACE>
<DATE>[1884].</DATE>
</PUBLICATIONSTMT>
</BIBLFULL>
</SOURCEDESC>
</FILEDESC>
<ENCODINGDESC>
<EDITORIALDECL>
<P>All quotation marks, dashes, and apostrophes have been transcribed as
entity references.</P>
<P>Any hyphens occurring in line breaks have been removed; all hyphens are
encoded as "-" and em dashes as &amp;mdash;.</P>
<P>All quoted sections that are italicized in the original are enclosed in
&lt;q&gt;; all other quoted sections are transcribed without encoding. All
text encoded as &lt;emph&gt; is to be rendered in italics unless specified
in the "rend" attribute. All names that appear in all caps are enclosed in
&lt;name&gt;.</P>
<P>The list of pamphlets following p. 14 has been omitted.</P>
</EDITORIALDECL>
<TAGSDECL>
<TAGUSAGE GI="ADDRESS" OCCURS="1"></TAGUSAGE>
<TAGUSAGE GI="ADDRLINE" OCCURS="2"></TAGUSAGE>
<TAGUSAGE GI="BODY" OCCURS="1"></TAGUSAGE>
<TAGUSAGE GI="BYLINE" OCCURS="1"></TAGUSAGE>
<TAGUSAGE GI="DIV1" OCCURS="1"></TAGUSAGE>
<TAGUSAGE GI="DOCAUTHOR" OCCURS="1"></TAGUSAGE>
<TAGUSAGE GI="DOCEDITION" OCCURS="2"></TAGUSAGE>
<TAGUSAGE GI="DOCIMPRINT" OCCURS="1"></TAGUSAGE>
<TAGUSAGE GI="DOCTITLE" OCCURS="1"></TAGUSAGE>
<TAGUSAGE GI="EMPH" OCCURS="8"></TAGUSAGE>
<TAGUSAGE GI="FRONT" OCCURS="1"></TAGUSAGE>
<TAGUSAGE GI="HEAD" OCCURS="1"></TAGUSAGE>
<TAGUSAGE GI="ORIG" OCCURS="1"></TAGUSAGE>
<TAGUSAGE GI="P" OCCURS="12"></TAGUSAGE>
<TAGUSAGE GI="PB" OCCURS="12"></TAGUSAGE>
<TAGUSAGE GI="PUBLISHER" OCCURS="1"></TAGUSAGE>
<TAGUSAGE GI="PUBPLACE" OCCURS="1"></TAGUSAGE>
<TAGUSAGE GI="TEXT" OCCURS="1"></TAGUSAGE>
<TAGUSAGE GI="TITLEPAGE" OCCURS="1"></TAGUSAGE>
<TAGUSAGE GI="TITLEPART" OCCURS="2"></TAGUSAGE>
</TAGSDECL>
```

```
</ENCODINGDESC>
<REVISIONDESC>
<CHANGE>
<DATE>1999-Oct-05</DATE>
<RESPSTMT>
<NAME>Perry Willett,</NAME>
<RESP>general editor.</RESP>
</RESPSTMT>
<ITEM>Standardized encoding to Level 4.</ITEM>
</CHANGE>
<CHANGE>
<DATE>1996-Aug-27</DATE>
<RESPSTMT>
<NAME>Margaret Parkes</NAME>
<RESP>editor.</RESP>
</RESPSTMT>
<ITEM>transcribed and encoded.</ITEM>
</CHANGE>
<CHANGE>
<DATE>1996-Aug-30</DATE>
<RESPSTMT>
<NAME>Perry Willett, </NAME>
<RESP>general editor.</RESP>
</RESPSTMT>
<ITEM>Finished TEI-conformant encoding and proofing.</ITEM>
</CHANGE>
<CHANGE>
<DATE>1996-Oct-19</DATE>
<RESPSTMT>
<NAME>Perry Willett, </NAME>
<RESP>general editor.</RESP>
</RESPSTMT>
<ITEM>fixed entity references to be SDATA</ITEM>
</CHANGE>
</REVISIONDESC>
</TEIHEADER>
<TEXT>
<FRONT>
<TITLEPAGE>
<DOCTITLE>
<TITLEPART>THE INIQUITY OF STATE REGULATED VICE.
   </TITLEPART>
<TITLEPART TYPE="sub">A SPEECH DELIVERED AT EXETER HALL,
   LONDON, ON FEBRUARY 6TH, 1884,</TITLEPART>
</DOCTITLE>
<BYLINE>By
```

<DOCAUTHOR>MRS. BOOTH,</DOCAUTHOR> Of the Salvation Army.
  </BYLINE>
<DOCIMPRINT>
<PUBPLACE>LONDON:</PUBPLACE>
<PUBLISHER>DYER BROTHERS,
<ADDRESS>
<ADDRLINE>AMEN CORNER,</ADDRLINE>
<ADDRLINE>PATERNOSTER ROW.</ADDRLINE>
</ADDRESS></PUBLISHER></DOCIMPRINT>
<DOCEDITION>May be ordered through Booksellers everywhere.
  </DOCEDITION>
<DOCEDITION>PRICE ONE PENNY.</DOCEDITION>
</TITLEPAGE>
</FRONT>
<BODY>
<DIV1 TYPE="text">
<PB>
<HEAD>THE INIQUITY OF STATE REGULATED VICE.</HEAD>
<P>At a large meeting at Exeter Hall, London, called to protest against the State regulation of vice in England and our Colonies, Mrs. Booth, of the Salvation Army, delivered the following speech. The resolution to which she spoke read as follows:&mdash;</P>
<P>&ldquo;That this meeting looks with confidence to the House of Commons, and to Her Majesty&apos;s Ministers, to complete the work already commenced, by the total repeal of the so-called Contagious Diseases Acts, and hopes to see the Government of our country cleared from all complicity with the traffickers in vice. It trusts that laws may be passed in the future having more regard to the equal treatment of men and women, and for the better protection of the young; and requests the Chairman to sign a Petition to this effect, on behalf of this meeting,
<PB ID="p4" N="4">
and send copies of the Resolutions to the Right Hon. W. E. Gladstone, M.P.; the Marquis of Hartington, the Earl of Northbrook, and Sir W. Vernon Harcourt, M.P.&rdquo;</P>
<P>Mrs. Booth said:&mdash; Mr. Chairman, Ladies and Gentlemen: I feel that I can most heartily move the resolution which you have just heard read. I can do so, because with its fundamental doctrine, I am agreed. The next best thing to doing the right, is to be willing to pause and retract when we have done wrong. I take it as a sign of nobility, either in an individual, or in a Government when a false step has been taken, either through inadvertence &mdash;or, as Mr.Gladstone says, &lsquo;through obscurity&rsquo;&mdash; for he says these Acts were introduced into the English Statute Book in obscurity. I take it as a sign of nobility, if one having made a false step is willing to retract it. (Cheers.) And therefore, I gratefully, as one of the women of England, acknowledge the action of the English Government in thus retracing its steps. And I also praise God fervently for the wisdom given to the Government in the

re-consideration of this question—and I earnestly pray, (and I am sure every pure-hearted man and woman will say ‘Amen’), that God will continue to give this wisdom to the Government, and will enable them presently to blot off from the Statute Book laws so infamous.</P>
<PB ID="p5" N="5">
<P>Apart from this rectifying action on the part of the Government, I must confess that the deepest feeling of my soul in rising to speak on this subject is that of intense <EMPH>shame!</EMPH> shame that it should be necessary at this period of our national history, to stand on this Exeter Hall platform to plead for the repeal of such measures as those you have discussed to-night.</P>
<P>I can only conceive of one greater shame possible, and that would be, to shrink from the necessity which has been imposed upon us.</P>
<P>I do not know how other friends feel, but I have felt almost ashamed that I have become only recently acquainted with this question. Having been engaged every day of my life in striving to destroy the roots not only of unchastity, but of all impurity, I considered that I was doing the best thing to promote this kind of purity—but when dear Mrs. Butler, some two years ago, sent me a pamphlet, I felt reproved that I had not acquainted myself with the matter sooner, for I feel that every true woman in England, who will really examine the question, must feel bound to give her influence towards the repeal of these abominable Acts. I have been told, and I dare say our friends on the platform have been told, that it is a disgrace for a woman to meddle with this question. But I say if measures are passed which are so obnoxious that it is a disgrace and abomination to discuss them—the
<PB ID="p6" N="6">
odium of such disgrace rests with those who instituted them. (Cheers.) And not with those who offer themselves as the butt of public ridicule and scorn in their efforts to get them repealed. (Cheers.)</P>
<P>For my own part I look forward with admiration and reverence on those noble few who have taken the lead in this movement, and especially on dear Mrs. Butler, who has endured the worst insinuations of bad men, and the contempt of uninformed or weak women, in carrying forward this agitation for repeal. I say all honour to them. Future generations will call them blessed. (Hear, hear.) Their experience has been to us a wonderful and beautiful exemplification of the truth that to the pure all things are pure. And <EMPH>nothing more so than the exposure of impurity for its destruction! </EMPH> May God bless the noble band who have been enduring for sixteen years ignominy, contempt, and misrepresentation, our Chairman amongst the number, and all who have helped them.</P>

...

</DIV0></BODY></TEXT></TEI.2>

The TEI is a most significant achievement in humanities computing and it is having an impact in wider circles. The TEI made a decision to use SGML when SGML was still relatively new, but the mid-1990s saw a rapid increase in the use of SGML as more companies recognized the need for machine-independent markup. The TEI's use of SGML provides a much better mechanism than any other encoding scheme for handling the complexities of scholarly texts in the humanities, for example the critical apparatus, marginal notes, changes of language and script, for which adequate encoding schemes have never previously been available. Notes can be linked to the main text as it is being searched and separate indexes can easily be made for the different languages in a multilingual text. The TEI has also developed mechanisms for encoding the results of linguistic analysis and other interpretative material (literary and historical), which permit more than one analysis to be given for a text, even if these analyses conflict with each other. More than anything, by encouraging a thorough analysis of the features in a text, the TEI ensures that encoders think seriously about the material they are encoding.

There are a few areas which are not treated so well in the 1994 version of the TEI guidelines. The TEI is poor on encoding for analytic bibliography, but tag sets for this could easily be added within the TEI framework as was demonstrated by Bauman and Catapano (1999). The TEI does not have specific recommendations for encoding newspapers, which are difficult since they represent a microcosm of many different types of material. There is a need for extension of the spoken text material and for types of literary analysis, especially for verse. SGML can also be used to surround images or other multimedia information, but this is another area where the TEI is not particularly strong, although it does have some mechanisms for pointing to positions within images, or to audio or video. It is only when researchers begin to use a set of guidelines that the need for extensions becomes apparent, but the TEI was designed in a modular way in order to facilitate further development. Some groups, for example the Model Editions Partnership, have used the TEI as a basis for their own guidelines which they have also made available on the Web (Chesnutt, Hockey, and Sperberg-McQueen 1999).

SGML does have one problem which is particularly apparent in humanities material. It tends to assume that a document is a single hierarchic structure and that each element nests neatly within another element. As we have seen in the example above (for COCOA), multiple parallel hierarchies are very common in existing texts. The TEI guidelines suggest that one way to solve this problem is to choose one main hierarchy for the text and to encode features apparent in other hierarchies as what it calls 'milestone' tags, that is, empty tags or tags which have no content, but simply mark a position in the text. This takes away some of the power of SGML, since an SGML parser cannot carry out any validation on a milestone tag. Various other solutions have been proposed (Barnard *et al.* 1988, 1995). In fact the SGML standard does include a function called CONCUR which is intended to handle multiple hierarchies. The syntax of this function is rather clumsy because it requires a DTD for each hierarchy, and thus the name of the appropriate hierarchy must be given with each element. It has been implemented in very few SGML-aware programs.

An alternative encoding scheme, which is rather like SGML, has been developed for the Wittgenstein Archives at the University of Bergen (Sperberg-McQueen and Huitfeldt 1999). Called MECS (Multi-Element Coding System), this encoding scheme permits overlap very neatly in the form (using the MECS syntax) of

<a/ xxxx <b/ yyyyy /a> zzzzz /b>

but at some cost to the user. Although MECS has what it calls a Code Declaration Table which declares the tags in a particular document, this does not provide any kind of document grammar like that of an SGML DTD. Therefore it is not possible to validate MECS markup in the same way as SGML. In their paper, Sperberg-McQueen and Huitfeldt discuss the relative merits of MECS and CONCUR and possible methods of conversion from one to the other. They finally recommend CONCUR because of the added processing power, but the examples appear clumsy when compared to the MECS format.

Other new developments in markup have centred around XML (Extensible Markup Language) (Bray, Paoli, and Sperberg-McQueen 1998). XML is subset of SGML which is designed to run directly on the Web. It makes it possible for Web documents to be encoded in markup tags which more closely reflect the nature of the documents and the features within them. Like SGML, XML is a syntax framework within which groups of users can define their own markup tags. It is expected that XML will run directly on the Web just as HTML does now. A number of other XML-related standards including a style-sheet language called XSL are being developed. With XSL it will be possible to program a Web browser to carry out many more functions on an electronic text than is now possible with HTML. Thus the manner in which the Web operates will begin to shift from the server, where most of the processing is now carried out, to the client (the user's computer). Web documents will be downloaded to the user's computer, where the user will be able to carry out many more operations on them. Developments in the XML world are moving very fast and it is pleasing to note that several of the ideas first promoted by the TEI have been taken up in XML. XML does not, however, address the multiple hierarchy problem.

Exactly what markup scheme to use depends very much on the nature of the project. For a digital library or large and long-term project, it makes sense to use SGML, or rather XML, for which there is likely to be more support. The TEI is a very good starting point for humanities material and can be used as a basis for the development of a specialized encoding scheme. However, the TEI uses some of the features of SGML which are not being implemented in XML and work is now in hand to create an XML-compatible version of the TEI. Software tools for processing SGML/XML are not trivial, and a project which uses SGML needs ready access to an SGML expert or to develop the necessary expertise. SGML also has the added advantage of not being tied to any particular program. Text encoded in SGML will outlast many computer systems and ensure that the investment remains in the data (Hockey 1999). The individual humanities scholar may be better working with a simpler markup scheme which is processable by desktop tools such as Concordance. It is not difficult to devise such a scheme and, if the basic principles of SGML/XML are understood, the scheme can be converted automatically to SGML/XML for the archival version of the material.

The level of interest generated by the TEI has been such that a whole new research area has grown up around markup theory and practice (Mylonas and Renear 1999). Some of the most significant contributions have been made by philosophers, and interested readers can follow the development of structured markup theory from the initial explorations made by Coombs, Renear, and DeRose (1987), to the ordered hierarchy of content objects (OHCO) theory developed by Renear, Durand, and Mylonas (1996) to Renear's (1997) three meta-theories of textuality. The OHCO theory (what Renear calls 'Platonism') works reasonably for new documents, particularly office documents and technical manuals where some control on the document structure is needed. The TEI community needed to encode the multiple hierarchies in existing documents and to treat text as structures of objects, thus giving rise to the second theory, Pluralism. Renear's third theory, Antirealism, sees texts as products of 'theories and analytical tools we deploy when we transcribe etc' (1997: 122). Huitfeldt has a number of problems with the TEI approach to encoding, arguing that 'there are no facts about a text which are objective in the sense of not being interpretational' (1994: 278). If our understanding of a text is fundamentally interpretational, there are some methodological problems with an SGML/XML-based approach which is fundamentally hierarchic. Pieces of hierarchies linked together may be a solution, but it is not clear yet how this might work out in practice. See also Biggs and Huitfeldt (1997) for a summary of these discussions and Buzzetti (1999) who reflects on the conceptual status of markup, speculating that it might be a sort of metalinguistic description, or an extension of text representation.

It is clearer now than ever that inserting markup in a text is an act of interpretation. This raises questions of what the interpretation is and therefore who is doing the markup. Perhaps the markup can be done by a keyboarding company if the typographic markup is followed exactly, with the expectation that it can be converted to a syntax if not the specifics of structured markup. But if somebody has made some kind of interpretation, the markup should record who made these decisions and why. Anyone who begins to put more than very simple markup in a text faces immediate questions and difficulties. See Sperberg-McQueen (1991) and Brown *et al.* (1997) for discussions of these issues in two very different areas; see also Greenstein (1991) for various problems associated with encoding historical data. Debates about markup will no doubt continue for a long time, but markup theory, especially that developed among the humanities computing community, is a research area which is leading to better understanding of knowledge representation and manipulation.

4 | Concordance and Text Retrieval Programs

Concordance and text retrieval programs form the basic tools for most kinds of text analysis. Much early work in literary and linguistic computing was based on these tools. Although user interfaces and hardware systems have made significant advances, since these early projects there has been much less development in terms of software functionality. Later chapters, especially Chapter 6, will look at some possibilities for analysing text beyond the level of the graphic word or sequence of characters, but here we will concern ourselves with the functions of some basic tools. In later chapters we will also examine some applications of these tools. Many of the issues concerning alphabetization, context units, and ambiguous symbols discussed in early papers on concordance making are still relevant today. Burton (1981a, 1981b, 1981c, 1982) gives an overview of concordance making up to 1981. Wisbey (1962) also gives some early history. Howard-Hill (1979) discusses several important aspects, but mostly from the perspective of concordance making on Renaissance English texts. For a further discussion of these issues and more examples see Sinclair (1991) and Hockey (1998).

What we shall call a 'batch' concordance program operates on a raw text, usually a plain ASCII file, and generates an analysis by carrying out a sequential search on this raw text for every user request. We shall see later that this method offers flexibility, but it is not feasible for large texts. Much text analysis nowadays is based on interactive searching rather than on batch concordances. Interactive retrieval programs are able to provide instant responses to search requests because they query an index which has been built earlier by a separate computer program. They assume that the index is built once and that every query operates on the same index. This index is in fact a kind of concordance designed for use by a computer program rather than by a human. Therefore most principles of concordance building are just as relevant for interactive retrieval programs. The decisions made in designing the computer programs which construct this index and then deliver portions of text in response to user queries are much the same as the decisions made in creating a batch concordance.

The tools discussed in this chapter are designed to carry out a detailed analysis of words, phrases, or other components of a text or collection of texts. In contrast with document retrieval programs, text analysis programs deliver the number of instances of the search word and present the user with information about the occurrences of the word, rather than the texts in which it occurs. Although there is some overlap in these applications, and this overlap has become easier to work with since the advent of SGML/XML-based markup systems, document retrieval programs are not really suitable for detailed text analysis, particularly of humanities material.

The most basic function of a concordance program is to generate a word frequency list (hereafter 'word list') giving a count of the number of occurrences of each word. The words are normally presented in alphabetical order or order of their frequency of occurrence. Figure 4.1 shows the beginning of a word list of Jane Austen's *Emma*. Here we see that the most frequent word *the* (5,204 occurrences) is followed closely

the	5204	Mr	1154	from	546
to	5186	his	1150	they	541
and	4878	at	1032	What	536
of	4292	so	972	this	526
I	3187	all	846	or	494
a	3126	could	837	Such	489
It	2529	would	820	much	486
her	2482	Emma	784	if	485
was	2400	him	771	said	484
she	2364	been	760	more	469
in	2174	no	741	an	463
not	2151	my	732	are	455
You	1999	Mrs	701	one	443
be	1975	on	691	them	436
he	1811	any	654	every	435
that	1800	do	637	Harriet	415
had	1626	Miss	602	than	415
but	1440	were	601	am	414
as	1437	me	583	thing	397
for	1347	must	571	Weston	388
have	1321	by	568	think	384
is	1243	will	559	well	384
With	1218	which	556	How	371
very	1212	there	551	should	371

FIG. 4.1. Part of a word frequency list of *Emma*

by *to* (5,186 occurrences) with *and* (4,878 occurrences) coming third. The list tails rapidly. The word list also gives totals, not shown here, indicating that there are 159,613 words in this version of *Emma*, but with only 9,320 different words. We see from a further frequency analysis that 2,990 words occur once, 1,079 occur twice, and 554 occur three times. General frequency counts will be discussed in more detail in Chapter 6, but the usual pattern of a few high frequency words with many low frequency words can be seen here. Perhaps also worth noting is the high position of *I* in the list, undoubtedly due to the large amount of dialogue in the novel.

A word index gives a list of words accompanied by a reference indicating where each word occurs in the text. This is the form which is most often described as a 'concordance' in the earlier concordances built before the advent of computers (McCarty 1993b). The nature of these references depends on the structure of the text, but they would normally be something like page and line number, or title of poem and line number, or act, scene, and speaker, or identification of speaker and transcript for spoken texts. Figure 4.2 shows part of a word index of *The Merchant of Venice*. Here the references are act, scene, speaker, and line number. As an aside, it appears that this program is able to sort roman numerals correctly. Normally these would be treated as letters, causing IX to appear before V, but with a little ingenuity this problem can be avoided.

```
hanging  2  II.II Launc. 12;        V.I Lor. 81
II.IX Ner. 82
                                     harder  1  IV.I Ant. 78
hangman's  1  IV.I Grat. 124
                                     hardly  1  III.III Ant. 35
happier  1  III.II Por. 161
                                     hare  1  I.II Por. 19
Happiest  1  III.II Por. 163
                                     hark  2  V.I Jess. 30; V.I Por. 97
happily  1  II.II Bass. 174
                                     harm  1  I.I Salar. 25
happiness  1  I.II Ner. 7
                                     harmless  1  IV.I Shyl. 54
happy  4  III.II Bass. 164;
III.II Por. 160; III.IV Lor. 42;     harmony  2  V.I Lor. 57;
V.I Steph. 32                        V.I Lor. 63

harbour  1  V.I Por. 282            harsh  1  IV.I Grat. 122

hard  10  I.II Por. 25;             has  2  II.II Gob. 90;
I.III Shyl. 163; II.II Launc. 26;   II.II Launc. 104
II.II Gob. 41; III.I Shyl. 67;
III.II Bass. 102; III.II Jess. 290;  hast  10  II.II Gob. 88;
IV.I Ant. 77; IV.I Ner. 145;        II.II Gob. 89; II.II Bass. 139;
```

FIG. 4.2. Part of a word index of *The Merchant of Venice*

```
                                   run       17
1  3  65  y of wholesome food, let them     run  about a great deal in the summer, a
1  7  98  t deceive yourself; do not be     run  away with by gratitude and compassi
1  9 115  h were otherwise of a sort to     run  into great length, by the eagerness
1  9 197  course of true love never did     run  smooth-- A Hartfield edition of Sha
1 13  46    all the benefit of a country   run,  and seemed to ensure a quick despa
1 13  57  friend. Let me entreat you to     run  no risks. Why does not Perry see he
2  6  48  e neighbourhood than from any     run  on the road; and his companions had
2  7 185    this. I am sure, rather than    run  the risk of hurting Mr. and Mrs. Co
2  8 460    up an idea, Mrs. Weston, and    run  away with it; as you have many a ti
2  9 156  " said the latter, "I am just      run  across to entreat the favour of you
2  9 165  e.-- Oh! then, said I, I must      run  across, I am sure Miss Woodhouse wi
2  9 166  odhouse will allow me just to     run  across and entreat her to come in;
2 16 172  e. Miss Fairfax, you must not     run  such risks.-- Liable as you have be
2 16 177    a day for your letters, than    run  the risk of bringing on your cough
2 18  60  ne lady, I assure you. Do not     run  away with such an idea." "Is not sh
3  7  60    broken bounds yesterday, and    run  away from your own management; but
3 13 232  ; but no flight of generosity      run  mad, opposing all that could be pro

                                   rung      1
1 15 142  " "Yes, do." And the bell was     rung, and the carriages spoken for. A f

                                   running   4
1  4 192  aiting; and Harriet then came     running to her with a smiling face, and
2  1 245  her." "I am afraid we must be     running away," said Emma, glancing at H
2  3 212  ar Jane, I believe we must be     running away. The weather does not look
3  7 298  lent; and Emma felt the tears     running down her cheeks almost all the

                                   runs      2
2  3 203  d. One takes up a notion, and     runs away with it. Mr. Dixon, you say,
3  5  83    air of probability sometimes   runs through a dream! And at others, wh
```

FIG. 4.3.   Part of a concordance of *Emma*

A concordance presents each occurrence of each word surrounded by some words of context and also normally accompanied by a reference. Figure 4.3 shows part of a concordance of Jane Austen's *Emma*. The entries are displayed in the keyword in context (KWIC) format where the keywords are aligned down the middle of the screen or page. The references to the left indicate the volume number, chapter number, and the line number within the chapter. In order to keep this example simple, the line numbers have been taken directly from the computer file and have been reset to 1 at the beginning of a new chapter. Line numbering is dealt with in more detail in Chapter 3.

The keywords or headwords in the concordance are the forms which appear in the word list or word index. On the surface it appears that it would be a very simple process for a computer to count or alphabetize words in a text. But two basic questions are raised here which are relevant for many other kinds of processing. They are: 'What is a "word"?' and 'What does "alphabetical order" mean?' As we will see, these questions are closely related to each other for computer processing. In order to alphabetize words a computer program has first to isolate each word and then to compare the words, letter by letter, and to rearrange them according to the appropriate alphabetical sequence of letters.

In a computer-generated word list, a 'word' is simply a sequence of letters, not a word according to what we expect from a dictionary definition. Figure 4.1 shows 397 occurrences of *thing*, but the word list also has 62 occurrences of *things* and 1 of *thing's*. These forms would obviously be closer together in the list if the words were in alphabetical order, but that would still not bring all the forms of some words together, for example *go* and *went* would still be a long way apart. In fact in this version of *Emma*, *go* occurs 132 times and *went* 46 times and we would also need to consider *goes*, *going*, and *gone* if we wanted to examine all forms of the verb *to go*.

Some of the words in Figure 4.1 have initial capitals and, obviously, some of these, such as *I*, *Emma*, *Miss*, are always capitalized. A few, such as *With*, *What*, and *Such*, are not normally capitalized except at the beginning of a sentence. The concordance program has almost certainly found instances of these three words with and without initial capitals and it must therefore make some decision about what form to display. Some programs allow the user to indicate whether all the words should have initial capitals or even be entirely in capitals. Others, such as this program, display the form which comes to the top at the end of the sorting process. It would be possible to program the computer to display the form without initial capitals if that one is found at all, but this might be problematic if the text contains proper names such as *Brown* or *White*, which also occur as words in their own right.

The definition of a word as a group of letters separated from other words only by spaces is much too simple for most purposes. Word separators need to include punctuation symbols which are not normally treated as parts of words for alphabetization, but may need to be handled in this way in some circumstances. Moreover, in many texts, 'words' do not only contain letters. Consider the following lines from *Hamlet* Act 3, Scene 3:

> Were thicker than itself with brother's blood,
> Is there not rain enough in the sweet heavens
> To wash it white as snow? Whereto serves mercy
> But to confront the visage of offence?
> And what's in prayer but this two-fold force,
> To be forestalled ere we come to fall,
> Or pardon'd being down? Then I'll look up;

These lines contain four instances of an apostrophe. In the word *brother's*, the apostrophe introduces the genitive *'s*. In *what's*, and *I'll*, it represents a contraction of two words *what is* and *I will*, the *I'll* form being very common in English. In *pardon'd*, the apostrophe is a contraction within a single word. There is also one hyphenated word *two-fold*. For automatic alphabetization, rules must be defined for the treatment of apostrophes, and, unless an exception list can be provided and acted upon by the program, or unless some markup is inserted for specific instances, the same set of rules must apply to all apostrophes. If the apostrophe was ignored for the purposes of sorting words, *brother's* would be treated as if it was the same form as the plural *brothers* and *I'll* would be treated as the same word as *ill*.

Similar questions arise with hyphenated words. Is *two-fold* one word or two? Should it be treated as if it was the same as *twofold*? And what would happen if it occurred in a prose text at the end of a line and was hyphenated because of typographic constraints? It would be possible for a program to reconstitute hyphenated words at the ends of lines, but true hyphens in compound words would either be lost, or would need to be provided in an exception list.

If hyphen and apostrophe were treated in the same way as punctuation characters which function as word separators, *I'll* would be listed as two words, *I* and the form *ll*, which does not make sense on its own. *What's* would be *what* and the nonsensical form *s*. *Two-fold* would be the two words *two* and *fold*. In most cases it makes best sense for hyphen and apostrophe in English to be treated as a kind of secondary sort key, often called diacritics. When words are being compared for alphabetization, these characters are only considered when all the other letters are the same. This would also cause forms such as *'tis* and *'twas* to be alphabetized under the letter *t*.

Accented characters in modern European languages also need special treatment for alphabetization. For example in French all the occurrences of the preposition *à* ought to appear immediately after all those of *a* (part of *avoir*) but before any word beginning *aa* or *ab*, and *élève* should be a separate form from *élevé*. It turns out that these characters can be treated as secondary sort keys in exactly the same way as hyphens and other diacritics.

Literary texts in particular can also include other characters embedded in words. These might be brackets surrounding editorial reconstructions, for example *a[nd]*, or denoting the expansion of abbreviations as in *Dec{ember}*. In this case these characters might need to be ignored when words are being compared for alphabetization, so that the occurrences of *and*, *a[nd]*, *an[d]*, *[a]nd*, *[and]*, and any other possible combination of *and* with embedded square brackets are all treated as the same word. This gives rise to a third type of character for alphabetization, often called 'padding' or 'non-sorting'. The headword *and* includes all the possible forms and, since only headwords appear in a word list, it would only be possible to see the different forms in concordance entries.

Letters cannot be alphabetized according to their native representation as bit patterns within a computer because upper and lower case letters are different in these representations. As we saw in the word list example above, upper and lower case normally need to be treated as equivalent for alphabetization, so that, for example, the word forms *the* and *The* are considered to be the same word even though they have different representations in the computer and for display. In fact this question of capitalization is a very common but specific instance of a more general issue of treating letters as equivalents for alphabetization which the computer can be programmed to do for any letters if the user so wishes.

Of course many languages do not follow the English alphabet order. A good concordance program should allow flexible alphabet definitions so that words can be sorted according to any order defined by the user. For example, a Greek alphabet might begin alpha, beta, gamma, delta, or *a, b, g, d* in a simple transcription form, although for ancient Greek it may need to allow for the many combinations of accents and breathing marks which are perhaps best treated as diacritics. Spanish may require doubled characters *ch, ll,* and *rr* to be separate letters of the alphabet so that, for example, *chico* appears after *cuatro*. It is not difficult to write a computer program to handle flexible alphabets, but it is surprising how few programs actually allow this.

The best programs perform some validation on the characters in a text and generate warnings when they encounter a character whose function has not been defined in any way. The first attempt to make a concordance of this text of *Emma* showed some instances of the character & in the text. A quick scan with a word processor indicated that this was part of &c. for *etcetera*. Placing & at the end of the alphabet causes all the instances of &c to appear at the end of the concordance. It is also surprising how many numerals are contained within texts, particularly informative texts such as newspapers. A first concordance attempt will often produce many 'words' which consist of numerals such as dates, for example *1997*, or forms such as *1st* or *8th* or *15–20*. The researcher must decide whether these are in fact to be treated as 'words' and then whether they should appear at the beginning or end of the word list. Many programs tend to place them at the beginning, which is disconcerting when the user first sees the list. Numerals are often also sorted as if they were sequences of letters, causing, for example, 103 to appear before 31 because 1 comes before 3.

Flexible alphabet definitions can be turned to other advantages. Sentences which end in certain features can be found by looking for punctuation preceded by the required feature or word. A search such as this can show the relatively high frequency of the word *thing* at the end of a sentence in *Emma*. Of the 397 occurrences of *thing* in *Emma*, 54 are followed immediately by a full stop. A further 10 precede a semi-colon and 7 precede a question mark. A good number of these forms are preceded by *every* or *any*, but the form *anything* occurs only twice and *everything* not at all. Of the 113 occurrences of *something*, only 1 is at the end of a sentence. The word *nothing* also occurs rather often at the end of a sentence with 20 of the 254 occurrences being followed by a full stop, a further 9 by a semi-colon, and 2 more by a colon. Of course a dot can also represent an abbreviation or a decimal point. In this case abbreviations are extremely unlikely, but if they are likely to occur, the easiest way to find them is to scan down a concordance in KWIC form.

Various options permit the retrieval of individual words. The simplest is of course the exact word itself, but the query may also include wild card (anything) characters. Unfortunately different programs offer a variety of different ways of expressing wild cards. The use of an asterisk (*) to denote any number of characters including none is common and well known to users of many computer systems. The query *at** finds any word beginning with *at* including the word *at*. The query *a*t* finds any word beginning with *a* and ending with *t* including *absent*, *acrobat*, and *at*. The query *a*t*e* finds any word beginning with *a*, with a *t* in the middle and ending with *e*, including *absolute, acquaintance, atone*, and *ate*. Another wild card character may denote any single letter. If this was a question mark (*?*), the query *b?d* would find *bad, bed, bid, bud*, but not *bead* or *betrayed*, and the query *b??d* would find *band, bird*, and *bead*. Yet another wild card character may denote at least one letter. If this was %, the query *a%t* would find *ant, acrobat*, and *absent*, but not *at*. Combining these options, the query *a?t%t*e* would find *anticipate, attentive, aptitude*, but not *attendance* or *architecture*.

What are called regular expressions provide a more sophisticated way of defining queries. Originally developed for computers running the Unix operating system, regular expressions have now been adopted by some other programs. For users new to regular expressions, the most important thing to remember is that an asterisk (*) does not mean any number of characters including none. It means zero or more occurrences of what comes before the asterisk. A full stop (period) means any single character and thus .* finds any number of characters including none. The regular expression to find any word beginning with *a* and ending with *t* is *a.*t*. The regular expression *b.d* finds *bad, bed, bid, bud,* but not *bead*. The regular expression *a.t..*t.*e* would be needed to find *anticipate, attentive, aptitude,* but not *attendance* or *architecture*.

Regular expressions provide more powerful features. These include ranges of characters where for example *[0–9]* means any digit from 0 to 9. Thus *a[0–9]* finds *a1, a2, a3* etc, *a[0–9]** finds *a* followed by zero or more digits, and *[a–z]01* finds any word that includes only lower-case letters and ends with 01. Square brackets are also used to denote alternatives. The regular expression *[bdg].*t* finds any word beginning with *b, d,* or *g* and ending with *t,* for example *bat, debit, got, beat, bright, disappoint,* and *government*. For more information on regular expressions see Lancashire *et al.* (1996: 58–60) and Friedl (1997).

Once the pattern features of a particular program have been understood, it is surprising how much useful work can be done without much extra effort. If the patterns find one or two unwanted words, it is much easier to delete these than to try to specify a much more complex program which might not work absolutely accurately in any case. Present participles in English can be found by a search for words ending in *-ing*. This will obviously include unwanted words such as *thing, something, anything, nothing, ring, wedding,* and *king*. Restricting the search to words of five letters or more would eliminate *ring* and *king,* but if the minimum number of letters is increased to six, we would also lose *doing, owing,* and *going*. Eliminating words ending in *-thing* would also lose *bathing* and *breathing* which we would want to keep. It is easy to spot these potential problems with a quick scan down the word list and a more accurate list of words can then be prepared for more detailed analysis.

Markup can obviously also be used to control the analysis. If appropriate markup were present, it would be possible to confine the analysis to only portions of a text. For example it might be appropriate to exclude quotations such as those from the Bible, or, if the text is in more than one natural language, to work separately with each of the languages. The analysis could perhaps also be applied only to dialogue or to narrative, or to certain characters within a play, or to certain types of verse within a large collection. A text analysis program operating on an SGML/XML-based markup scheme can also make use of the hierarchic structure, for example in a collection of many different kinds of historical documents to analyse quotations only when they are contained within diaries.

The words may be sorted according to different criteria, each of which can help to give a different view of the text. A quick scan over a word list in alphabetical order is usually sufficient to see the different

				bold	3
II.II	Bass.	173	art too wild, too rude and	bold	of voice
II.VII	Mor.	73	Had you been as wise as	bold	
III.II	Bass.	185	O, then be	bold	to say Bassanio's dead

				cold	4
I.II	Por.	18	a hot temper leaps o'er a	cold	decree
II.II	Bass.	178	To allay with some	cold	drops of modesty
II.VII	Mor.	74	are you well; your suit is	cold	
II.VII	Mor.	75		Cold,	indeed; and labour lost

				enfold	1
II.VII	Mor.	70	Gilded tombs do worms	enfold	

				unfold	1
II.IX	Arr.	10	First, never to	unfold	to any one

				gold	15
I.II	Ner.	29	d in these three chests of	gold,	silver
I.III	Ant.	95	Or is your	gold	and silver ewes and rams
II.IV	Lor.	30	What	gold	and jewels she is furnish'
II.VII	Mor.	4	The first, of	gold,	who this inscription bear
II.VII	Mor.	36	more this saying graved in	gold	
II.VII	Mor.	53	times undervalued to tried	gold	
II.VII	Mor.	55	Was set in worse than	gold.	They have in England
II.VII	Mor.	57	Stamped in	gold,	but that's insculp'd upon
II.VII	Mor.	66	All that glitters is not	gold	
II.IX	Arr.	19	To my heart's hope!	Gold;	silver; and base lead
III.I	Shyl.	103	my	gold	again: fourscore ducats at
III.II	Bass.	101	est. Therefore, thou gaudy	gold	
III.II	Por.	307	quiet soul. You shall have	gold	
V.I	Lor.	59	aid with patines of bright	gold	
V.I	Grat.	147	About a hoop of	gold,	a paltry ring

FIG. 4.4. Part of a reverse concordance of *The Merchant of Venice*

forms of a word and perhaps also to help refine the alphabet definitions. In a word list in frequency order, the once-occurring words may include misspellings or other errors. A frequency list also shows the need for a second sort key. Since there are many low-frequency words occurring once, twice, etc., all the words of the same frequency need to be sorted into alphabetical order as well. A reverse sort (assuming an English alphabetical order) gives words sorted on their endings, beginning with words ending in *a*, then with *b* etc. This can be very useful, especially for inflected languages and for rhyme schemes in verse. The repetition of words ending in *-old*, especially at the ends of lines, by the Prince of Morocco in *The Merchant of Venice* can be seen even from the short reverse concordance example in Figure 4.4.

The format and layout of the concordance entries can be controlled in several ways and sensible choices can reduce the amount of hand-editing or further processing of results to a minimum. The amount of text in the citation or context, as we shall call it, of each concordance entry can be defined in terms of logical units of text, for example lines, sentences (if these are tagged), speeches. It can also be specified in terms

```
                                       very    50
1 209 lor's advantage; she knows how very acceptable it must be, at Miss Tayl
1 216 joy to me," said Emma, "and a very considerable one--that I made the m
3 564 ding in the parish of Donwell-- very creditably, she believed--she knew
1 162 ." "But you must have found it very damp and dirty. I wish you may not
3 511 school was in high repute--and very deservedly; for Highbury was reckon
1   7 n mistress of his house from a very early period. Her mother had died t
2 410  there was such comfort in the very easy distance of Randalls from Hart
3 551 , but she found her altogether very engaging--not inconveniently shy, n
1 181 h. "I am afraid I am sometimes very fanciful and troublesome." "My dear
2 395 eston had, of course, formed a very favourable idea of the young man; a
2 373 nd his fond report of him as a very fine young man had made Highbury fe
1  13  as a governess than a friend, very fond of both daughters, but particu
3 522 ladies whom Emma found herself very frequently able to collect; and hap
2 381  his father's marriage, it was very generally proposed, as a most prope
1 128 s is so obliged to you!" "I am very glad I did think of her. It was ver
2 424 poor Miss Taylor! She would be very glad to stay." There was no recover
1 130  and I am sure she will make a very good servant: she is a civil, prett
3 561 om she had just parted, though very good sort of people, must be doing
1 250 le day, 'I think it would be a very good thing for Miss Taylor if Mr. W
1 282 y young man, to be sure, and a very good young man, and I have a great
3 535 n, on account of her beauty. A very gracious invitation was returned, a
2 391  Weston? I understand it was a very handsome letter, indeed. Mr. Woodho
1 157 se gratefully observed, "It is very kind of you, Mr. Knightley, to come
3 571 n interesting, and certainly a very kind undertaking; highly becoming h
3 600 you to a little bit of tart--a very little bit. Ours are all apple-tart
1   4 ty-one years in the world with very little to distress or vex her. She
1 128 lad I did think of her. It was very lucky, for I would not have had poo
1 278 eir hands to-day, he looked so very much as if he would like to have th
1  96 fferently from himself, he was very much disposed to think Miss Taylor
3 526 r father look comfortable, and very much pleased with herself for contr
3 449 ciety in his own way. He liked very much to have his friends come and s
1  19  together as friend and friend very mutually attached, and Emma doing j
1 146 ght-and-thirty, was not only a very old and intimate friend of the fami
3 477 ormer vicar of Highbury, was a very old lady, almost past every thing b
3 544 hool there with her. She was a very pretty girl, and her beauty happene
1 132 eys and asks me how I do, in a very pretty manner; and when you have ha
1 282 im a service." "Mr. Elton is a very pretty young man, to be sure, and a
3 478  with her single daughter in a very small way, and was considered with
3 598 u need not be afraid, they are very small, you see--one of our small eg
3 596 e of these eggs. An egg boiled very soft is not unwholesome. Serle unde
1 113  must go and pay wedding visit very soon." "My dear, how am I to get so
1 203 , Mr. Knightley, she is really very sorry to lose poor Miss Taylor, and
1 123 . And as for James, you may be very sure he will always like going to R
1 180 were not by." "I believe it is very true, my dear, indeed," said Mr. Wo
3 566  be coarse and unpolished, and very unfit to be the intimates of a girl
3 575 hat the evening flew away at a very unusual rate; and the supper-table,
3 587 is conviction of suppers being very unwholesome made him rather sorry t
3 534 l of seventeen, whom Emma knew very well by sight, and had long felt an
1 280 d office done for him! I think very well of Mr. Elton, and this is the
3 482 rried. Miss Bates stood in the very worst predicament in the world for
```

FIG. 4.5. Right-sorted concordance of 'very' from *Emma*

```
                                   very    50
1 216    joy to me," said Emma, "and a very considerable one--that I made the m
1 282 y young man, to be sure, and a very good young man, and I have a great
2 373 nd his fond report of him as a very fine young man had made Highbury fe
3 575 hat the evening flew away at a very unusual rate; and the supper-table,
1 250 le day, 'I think it would be a very good thing for Miss Taylor if Mr. W
3 535 n, on account of her beauty. A very gracious invitation was returned, a
3 571 n interesting, and certainly a very kind undertaking; highly becoming h
2 395 eston had, of course, formed a very favourable idea of the young man; a
1   7 n mistress of his house from a very early period. Her mother had died t
3 478 with her single daughter in a very small way, and was considered with
1 132 eys and asks me how I do, in a very pretty manner; and when you have ha
1 282 im a service." "Mr. Elton is a very pretty young man, to be sure, and a
1 130 and I am sure she will make a very good servant: she is a civil, prett
1 146 ght-and-thirty, was not only a very old and intimate friend of the fami
3 600 you to a little bit of tart--a very little bit. Ours are all apple-tart
3 477 ormer vicar of Highbury, was a very old lady, almost past every thing b
2 391 Weston? I understand it was a very handsome letter, indeed. Mr. Woodho
3 544 hool there with her. She was a very pretty girl, and her beauty happene
3 551 , but she found her altogether very engaging--not inconveniently shy, n
1 128 s is so obliged to you!" "I am very glad I did think of her. It was ver
3 526 r father look comfortable, and very much pleased with herself for contr
3 511 school was in high repute--and very deservedly; for Highbury was reckon
3 566 be coarse and unpolished, and very unfit to be the intimates of a girl
3 598 u need not be afraid, they are very small, you see--one of our small eg
1 123 . And as for James, you may be very sure he will always like going to R
2 424 poor Miss Taylor! She would be very glad to stay." There was no recover
3 587 is conviction of suppers being very unwholesome made him rather sorry t
3 596 e of these eggs. An egg boiled very soft is not unwholesome. Serle unde
3 564 ding in the parish of Donwell-- very creditably, she believed--she knew
1  13 as a governess than a friend, very fond of both daughters--but particu
1  19 together as friend and friend very mutually attached, and Emma doing j
3 522 ladies whom Emma found herself very frequently able to collect; and hap
1 209 lor's advantage; she knows how very acceptable it must be, at Miss Tayl
1 180 were not by." "I believe it is very true, my dear, indeed," said Mr. Wo
1 157 se gratefully observed, "It is very kind of you, Mr. Knightley, to come
1 162 ." "But you must have found it very damp and dirty. I wish you may not
3 534 l of seventeen, whom Emma knew very well by sight, and had long felt an
3 449 ciety in his own way. He liked very much to have his friends come and s
1 203 , Mr. Knightley, she is really very sorry to lose poor Miss Taylor, and
1 278 eir hands to-day, he looked so very much as if he would like to have th
1 181 h. "I am afraid I am sometimes very fanciful and troublesome." "My dear
2 410 there was such comfort in the very easy distance of Randalls from Hart
3 482 rried. Miss Bates stood in the very worst predicament in the world for
1 280 d office done for him! I think very well of Mr. Elton, and this is the
3 561 om she had just parted, though very good sort of people, must be doing
1 113 must go and pay wedding visit very soon." "My dear, how am I to get so
1  96 fferently from himself, he was very much disposed to think Miss Taylor
1 128 lad I did think of her. It was very lucky, for I would not have had poo
2 381 his father's marriage, it was very generally proposed, as a most prope
1   4 ty-one years in the world with very little to distress or vex her. She
```

FIG. 4.6.   Left-sorted concordance of 'very' from *Emma*

love   56

Ant.	I.I	154	time / To wind about my	love with circumstance; / And out
Ant.	IV.I	282	Bassanio had not once a	love. / Repent but you that you s
Ant.	IV.I	411	ed, over and above, / In	love and service to you evermore
Ant.	IV.I	447	et his deservings and my	love withal / Be valued against y
Bass.	I.I	131	he most, in money and in	love, / And from your love I have
Bass.	I.I	132	in love, / And from your	love I have a warranty / To unbur
Bass.	IV.I	65	l the things they do not	love
Bass.	III.II	155	fear the enjoying of my	love: / There may as well be amit
Bass.	III.II	157	fire, as treason and my	love
Bass.	III.II	252	en I did first impart my	love to you, / I freely told you,
Bass.	III.II	322	your / pleasure: if your	love do not persuade you to come,
Duke	IV.I	24	ith human gentleness and	love, / Forgive a moiety of the p
Grat.	I.I	88	thee what, Antonio-- / I	love thee, and it is my love that
Grat.	I.I	88	love thee, and it is my	love that speaks-- / There are a
Grat.	V.I	145	/ Since you do take it,	love, so much at heart
Grat.	IV.I	295	wife, whom, I protest, I	love: / I would she were in heave
Grat.	III.II	205	was dry / With oaths of	love, at last, if promise last, /
Grat.	III.II	207	r one here / To have her	love, provided that your fortune
Jess.	II.VI	29	Lorenzo, certain, and my	love indeed, / For who love I so
Jess.	II.VI	30	y love indeed, / For who	love I so much? And now who knows
Jess.	II.VI	36	ed of my exchange: / But	love is blind and lovers cannot s
Jess.	II.VI	43	an office of discovery,	love; / And I should be obscured
Lor.	V.I	13	d sea banks and waft her	love / To come again to Carthage
Lor.	V.I	20	w / And with an unthrift	love did run from Venice / As far
Lor.	V.I	28	tle shrew, / Slander her	love, and he forgave it her
Lor.	II.VI	28	Lorenzo, and thy	love
Lor.	II.VI	52	Beshrew me but I	love her heartily; / For she is w
Mor.	II.I	6	s make incision for your	love, / To prove whose blood is r
Mor.	II.I	9	ear'd the valiant: by my	love I swear / The best-regarded
Mor.	II.VII	34	But more than these, in	love I do deserve. / What if I st
Ner.	I.II	32	t /one who shall rightly	love. But what warmth is /there i
Ner.	II.IX	101	Bassanio, lord	Love, if thy will it be
Por.	I.II	63	forgive him, for if he /	love me to madness, I shall never
Por.	V.I	170	your flesh. / I gave my	love a ring and made him swear /
Por.	IV.I	424	And, for your	love, I'll take this ring from yo
Por.	IV.I	426	ke no more; / And you in	love shall not deny me this
Por.	III.II	110	d green-eyed jealousy! O	love, / Be moderate; allay thy ec
Por.	III.II	129	tells me, but it is not	love, / I would not lose you; and
Por.	III.II	153	ere is mingled with your	love
Por.	III.II	168	one of them: / If you do	love me, you will find me out. /
Por.	III.II	173	presage the ruin of your	love / And be my vantage to excla
Por.	III.II	181	ence, but with much more	love, / Than young Alcides, when
Por.	III.II	314	are dear bought, I will	love you dear. / But let me hear
Por.	III.II	324	O	love, dispatch all business, and
Por.	III.IV	13	do bear an equal yoke of	love, / There must be needs a lik
Por.	III.IV	34	position; / The which my	love and some necessity / Now lay
Por.	III.IV	71	ourable ladies sought my	love, / Which I denying, they fel
Salar.	I.I	47	Why, then you are in	love
Salar.	I.I	49	Not in	love neither? Then let us say you
Salar.	II.VIII	43	ot enter in your mind of	love: / Be merry, and employ your
Salar.	II.VIII	45	and such fair ostents of	love / As shall conveniently beco
Serv.	II.IX	92	likely an ambassador of	love: / A day in April never came
Shyl.	I.III	139	s with you and have your	love, / Forget the shames that yo
Shyl.	I.III	172	ot, adieu; / And, for my	love, I pray you wrong me not
Shyl.	II.V	13	I go? / I am not bid for	love; they flatter me: / But yet
Shyl.	IV.I	46	et? / Some men there are	love not a gaping pig; / Some, th

FIG. 4.7. Concordance of 'love' in *The Merchant of Venice* sorted by character

of the number of characters or number of words, or simply to fill up the available display space. The keyword in context (KWIC) format, as-shown in Figure 4.3, is the most useful for scanning a set of entries. Here the context fills the available space across the screen or page. This kind of context makes most sense for a prose text, but perhaps not broken in the middle of a word at the beginning and end as has happened here. A click on one line of context can expand that context to some other amount of text, perhaps to fill the screen or to the end of the current page, chapter, or other unit, provided that these units are identified within the text.

The context entries for each word are normally displayed in the order in which they occur in the text, but other options are possible. Figure 4.5 shows a concordance of the word *very* from the first three chapters of *Emma*, but this time the entries are not displayed in the order that they occur in the text, but are sorted according to the words to the right of the keyword *very*. This format, known as a 'right-sorted concordance', has the effect of bringing together all the instances of *very* followed by the same phrase or sequence of words, for example in *very much, very good, very well*. When the occurrences are sorted according to the left of the keyword (a 'left-sorted' concordance), different sequences emerge, as is shown in Figure 4.6, where *a very* and *the very* are frequent.

The contexts can also be sorted according to the references. This function is better illustrated by a play where each character's usage of a particular word can be identified. Figure 4.7 shows the 56 concordance entries for the word *love* in *The Merchant of Venice* sorted by character in the play. We can see from this example that Portia uses the word the most often, but to see whether this is significant or not, we also need to know what proportion of the total number of words in the play are spoken by Portia. This and other simple statistical methods are examined further in Chapters 6 and 7. The concordance is thus used to provide basic data for further analyses. This example shows another option for verse text, that is, to display contexts longer than a single verse line, but to indicate where the line breaks occur, in this case by inserting a slash character. Other programs display the headword in bold within the contexts or use colour, which can add another dimension to viewing results on a screen.

Concordances can be displayed very neatly on the World Wide Web. Rob Watt's Concordance program includes a facility to generate Web concordances following the model of his earlier Web concordances (Watt 1999; n.d.). Concordance offers several options for the layout of the Web pages, but the one it chooses to provide if no further instructions are given is more than adequate. It uses four frames. A frame along

```
                                   as chaste as    1
Por.     I.II  104 d as Sibylla, I will die   as chaste /as Diana, unless I be o

                                   as easy as     1
Por.     I.II  12              If to do were   as easy as to know what were good

                                   as fair As     1
Por.     II.I   20 owned prince, then stood   as fair / As any comer I have look

                                   as false As    1
Bass.    III.II 83 ds, whose hearts are all   as false / As stairs of sand, wear

                                   as far as      2
Launc.   II.II 104 erve not him, I will run   as far as God has /any ground
Lor.     V.I    21 ve did run from Venice /   As far as Belmont

                                   as liberal as  1
Por.     V.I   229 for me, / I will become   as liberal as you; / I'll not deny

                                   as many as     1
Launc.   III.V  20 stians enow before; e'en   as many as could well / live, one

                                   as much as     7
Arr.     II.IX  35 ho chooseth me shall get   as much as he deserves:' / And wel
Arr.     II.IX  49 ho chooseth me shall get   as much as he deserves.' / I will
Arr.     II.IX  57 o chooseth me shall have   as much as he deserves.' / Did I d
Mor.     II.VII  7 ho chooseth me shall get   as much as he deserves;' / This th
Mor.     II.VII 23 ho chooseth me shall get   as much as he deserves.' / As much
Mor.     II.VII 24   much as he deserves.' /   As much as he deserves! Pause ther
Mor.     II.VII 31 k disabling of myself. /   As much as I deserve! Why, that's
```

FIG. 4.8. Part of a concordance of the phrase 'as . . . as' in *The Merchant of Venice*

the top of the page holds the letters of the alphabet as clickable boxes. A click on a letter displays the list of words beginning with that letter in alphabetical order in a frame on the left. All the words are linked to their concordance entries. A click on a word brings up one-line concordance entries in another frame, together with a reference which is also a link. A click on the reference displays that part of the text in the fourth frame. These interactive Web concordances can be particularly effective for learning about concordances as well as about a particular text or set of texts.

Concordance programs can also be used to search for phrases or sequences of words. Figure 4.8 shows a concordance of the phrase *as . . . as* in *The Merchant of Venice*, again sorting the concordance entries by references to show the use by characters in the play. The headwords are sorted as if the phrase was a single word. Using the pattern options this facility can be used in simple ways to search for some kinds of alliteration or for idioms which are close to each other but not exactly the same words.

Text analysis programs can also be used to generate collocations, which show pairs of words which co-occur frequently. In the simplest case a program can be instructed to find all the words which occur within a given number of words of the collocate node or key. Figure 4.9 shows the collocates *pound* and *flesh*, and *flesh* and *blood* in *The Merchant of Venice*. Here the program has been instructed to find all the places where any word beginning with *pound* is followed within seven words of any word

```
                                        pound flesh    10
     I.III Shyl. 151 e nominated for an equal  pound / Of your fair flesh, to be
     I.III Shyl. 167 n of the forfeiture? / A   pound of man's flesh taken from a
   III.III Ant.   35 t I shall hardly spare a   pound of flesh / To-morrow to my
      IV.I Duke   22 o penalty, / Which is a     pound of this poor merchant's fle
      IV.I Shyl.  98 o do I answer you: / The   pound of flesh, which I demand of
      IV.I Por.  234 is the Jew may claim / A   pound of flesh, to be by him cut
      IV.I Por.  296               A   pound of that same merchant's fle
      IV.I Por.  304 e words expressly are 'a   pound of flesh:' / Take then thy
      IV.I Por.  305  thy bond, take thou thy    pound of flesh; / But, in the cut
      IV.I Por.  326 ss nor more / But just a   pound of flesh: if thou cut'st mo


                                        flesh blood     5
     II.II Gob.   87 celot, thou art mine own   flesh and blood. / Lord worshippe
    III.I Shyl.  32             My own   flesh and blood to rebel
    III.I Shyl.  34 I say, my daughter is my   flesh and blood
     IV.I Bass. 112  / The Jew shall have my   flesh, blood, bones and all, / Er
     IV.I Por.  324 pare thee to cut off the   flesh. / Shed thou no blood, nor


                                        flesh bloody    1
   III.III Ant.   35  hardly spare a pound of   flesh / To-morrow to my bloody cr
```

FIG. 4.9. Collocates 'pound' and 'flesh' in *The Merchant of Venice*

beginning with *flesh* and where any word beginning with *flesh* is followed within seven words of any word beginning with *blood*. The results show the phrase *pound of flesh* but with four variants of it where extra words are inserted between *of* and *flesh*. These four examples would not have been found with a search for the phrase *pound of flesh*. Similarly the co-occurrences of *flesh* and *blood* are not all in the phrase *flesh and blood*.

Some concordance programs can generate a list of all the collocates of a given node and list them by position to the left and right of the node. They do this, for example, by showing all the collocates one word to the left or right, then two words to the left or right, and so on up to the chosen span of words. Many of the collocates will be common words such as *the*, *and*, *of*, etc. and it may be possible to specify these as a list of collocates to be ignored.

After this overview of the functions of basic text analysis tools, we can return to a discussion of the relative merits of interactive retrieval and batch processing. Interactive retrieval programs are faster, especially for large texts, but many do not offer a full range of searches. When a query is made, the program jumps straight to that word in the word list and can respond immediately. However, the ability to do this limits the range of searches which can be carried out. A query beginning with a wild card character, for example to look for words ending in certain characters, may not be possible unless a reverse index has also been built. The program will either indicate that this search is not possible or the search will take a long time because the search is being carried out sequentially on the entire list of words. Search terms that include diacritics and non-sorting characters are unlikely to be possible unless these forms have all been indexed separately, but even then a decision must be made on how to treat all non-sorting characters at the time of building the index.

Beginners who are working on their own material often find that it takes some time to achieve useful results with programs that work with pre-defined indexes. It is necessary to run the index-building program before any analysis can be carried out, which essentially means doing the difficult things first. More often than not, the index will need to be rebuilt several times before some accurate and useful analyses can be done. Moreover, if any changes are made to the text—and of course text analysis tools are very useful for finding the inevitable errors or inconsistencies—the index must be rebuilt. Searches for punctuation or other similar features can only be carried out if these features have been indexed.

Large-scale, multi-user, on-line text retrieval systems are only feasible with pre-built indexes. Libraries which are developing electronic text collections for on-line searching must therefore make decisions at the outset about what retrieval facilities they are going to provide and then build the indexes accordingly. This places some responsibility on the person handling this work, who needs to try to anticipate all the kinds of questions which an unknown group of users wants to ask. In practice most electronic text collections tend to offer a more limited, word-based set of search facilities geared towards finding all the places where a particular word or combination of words occurs. Some large systems, following the pattern of document retrieval systems, omit common words, but with the capacity of modern computer systems there seems little point in doing this now. Common words are important in concordances used for language teaching, corpus analysis, lexicography, and for stylistic studies. Moreover, there is a danger that some common words, for example the auxiliaries *will* and *might* in English, are homographs of other words which should not be omitted.

In general, then, a batch concordance offers more flexible queries but is only feasible when the text is not very large. The exact amount of text that can be analysed effectively with a batch concordance depends on the actual program, the memory and disk drive capacity of the computer being used, and the nature of the analysis. Most Windows-based text analysis programs operate in this way and can be effective for many humanities applications. Simple approaches can go a long way towards providing useful results which can then be refined with further analysis or with a word processor or some other software.

5 | Literary Analysis

Computers can assist with the study of literature in a variety of ways, some more successful than others. Like other applications discussed in this book, the computer is best at finding features or patterns within a literary work and counting occurrences of those features. If the features which interest a scholar can be identified by computer programs, the computer will provide an overall picture which would be impossible to derive accurately by manual methods. It can also pinpoint specific features within a text or collection of texts and lead the researcher to further areas of enquiry. It is often best treated as an adjunct to other research methods. Even a concordance of a text can serve as a valuable reference tool for many purposes, and repeated delving into a text can help to throw new light on questions of interpretation. Computer-based tools are especially good for comparative work, and here some simple statistical tools can help to reinforce the interpretation of the material. These studies are particularly suitable for testing hypotheses or for verifying intuition. They can provide concrete evidence to support or refute hypotheses or interpretations which have in the past been based on human reading and the somewhat serendipitous noting of interesting features. Milic (1991) and Potter (1991) provide surveys of statistical analysis of literature.

The use of computers in literary studies is an area which has attracted a good deal of criticism, most notably by Fish (1980). Much of this criticism has been directed towards the computer-based study of style. Scholars are unhappy about the apparent quantification of literature, and have taken issue both with what is being quantified and with the interpretation of the results. Some critics are deeply suspicious of numbers, which they feel are alien to their normal way of working, yet even simple counts can help to reinforce a feeling about a text or show that what intuitively seems rare or very frequent is not in fact so. There has also been some tendency to regard the computer as a kind of black box out of which will come tables of numbers which themselves will, or will not, depending on the attitude of the scholar, illuminate aspects of literature. The computer is merely a tool. It can do some things very well, but much should be left to the judgement of the scholar, both to situate the project in the broader range of scholarship on the particular topic and to interpret the results within the context of other research. There has also been some tendency to approach literary computing from the perspective of 'What shall I do with the computer?' rather than 'Can the computer help me with this problem and how?' Some projects that might fit into the former category have not served to enhance the role and reputation of computer-aided literary research.

This chapter will attempt to cut through this criticism of literary computing to survey a number of projects and methodologies, most of which have been carried out by literary scholars. It is not the place of this book to examine these projects in the light of current trends in literary criticism. Readers can make these judgements for themselves. The chapter will investigate methodologies which have helped to throw new light on and to derive new knowledge about works of literature, and it will draw attention to pitfalls and problems. Many of these projects are based on concordance and word-count applications, but, as we shall see, computers can help to study sound patterns in verse and the structure of some kinds of dramatic works.

It has long been thought that computers could help to find echoes from one author or text in another, but this of course depends on the nature of the echoes. An exact match of sequences of words is easy to find, but there have been various approaches to try to search for partial matches. A lemmatized text makes this easier but can still only provide a partial solution. The methodology for Raben's ([1965]) study of the influence of Milton on Shelley is described in Goodman and Villani ([1965]). Although this was a study on verse, it was carried out using sentences as the base unit for comparison. The texts were lemmatized with machine aid and, working from concordances but excluding common words, the program created lists of individual pairs of sentences which had one word in common. It then generated all pairs of sentences which contained the word before eliminating single occurrences, leaving sentences where more than one word matched. The sentences were then sorted to show the ones with the largest number of words in common. Raben could then examine the results to find sentences which interested him. Although rather crude, this methodology was reasonably effective, and Raben's paper shows many places where he found influences. Some of the statistical tools now being used for corpus linguistics might improve the methodology (see Chapter 6), but the system devised by Raben and his programmers was well understood and could be applied today. A simpler process of making a concordance of two texts together would yield some influences, but this would be more effective if the user had specific words or phrases in mind rather than scanning a large set of results.

Writing over thirty years later, Bucher-Gillmayr (1996) reports on similar methodology to look for allusions to the New Testament in other texts, especially the late twentieth-century German lyric poems of Christine Busta. Like Raben, Bucher-Gillmayr also worked with lemmas, which were also weighted for their significance. Some hand tagging was done for words which were likely to establish a link. She first found every word in the poems which matched a biblical word, then also searched for sequences of two or three words, then for these sets of words but in a different order. Verbatim quotations are easy to find by this means, but she was also able to find what she calls 'loose combinations' (Bucher-Gillmayr 1996: 3). She then tried another approach, looking in larger areas of the New Testament (blocks of 200 words) to find those where there were at least five lemmas in common with one poem.

Heinemann (1993) discusses the role of the TACT program in helping find echoes in an Old French text where there is 'an often elaborate play of variation in the echoes' (1993: 191). His method is much more interactive, relying on first browsing the word list or reading the poem, and then exploring the TACT databases to look at specific instances. Heinemann was principally interested in where these echoes occurred, whether they were close to each other or far apart, and also their relation to the logical structure of the poem, what he calls the 'weaving of components' (1993: 193). This kind of study requires some detailed structural markup of the poem, and it is then possible to produce density diagrams showing the relationship of the echoes to the structural boundaries. He notes that the 'literal-minded' approach of the computer-based tools encouraged him to look explicitly at both components of an echo (the variable and the constant) (1993: 200). See also Heinemann (1991) for more discussion. It is thus easy to see how these tools can help with an investigation of any material which is formulaic or repetitive. A lemmatized version of the text is better for some material, but the time taken to create the lemmatized version must be weighed against the added benefit. These approaches tend to be more successful with verse because of its more rigid structure. But for all of them, the computer's role is only partial. It can draw attention to some possible echo and allusions. Some kinds of echo might be much more difficult to find by computer program, and of course for all of them finding echoes is only a prelude to interpretation and analysis.

Lancashire has investigated what he calls 'phrasal repetends' in a number of different texts from Chaucer to Margaret Atwood (Lancashire 1993a, 1993b, 1993c, 1996b). His approach is closer to the collocation analysis of the corpus linguists, but it also uses fixed order sequences of words (phrases). Using the TACT program he is able to examine the collocates of certain words and begin to use the results of this to postulate the cognitive processes or long-term memory of the author, what he calls 'cognitive stylistics' (Lancashire 1995). Lessard and Hamm (1991, 1996) show how a computer program can identify repeated structures in Stendhal. Their first explorations were carried out using the Oxford Concordance Program to find the repetitions directly, but eventually they found it useful to design and develop their own procedures which operated on a right-sorted concordance generated by OCP. They looked at the frequency of repeated strings, and also at the distance between repetitions, for example within the same syntactic framework, within one page where they will be remembered by the reader and also repetitions which are a long way apart and the possible implications of this for the reader.

A study of vocabulary can also contribute to an investigation of genre. This kind of approach is methodologically very similar to the work on variation in spoken and written texts carried out by Biber (1988) and discussed in Chapter 6, but the context or literary analysis leads to a different emphasis in interpretation. Craig (1991) investigated the use of plural pronouns in thirteen plays by Shakespeare and thirteen plays by Jonson in an attempt to see how they can be used to distinguish genre. His study concentrated on the Roman plays, using others as a comparison. The pronoun *you* was discounted because it might be singular, and *we* was tagged to eliminate the royal *we*. Craig demonstrated a heavy use of five plural pronouns in the Roman plays, notably *our*, which he explains by the emphasis on group and political activities in these plays. The Roman plays all exhibit this feature, but the plural first person pronoun does not clearly separate the tragedies and the Roman plays. The rate of occurrence of *our* and *we* is low in *Othello*, but higher in *Macbeth*, where Craig notes that 'people act together' (Craig 1991: 185). In the test which he set himself (described in more detail in Chapter 7), Burrows (1992a) was able to derive genre information from four tables giving the raw counts of the fifty most common words in four texts. The high frequencies of *I, you, he, she*, and the verb *said* indicated correctly that these texts are novels. An examination of the segments within the texts also showed where dialogue is prominent.

Burrows's much longer study of the novels of Jane Austen is one of the few full length monographs based on computational approaches

(Burrows 1987). His basic argument is that the thirty most common words (eight personal pronouns, six auxiliary verb forms, five prepositions, three conjunctions, two adverbs, the definite and indefinite articles, and *to, that, for,* and *all*) have been almost completely neglected in the study of these novels, but that these words can shed light on the relationships between narrative and dialogue, on characters, and also between novels and novelists. 'It is a truth not generally acknowledged that, in most discussion of works of English fiction, we proceed as if a third, two-fifths, a half of our material were not really there' (Burrows 1987: 1). The study is based on concordances of the six Austen novels, plus *Sanditon* and *Sanditon by Jane Austen and Another Lady*, Georgette Heyer's *Frederica*, Virginia Woolf's *The Waves*, Henry James's *The Awkward Age*, and E. M. Forster's *Howards End*. The control texts were chosen because of their diversity, and were used in the study for broader investigations of narrative and dialogue. The texts were marked up to allow for contracted forms and separation of some homographs, but for the purposes of the study the dialogue is encoded 'in the manner of a playscript' (Burrows 1987: 9), that is, each piece of dialogue is identified by who is speaking it. Burrows had to make some decisions about material which comes between dialogue and what he calls 'quasi-indirect speech' (1987: 10). He also encoded what he called 'character narrative' where the narrator resorts to the 'free indirect style' (1987: 10). His investigation centred on the forty-eight characters in the Austen novels who speak more than 2,000 words and, for the basis of comparison, all the calculations were based on the rate per 1,000 words.

Much of the book is organized by various statistical methodologies rather than by an analysis of the characters in the novels, but it is easily possible to extract the 'criticism' from the 'computation'. An investigation of pronouns illuminates some of the differences between the characters, but for comparative purposes Burrows found that the chi-square test which he used first was able to separate the central characters but not the others. More interesting are the results from various correlations where pairs of characters were compared. A comparison between Darcy and Elizabeth (1987: 82–3) shows that they are fairly similar, but that Elizabeth uses *do* much more than Darcy. A multi-dimensional approach for *Mansfield Park* shows the isolation of Lady Bertram and the high correlation between the other characters except for Fanny. The culmination of his investigation of external character relationships is a diagram showing the relationships and distances between all the characters (1987: 130). In one direction this measures their divergence from Emma, who has by far the largest share of the dialogue in the novels. Burrows interprets the other dimension as 'a gradual transformation from garrulousness and intellectual indiscipline, through a middle area of civil and articulate speech-habits, to formality and dignity, and onward to pomposity' (1987: 132).

Burrows then concentrates some of his investigations on the hero and heroine in each novel, where he shows a greater contrast between Henry and Catherine than between Emma and Mr Knightley or Anne and Wentworth. Further studies are able to separate the Austen novels from the control novels on some features, but the narrative in all of them is closer together than to any of the dialogue. A similar methodology can be used to trace the development of the major characters through each of the novels: Austen's characters show more variation than the characters in the controls. There is much more to Burrows's work, which he describes as an experiment in method as well as a study of the novels. The statistics are not difficult and the whole is readable. In fact his investigations and the results that they produce unfold like a story, with each new tool adding to what has been found before.

In his first chapter, Burrows uses the rates of occurrence of four words (*the, of, not, I*) to illustrate how he presents his figures (Burrows 1987: 3). Even this small example showing Henry Tilney, Catherine Morland, and Isabella Thorpe is illuminating. In each case the rate of usage by Henry is very different from that by Catherine, with Isabella closer to Catherine than to Henry. Isabella and Catherine use *I* more than twice as often as Henry. Henry has the lowest rate of occurrence of *not*, and the highest of *the* and *of*. Elsewhere Burrows's investigation focuses on gender, but other scholars have also looked at computer-based tools to look at gender questions in literature. Merideth (1989) examined the dialogue of the heroines in three novels by Henry James, contrasting the heroine in each novel with one male character. She looked at incidences of questions, imperatives, exclamations, pauses, fragments, conditionals, definitions, negatives, universals, adverbs, and comparisons (1989: 192). She found that Daisy Miller uses few questions and definitions, but many exclamations, perhaps supporting traditional criticism of the novel where Daisy is portrayed as weak. The findings also support traditional views of Isabel in *Portrait of a Lady*, where she has many negatives, but asks more questions. In *The Bostonians*, Verena has fewer questions, and weaker ones, and she also uses more conditionals (1989: 199–200).

Irizarry (1992) carried out her investigation of gender-related idiolect on two contemporary Mexican writers (one male and one female) writing about gender issues. She studied approximately 11,000 words of each author, which is a manageable amount of material for some hand-editing or checking of results. Various criteria were used in the study and Irizarry relates each of these to other research based on them. She was also able to compare some of her results with a larger corpus which she had prepared for another project. Sentence length was problematic because of the definition of a sentence, but she was able to establish that the female uses more questions and longer questions, reflecting hesitation and a lack of assertiveness. The male has more adversatives, but the female has a wider vocabulary. Following Burrows she examined *we*, which exists only in the masculine and general form *nosotros* in Spanish. The female uses this much less (1992: 109–11). Words of compassion, which were initially taken from a thesaurus, only appear in the female's work (1992: 111). Diminutives are more common in the female's work (1992: 111). The male's use of space and place refers to broader places, with less about enclosed spaces and home, and more about travel, with more mention of place-names (1992: 112). The male uses more words like *always* and *absolutely* to denote 'emphasis and authority' (1992: 112), and more negatives as the first word of a sentence. The male also uses expressions of certitude and truth more (1992: 113), and other expressions of assertion at the beginning of sentences (1992: 113). The female has a more hesitant way of suggesting something. Irizarry's study is thorough and it is also recommended for her insightful comments on her methodology and the results.

Lexical and vocabulary studies can also be used to investigate themes, imagery, and the like. Care needs to be taken with these studies since the computer can only find specific instances of words or phrases, unless the text has been encoded with interpretative material, which can be a lengthy process or reflect one scholar's viewpoint which must then be explained carefully. These studies are obviously most fruitful when specific words are used intentionally. Sometimes rather too much can be read into the results, particularly when density analysis or other statistical analyses are carried out on vocabulary counts. The more useful studies are firmly related to traditional criticism on the material. A dictionary or lexical database of synonyms or words denoting specific themes can facilitate this kind of study. Scholars have built their own databases for specific applications, often constructing *ad hoc* lists of words and drawing on existing synonym dictionaries, and also operating with lemmas rather than individual forms. In effect these databases are smaller and specialized versions of the lexical databases used in computational linguistics and discussed in Chapter 9. It would be interesting to see how effective they might be for literary studies and to speculate whether it would be possible to build a general-purpose lexical database for literary analysis, which would need multiple interpretations for many terms.

Fortier has been developing tools for thematic analysis of French literature over a long period (Fortier and McConnell 1973). In Fortier (1989) he shows how the theme of violence is used most often in the African section of Céline's *Voyage au bout de la nuit* (1989: 86), but not in the war chapters. He has used concordances, for example to look at mythic dimensions in Malraux (1989: 88), and has also examined associations of sickness and health in Gide's *L'Immoraliste* (Fortier 1996). Some of this work is similar to the kind of content analysis carried out in the social sciences, but there seems to have been little overlap in discussion and assessment of methodologies. Researchers in the social sciences are more interested in concrete data from which they can extrapolate trends of various kinds. The material which they analyse is less likely to be deliberately ambiguous or metaphoric in the way that literature is, but the methodologies are basically the same.

Ide based her investigation of imagery in Blake's *The Four Zoas* on an analysis of specific terms and their occurrences within the structure and thematic dimensions of the poem (Ide 1986, 1989). The intention was to attempt to identify spatial relationships between images to help clarify Blake's symbols and system of relationships. Ide argues that even figurative use of some of the image terms, for example *fire* and *ice*, convey something of the image (Ide 1989: 125). She built up a set of image categories using word lists and a dictionary of symbols, and then identified occurrences of these within the poem. She also developed a method for dealing with synonyms (Ide 1986: 500). She further discusses the problem of images which consist of more than one word, where, for example, 'Robes of blood' can be treated as *robes* and *blood* separately, and then associatively (1986: 501). She was able to identify areas of high and low image concentration, and where specific images, for example sea or fire, occur very frequently. High incidences of images overall can then be compared with the poem's logical sections. The patterns of images are represented graphically, showing peaks and troughs for high and low incidences. When they are computer-based, investigations of this kind can easily be repeated many times using different sets of terms or images, and in relation to different areas of the text. Smith uses similar tools to look at various themes in Joyce, linking the density of the theme with the content, but also stressing that the critic must then interpret the results (J. B. Smith 1973; 1989).

As part of his larger study of Milton, Corns (1982) discusses imagery in the Milton tracts in some detail, but he also had problems in defining imagery in reasonably exact terms. He settled on 'a generic term for simile, metaphor, and other structures of comparison, such as those introduced by "as if" or by "as ... (high/happy/small/etc.) ... as"' (43), but even with this fairly general definition he was able to find more examples than he could by intuition. Again a concordance or word list gives a way in to the text which the scholar can then examine from different perspectives. Corns found many examples of biblical imagery which he notes distinguishes Milton's early work from his later work and from other texts from the same period which he used as controls.

Corns's work is also useful because of the way he situates it within the broader context of Milton criticism. He is able to refute some earlier work which was based on less rigorous methodologies. In his first study he contrasted Milton's early (1641–2) anti-prelatical tracts and late (1659–73) final pamphlets with some non-Miltonic material of the same period, and then applied the same techniques to Milton's tracts of 1643–5 and 1649 and to some non-Miltonic material of this period. He examined a variety of features, including word frequencies, which he related to context, noting the wider vocabulary in passages discussing many concepts or rich in imagery.

The electronic *Oxford English Dictionary* was not available at this time, but it would have been a great help to Corns, especially when looking at other features of lexis, for example Latinate words. The *OED* is based on written material and so would be less useful for examining colloquialisms. Corns also investigated neologisms in the poetry, by comparison with the *OED*, and found many compounds around person-ification. *Paradise Lost* also exhibits some unusual kinds of collocation, for example the materiality of insubstantial things such as air and light, and the inanimate or abstract where the animate would be expected.

Corns hand-coded some sentences for part of speech tagging and was able to derive patterns from larger samples than the earlier critics, who did not use computers to tabulate their results. His study of Milton's sentence structure (Corns 1990) looks at sentence length and structure in verse, where obviously sentences need to be related to the lineation. Corns also discusses his definition of a sentence:

I consider a unit of text to be a sentence if it is grammatically complete, can be terminated without leaving grammatically incomplete fragments in residue and makes good sense. The final semantic requirement introduces a certain theoret-ical inelegance, in that it invokes the semantic level in analysis of syntax, and it points, too, to the inevitable introduction of a certain limited subjectivity and the possibilities for disagreement. (1990: 12)

Corns is able to establish that Milton has a higher incidence of long sentences than do his control texts, except for the minor poems, and that these sentences also have more syllables in their words (1990: 14–15).

In contrast, Milton's short sentences have many monosyllabic words (1990: 16).

Word searches and collocations can provide a route into other kinds of investigation, and here we note just two very different studies. Miall (1992) examined various collocations in Coleridge's notebooks, with a particular emphasis on words associated with emotion, which he could then relate to a discussion of Coleridge's understanding of psychology. Some words were used very differently in Coleridge's poetry. An examination of the collocates over time also revealed differences and helped to show 'how important Coleridge's thought about emotion was in developing his mature literary and philosophical theory' (1992: 11). Miall found, for example, that *body* was a frequent collocate of emotion words in the middle period, and *love* and *heart* were frequent around 1807. Rommel (1995) looked at *Robinson Crusoe* in the light of criticism which says that the novel is more like a true report than an imaginary story. He concentrated on words connected with time and place and was able to show a high incidence of these where a frame of reference is being established. Temporal and topographical references overlap in the same 'narrative unit' to help the reader get orientated (1995: 283). But a close analysis showed that time and place references are very often vague and approximated. Rommel's view of these vague references is that they make the narrator's report sound more credible, and that they also help overall to give the impression of a report.

Opinions vary about approaches towards the deeper analysis of literary texts. Most scholars tend to favour the 'fishing expedition' approach, where repeated searches in a text can help to draw attention to new features and new interpretation. The text is marked up only for basic structural information so that the location of the features can be noted. If the features are to be used later for other analyses, they are stored separately from the text in a file of categories, or as rules which a program can use. In this way, the text is not cluttered with detail with which another scholar may not agree. An alternative approach is to embed interpretative information directly in the text with more detailed markup. This makes it easier to carry out searches directly on the markup and, depending on the program being used, to deliver the results in a more readable form to a wider audience. Once markup extends beyond the very basic structural components of page, section, book, line, etc. it becomes more interpretative and more dependent on the view of the particular scholar. It is possible to envisage a text with multiple and conflicting literary interpretations embedded in it with tools to enable users to contrast the views, but no such electronic object appears to have been created, nor are there any tools to handle it effectively.

Some of the most complex literary tagging is found in McCarty's Analytical Onomasticon of Ovid's *Metamorphoses* (McCarty, Wright, and Suksi n.d.). The *Metamorphoses* is a collection of interrelated stories involving mythological persons. The whole is interwoven to a great extent, what Ovid calls a 'perpetuum carmen', where the persons appear and reappear in different forms. McCarty has created an electronic text of the 12,000-line 78,000-word poem which uses various levels of tagging to identify persons and references to persons (McCarty 1991, 1993b, 1996). The tagging was created for the TACT program and is not SGML-conformant, although it would be possible to convert it to some SGML-based structures. The tagging focuses on names and other references to persons and McCarty had thus first to define all of these. Each line of the text is followed by a line of tagging for each name or reference to a person within the line. Put simply, the tagging will bring together references to the same person and help to construct a kind of composite representation of each person.

The methodology itself helps to illuminate the poem but is time-consuming. The narrow definition of a name is not enough to identify persons. Names include proper names, patronyms, circumlocutions, and groups (including anonymous individuals). They also include nouns, relative clauses, and pronouns which refer to persons, including the pronoun implicit in the verb in Latin, and also attributes of persons (body parts, clothing, equipment, states of mind, etc.). These occur at an average rate of four per line, all of which are tagged for a standard form of the name, and an indication of the type of tag (proper name, nominal, attribute, pronoun, etc.). McCarty had to create his own definitions for a person in order to assign the standard form of the names. This in itself required a set of definitions for what he calls 'monstra', unnatural beings, and also rules for dealing with two or more people acting as one, or two individuals with the same name. It also highlighted a number of problems, for example, *sol*, 'sun' and *Sol*, 'sun-god', where the capitalization is provided by modern editors and where Ovid's intentions were perhaps deliberately ambiguous. In the tagging the quoted text is reassembled in a form suitable for computer-processing with a lemmatized form of the word.

From the following example:

```
Cum pater ignarus Cadmo perquirere raptam
when the ignorant father orders Cadmus to search for the snatched girl
=Agenor=pater/Cadmus/_ignarus, =Cadmus
=Europa=rapta / Jupiter
```

(McCarty 1996: 249)

it is possible to identify all instances of Agenor (the father of Cadmus), to find all the persons who are labelled as ignorant, that is, *ignarus* in all its inflected forms, and to note all the persons who are snatched and by whom. McCarty gives many other instances, including parts of the body, battles, hunting, etc. The Onomasticon also includes a thesaurus which can be translated into categories for the TACT program.

This project has produced a new kind of tool to assist in the study of the poem, but it has led to questions about exactly what kind of tool it is. McCarty calls it an 'electronic edition' (1996: 240), but the detailed interpretative tagging makes it very different from other works which are called editions. It is perhaps more of a reference work, but a reference work which depends very heavily on the interpretation of one person. It has applications as a tool to aid the study of other Latin poetry, and perhaps tools for the study and analysis of other Latin poets could draw on this tagging. One major contribution of this project have been McCarty's insights into what is involved in the detailed interpretative tagging of literary material. It is fraught with questions of interpretation at all levels, and therefore with the need to justify the interpretations that are made. It forces the scholar to interact with the text at a very detailed level and to wrestle with ambiguities of various kinds. A project of this kind has to be carried out in order to understand what it entails. Parallels can be drawn with research in linguistic tagging where lighter tagging and some ambiguities are now being left in the text. But further exploration linking the tagging to a metrical interpretation of the text might shed new light on the results.

The ability of the computer to find and tabulate patterns makes it an invaluable tool in the study of undeciphered languages or scripts. The computer will not of course be able to decipher the language, but it can arrange and rearrange sequences of characters in many ways and thus help the scholar identify patterns of usage which might lead to a better understanding. An appropriate and consistent encoding scheme is essential for this kind of project. Related or similar material, if available, can also be used for reference. This approach was adopted in a study of the Linear A tablets where reference was made to a lexicon of Linear B. This was used to test hypotheses about the interpretation of certain signs by making parallels with occurrences in Linear B (Packard 1971). Packard carried out further analyses, tabulating the Linear A and Linear B material in many different ways (Packard 1974a). He was also able to make some further projections derived from hypothetical new assignments of signs in Linear A. These computer-generated readings could then be compared with Linear B to try to identify any that might represent plausible interpretations. Hart (1983) reports a somewhat similar analysis of writing and phonology in cuneiform Hittite carried out with the assistance of computer programs.

The computer's ability to find and tabulate patterns has been exploited further in the study of sound and metre in poetry. For some languages and verse forms, especially where the spelling corresponds with the sound or where the metre is very regular, it is possible to write computer programs to perform the scansion. For others scansion and other sound patterns can be built up with machine aid, or even created entirely by manual methods, and then subjected to machine analysis. While tabulation of the results is itself informative, some scholars have also moved on to propose various measures of sound patterns. Distributions are subject to the same problems as in attribution studies (see Chapter 7) since not enough is known about the underlying distribution of sound. The overall picture provided by tabulations accompanied by a discussion of unusual passages or lines serves most purposes well. The analysis of sound and metre seems to be a very obvious application for computers, especially as verse is generally more structured than other types of text and can thus provide a framework within which to operate. But, with the exception of Robey's work on Italian narrative verse and Laan's study of Euripides (see below), surprisingly little work appears to have been carried out recently.

Greek is a language where phonology and orthography correspond well and thus where useful data can be obtained by counting and tabulating letter frequencies. A study of sound patterns in Homer was based on a tabulation of 'sound densities', that is, the number of lines containing 0, 1, 2, 3, 4, 5, etc. occurrences of each letter (Packard 1974b). The sounds are also grouped into their major categories of liquids, labials, gutturals, and dentals. From this Packard was able to investigate those lines which have unusual densities of soft or hard sounds, which he does by also contrasting his findings with those of traditional scholars working with hand counts or intuition. The accuracy of his computer-based counts highlighted several instances where scholars working by traditional means had noted unusual occurrences, but which, in fact, turned out to be fairly common. Packard also investigated unusual clusters of consonants, again highlighting some unusual occurrences. He concludes his paper by proposing a kind of harshness measure, where harsh sounds receive a numerical value which is a high positive weighting and soft sounds receive a high negative weighting. This is used to locate lines with a high harshness value by summing the harshness values for each letter in the line, multiplying the result by 10 and then dividing the result by the number of sounds in the line. He admits that this is a 'primitive measure' (Packard 1974b: 258), and applying it to sequences of lines which have high harshness values drew his attention to some genuinely harsh topics in the text but identified others which did not especially call for harshness. The measure can also be used to locate juxtapositions of harsh and soft lines. This kind of measure, although primitive, can help to isolate interesting features, and it is very easy to recompute it with different weightings to see whether new values make any changes to the overall picture.

Robey's first foray into computer-aided study of verse was an analysis of sound and sense in the *Divine Comedy* (Robey 1987). After some preliminary attempts to use OCP to identify and count alliterations, he devised a computer program which could take advantage of the correspondence between sound and spelling in Italian. His program also handles various problems associated with double letters. The text was pre-edited to deal with the few exceptions, and, of course, once it is known what these might be, other programs can search for instances of these forms in the text. Robey used the SPITBOL programming language, which is particularly good for this kind of analysis. SPITBOL, a faster version of SNOBOL, has excellent facilities for building up patterns, both simple and complex, and then for storing and counting incidences of these patterns as the program passes through the text (Hockey 1985). In this paper Robey discusses the distribution of vocalic alliterations, both with each vowel treated separately and then with *e* and *i*, and *o* and *u* taken together – a process which would require only a very simple modification to the program. Other programs helped him investigate initial phonemes and various combinations of alliterations. See also his analysis of alliterations in Dante, Petrarch, and Tasso (Robey 1988).

For languages where sound and spelling do not correspond well, it is necessary first to make a phonological transcription of the text. There are two approaches to doing this. One consists of simply hand coding every line, which might be reasonable for a small amount of text. It makes sense to retain the original as well, if at all possible, so that the original rather than the coded form can be displayed in the results. The process of creating the transcription can be speeded up by beginning with a word list of the text in which each word occurs only once. The coding can be associated with each word in the word list, forming a kind of dictionary of phonological representations. A program can then pass through the text, deriving the coding for each word from the dictionary and inserting it in the text. Depending on the nature of the material, a program like this might best be run interactively. Where multiple interpretations of a word are possible, the user can choose between them. Chisholm (1976) adopted this approach for his study of German verse, where he devised a rule-based system for identifying syllable boundaries, also programmed in SNOBOL. The result was a phonological transcription of the text from which he was able to display 'frames' showing repeated syllables in their metrical positions.

Two different methods have been used for the identification of metrical patterns. In languages such as Latin and Greek where the metre depends on length of syllable, it is possible to identify some metrical forms automatically. Considerable success is reported in the automatic scanning of Latin hexameter verse, and Ott (1973b) describes the rules built into his algorithm in some detail. Briefly, the program identifies all the syllables which are long by inspecting the consonants following each vowel. It then attempts to fill in the rest of the scansion making sure that it fits the hexameter pattern of six feet of spondees or dactyls with the sixth foot always containing two syllables. The program can detect elisions, but in some cases it has difficulties with double vowels. Its method of dealing with difficult lines is simply to offer several scansions and expect the researcher to choose the correct one. Ott also found it necessary to check all the scansions, although the program proposed very few wrong ones. The scansions can then be related to other features. In his system each line is accompanied by a set of numeric codes indicating word end, elisions, hiatus, word accent, and punctuation. Ott notes that 'nearly everything of metrical interest can be compiled by relatively simple programs' from these codes. He published some of them in print form (see for example Ott 1974), but one can now imagine an interactive system where users, possibly students, could query this database of scanned text to find, for example, monosyllabic words at the ends of lines, or elisions in unexpected positions. Indeed some of Ott's printed publications were accompanied by a set of punched cards so that readers could apply their own analyses to the material. Packard also devised a program for scanning Greek hexameters which operated on similar principles, although Greek is somewhat easier because it has the long vowels eta and omega (Packard 1976).

Other Greek metres are more difficult to handle because of the wide variety of forms. One possible approach is to build up a dictionary of metrical forms in a similar manner to the phonological forms used by Chisholm and then to use a program which is also aware of the metrical form to attempt to scan each line. This was apparently the method adopted by Philippides (1984) in her study of the iambic trimeters in six plays of Euripides. Unfortunately, although she acknowledges in the preface that the computer 'served as an assistant throughout the study' (1984: p. vi), she says little more about the methodology, except to note that her programs were also written in SNOBOL. She notes that the 'computer was programmed to produce automatically much of the metrical scansion' and was also 'able to assist in the subsequent analysis of the meter' (1984: p. vi). Since her investigation concentrated on resolution, that is, words that 'would not otherwise fit metrically into the iambic trimeter line' (1984: 47), one can assume that the scansion was a combination of human and machine analysis. She found a high incidence of resolution in the prologues, and also in the language of those characters who are associated with action, what she calls 'excitement' (1984: 55). Minor roles and the Chorus exhibit less resolution. An examination of the individual words that cause resolution shows a great increase in some types in the three later plays which she examined.

Another computer-based approach to the chronology of Euripides concentrates on elisions in the iambic trimeters, but this is situated in the context of stylometry and the need to create overall descriptions of many features (Laan 1995). Preliminary results from this study show a small increase in the number of lines with elision from the *Medea* to *Orestes*, but a greater increase in the total amount of elision. Another approach to using sound to investigate the chronology of a Greek dramatist is reported by Craik and Kaferly (1987), where vowel-to-consonant ratios were examined in the seven plays of Sophocles, especially in the initial position. Their study showed a high proportion of initial vowels in the earlier plays and a trend towards more initial consonants in the later plays.

Fewer computer-based studies appear to have been carried out on English verse, but there have been some investigations of iambic pentameters which it is possible to scan semi-automatically, especially when working with a dictionary of metrical forms or a phonological transcription of the text. In their analysis of some of Hopkins's verse, Dilligan and Bender (1973) show how the scansion of each line can be derived by a program which records stress, punctuation, number of syllables, possible elisions, and assonance and alliterations. Once these features have been recorded, a mass of information can be tabulated. Their examples include positions where assonance and alliteration occur, and the places where function words receive some stress. Elsewhere, Dilligan and Lynn (1972) discuss more general questions of computers and prosody, particularly in relation to lines which appear to violate the rules. In her section of the paper, Lynn reports on an experiment with Chaucer where variations in spelling could be handled at the transcription phase.

Rhyme schemes are perhaps a more obvious application, particularly in languages where the spelling and sound have good correspondence. The rhyme indexes of Early German texts produced by Wisbey (1971) were derived from reverse concordances. Wisbey envisaged that these could be used as a reference tool, for example to look at abstract nouns in the rhyming position or to compare with other authors (1971: 33). If the rhyme scheme is regular enough, a computer program can identify and tabulate all the rhymes. Robey developed another set of SPITBOL programs to examine rhymes and rhyme words in a corpus of epics of the Italian Renaissance. He describes how the main program operates by matching characters, starting at the end of the words that rhyme together in each eight-line stanza (Robey 1990: 98). His program marks possible anomalies which he can then check by hand. He reports fewer than fifty errors in 38,746 lines of Ariosto's *Orlando Furioso*. From this analysis he comments on the types of rhymes, high incidences of rhyme types, and high numbers of different rhyme types in the four authors. He also notes how the computer can help with a study of what he calls 'equivocal rhymes (the rhyming together of two or three words with the same form, but different meanings or functions)' (1990: 108).

These investigations of sound patterns become more complete when several features are analysed together, making it possible to examine the interplay of different features. In a small way the study by Dilligan and Bender conducted almost thirty years ago shows the value of this, as did, on a larger scale, Ott's system for Latin hexameters. Both these systems were developed long before good facilities for interactive computing became available, but the methodological principles for deriving the scansions and investigating and tabulating the interplay of different features are very sound and could easily be implemented in a Windows or Web environment. Robey has developed his work on the *Divine Comedy* much further by producing a version of the text which incorporates word accent and syllable structure (Robey 1993). He was able to define a series of rules which could identify about 80 per cent of word accents, but concluded that the programming effort for defining more rules would not be worthwhile because manual checking would in any case be necessary. He also chose not to use a dictionary or electronic word list approach to marking the accents, because the accent structure of a word is always affected by the function of the word and its context and would thus need to be checked manually. Instead he wrote a SPITBOL program which was used in the interactive scanning of the *Comedy*. The program first applied the rules he had defined and offered a preliminary scansion with some comments. He could then verify and correct the scansion interactively. Any changes made by manual editing were recorded by the program and could thus be retrieved the next time that the same word was encountered. The results from a preliminary analysis are reported in Robey (1999).

Some researchers have begun to investigate whether the regularity and formal properties of metrical forms and scansion can be implemented in a more rigorous manner which might be more amenable to the kinds of verification made possible by computer science techniques. One possibility explored by de Jong and Laan (1996) was to build what they call 'a grammar of Greek verse'. In this approach the rules are kept separate from the program and what is called 'a parser generator' builds the parsing or analysis process from the rules and then applies it to the text. Any changes to the rules can be made without changing the program, thus eliminating the possibly widespread consequences of this. An alternative approach is somewhat similar to the neural networks discussed briefly in Chapter 7. Hayward (1996) calls this 'a connectionist model'. Very briefly, the syllables in a line of poetry (in his case an iambic pentameter) are considered as a series of units which interact with each other. Each syllable is in fact considered as six different units, thus there are sixty possible units in a pentameter line. The model cycles through the line updating the amount of stress for each syllable according to its relationship with the other units in the line until a kind of steady-state scansion is achieved. Hayward shows several examples of unmetrical lines which the model can distinguish. It would be interesting to apply this to other metres, but it is not clear what the model would do when the number of syllables in a line is not fixed.

Computers can also assist the study of the structure of dramatic works. If the text has been marked up sufficiently it should be possible to investigate the relationships between characters, when they are and are not on stage, in relation to the usual structure of acts and scenes. The commonly used structures of acts and scenes in Shakespeare were not particularly clear to Elizabethan theatre-goers, who would be more likely to see structure in terms of shifts from prose to verse, from balcony to stage level, or from song to dialogue, or of when a new character enters or exits (Steele 1991: 15). In his research, carried out with the assistance of the TACT program, Steele was able to derive an outline of who is on stage at any one time. This method could be further enhanced to model who is speaking and to whom, and to investigate the relationships between the characters. Ilsemann (1995) also discusses a program which analyses the structure of plays. The program identifies who is speaking, the length of speeches, the relationships between characters on stage at one time, and the distribution of their speeches through the play, all of which can be represented by some useful graphics. The example he uses is Lillo's *The London Merchant*, where he finds only few people on stage at one time and also some very long speeches for the main characters, which emphasize their dominance.

The kind of analysis carried out by Burrows on the Austen novel could equally well be applied to drama. Potter (1981, 1989) has also attempted to investigate the structure of some modern plays and the characters within them by the use of syntax, and exclamations and questions. Some of these analyses may at first appear shallow, but they could well work together with other approaches to studying the same plays and supplement other hypotheses or findings.

There are many other examples of computer-based techniques for the study of literature, but all follow similar patterns. The computer is best as an invaluable assistant. It can provide the kind of overall picture which would not be possible by any other means. Features which are easily identified and counted by computer may not necessarily be meaningful or may only provide a partial picture, but even a partial view may be useful provided that the interpretation of the picture acknowledges the limitations. A fuller view can be more helpful, but there are still dangers in investigating and counting vocabulary without making allowances for negatives, idioms, and metaphors, all of which can distort frequencies. In the most useful studies, researchers have used the computer to find features of interest and then examined these instances individually, discarding those that are not relevant, and perhaps refining the search terms in order to find more instances. They have also situated their project within the broader sphere of criticism on their author or texts, and reflected critically on the methodology used to interpret the results, avoiding the 'black-box' tendency of some projects to produce tables of numbers without any serious assessment of what those numbers might mean.

6 | Linguistic Analysis

The use of concordances and other computer-based tools for linguistic analysis developed rapidly in the 1990s and is now generally known as corpus linguistics. Simple text analysis tools of the kind we examined in Chapter 4 can provide evidence of many linguistic features within a corpus or collection of electronic texts. Word class tagging and other forms of annotation can enhance these corpora, offering more sophisticated analyses, but this chapter will first concentrate on what can be done with simple concordance tools. Most of the applications discussed in this chapter are based on language corpora, but they are just as relevant for specific literary or other humanities texts. Chapter 2 surveys some corpora in common use and discusses options for the design and development of a linguistic corpus.

As we have already seen, computer-based corpus linguistics began with the compilation of the Brown Corpus at Brown University in the early 1960s. However, Chomsky's preference for linguistic 'competence' as opposed to 'performance' had a profound influence on linguistics in North America for over two decades. His argument that a corpus can never provide evidence for all possible linguistic features turned many people away from corpus linguistics and towards working with invented sentences and native speakers' intuition. There were a few exceptions, notably Biber, whose work will be discussed below, but most North American linguists avoided corpora for a long time in favour of working with 'toy sentences' and intuition. 'Performance' relies on evidence which is best provided by a corpus, and scholars elsewhere, notably in Europe, continued to argue in favour of real evidence. For English language corpora, Geoffrey Leech and his group in Lancaster, and John Sinclair and his group in Birmingham, led the way in Britain. Both groups published accounts of their work in 1987, discussing their approaches to compiling corpora and their analysis tools (Garside, Leech, and Sampson 1987; Sinclair 1987). Stubbs (1993) traces the development of corpus linguistics in Britain, concentrating on the influence of John Sinclair. Leech has argued in favour of corpora on many occasions, but see especially Leech (1987, 1991, 1992) and Leech and Fligelstone (1992). Other historical surveys can be found in Kennedy (1998: 8–9), McEnery and Wilson (1996: 17–18), and Svartvik (1996). The 1991 Nobel Symposium was devoted to corpus linguistics, and the proceedings (Svartvik 1992) are a useful survey of the range of issues under debate at that time.

Examples of corpus use are far too numerous to mention them all in this book, but just one or two samples of each will suffice to illustrate the possibilities. In some cases I have found it interesting to attempt to reproduce some of the results using the BNC sampler. A corpus can serve as a reference tool in the study of other material. A detailed study of *utterly* is reported by Louw (1993). He used the Cobuild Bank of English as a kind of reference tool in a study of irony in what he calls 'collocative clash' (1993: 159) in relation to two poems by Larkin, where, in one case, the phrase 'Utterly unlike the snow' appears. *Utterly* has a bad connotation in most of the Cobuild examples. There are only twelve occurrences in the BNC sampler, and all but one also have a bad connotation. These include *utterly meaningless, utterly stupid, utterly disgraceful, utterly and profoundly miserable.* Louw also notes the negative pursuits of *bent on.* There are only two examples of this in the BNC sampler but both support his view. He concludes his paper by speculating that his findings might be of interest to what he calls 'the persuasion industry', that is, advertising, where the use of certain words immediately sends signals to the reader. The use of intensifiers in Cobuild has been studied by Partington (1993), particularly in relation to language change. He comments on the delexicalization of *terribly.* Examples from the BNC sampler support this with *terribly sorry, terribly polite, terribly important, terribly bored,* and even *terribly yellow* (of teeth). Most of these come from the spoken part of the corpus. Partington also notes that *heavily* is no longer associated with weight. In the BNC sampler *heavily* is preceded by *depend, invested, drinking,* and followed by *used, concentrated, discounted, mottled. Highly* is associated with emotions and feelings. Examples in the BNC sampler include *highly delighted, highly successful, highly suspicious,* and *highly likely.*

It has long been noted that corpora are invaluable for the study of phrasal verbs where a right-sorted concordance can show all the particles that occur after a verb and bring together all the uses of each particle. Chapter 5 of Sinclair (1991) investigates the phrasal verbs introduced by *set* in the Cobuild Bank of English. Each of these is followed or preceded by its own particular pattern. Sinclair notes for example (1991: 74–5) that the subject of *set in* is usually something unpleasant or negative such as *rot, anticlimax, disillusionment,* or *vicious (circle).* In the BNC sampler, examples of the subject of *set in* include *frosts, disillusion,* and *panic.* The form *set about* is followed by an *-ing* form in something like 'set about doing something', but preceded by connotations of uncertainty, for example *the faintest idea* (1991: 76). The form *set off* is most often used in connection with starting a journey (1991: 76), but it also is used to start something where the object is almost always something new and has the indefinite article *a,* for example *set off a train of thought* (1991: 77). The most frequent use of *set out* is not starting a journey, but signifying intention and is followed by an infinitive clause (1991: 77). Other particles after *set* include *about, apart, aside,* and *up.* This kind of application helps to enhance our understanding of particular verb forms and the situations in which they are used. It also highlights the benefits of studying words in their contexts, not in isolation as literary projects tend to do.

The editors of the Cobuild grammar series derive all their examples from the Bank of English. In his introduction to the *Cobuild English Grammar,* Sinclair notes that all the examples are drawn from the Bank of English (Sinclair 1990). He argues strongly for the use of hard evidence ('there is no justification for inventing examples' (1990: p. xi) and cites as an example of a simple subject–verb clause 'Trains stopped', which is a genuine example and communicates the structure much better than the invented 'Birds sing'.

Large corpora yield very many occurrences of common words, but language learners often have difficulty with some of these words. A common problem is the use of the article, which must occur many thousands of times in the Bank of English. The editors of the Cobuild grammar have trawled these to include a range of instances of different usages of *the* (Sinclair 1990: 43–8) and *a* and *an* (1990: 54–5). G. Francis (1993) discusses the data-driven approach to grammar at Cobuild, and cites many examples where evidence from the Bank of English contradicts the descriptions in other grammars. She looks at introductory *it* when preceded for example by *make* and *find.* A search for the phrase *find it* and *make it* in the BNC sampler confirms her findings that these phrases are often followed by choices between something easy and something difficult. Many more examples could be cited here, but it is easy to see how these examples can be derived by inspecting a concordance of a phrase, or a right- or left-sorted concordance of a particular word.

Corpora are now recognized as invaluable tools for learners. Tribble and Jones (1990) give several applications of concordances in the classroom. They show first how concordances can be used to inspect learner texts for misuses of words, problems with style and register, lexical errors, and also to examine word order, prepositions, tense, and articles. But they also note how difficult it is to study words or other features which are missing. They describe how concordances can be used as a kind of 'fill in the blank' exercise where students fill in a missing keyword based on an examination of the surrounding context. Their examples include the differences between *said* and *told*, or *look*, *see*, and *watch*, and the use of *like*.

Mindt (1996) describes how corpora can be used to help shape the syllabus for learners of English in Germany. He notes that the ten most frequent verbs in British and American English account for more than 45 per cent of all irregular verbs (1996: 233). It is easy to compare corpus evidence to the order of the introduction of material in language textbooks. Mindt's example here is modal verbs where textbooks introduce *can*, *may*, and *must* first, and *will* only later. But in the corpora he studied, *will* is the third most frequent modal after *would* and *can* (1996: 235). This is because *will* is mostly used to express the future and occurs very often in spoken material. Mindt also noticed differences between American and British English in expressing the future. Most German textbooks do not mention *shall* as a means of expressing the future, but this is found more frequently in British English, especially preceded by *I*. The BNC sampler supports this with 192 examples of *I shall* and 206 of *I will*. A scan through the other examples of *shall* also brings up *we shall* (70 instances), *shall we*, and *shall I*. Other instances occur in legal language, for example, *committee members as shall be determined by a general meeting*.

The TACT program was used by Wooldridge (1991) to aid learners of French in a first-year undergraduate course. Students used a Maigret novel to examine the difference between *savoir* and *connaître* or when to use *de* and when to use *à*, and more generally when to use the article. The students come to recognize thematic or typical items of vocabulary, for example, Maigret lighting his pipe (1991: 77), and can then look at words associated with *lighting* and *lit*, and relate this to other objects that can be lit (1991: 80). Wichmann *et al.* (1997) contains a variety of papers on the use of corpora in teaching and learning, including German, French, Welsh, child language acquisition, speech and prosody, and literary analysis. See also the papers in Granger (1997).

Texts that are tagged with demographic or other sociolinguistic variables can be used as a basis for comparative sociolinguistic studies. Nevalainen and Raumolin-Brunberg (1996) is a collection of papers describing work based on the Corpus of Early English Correspondence. This corpus was compiled at the University of Helsinki and it consists of 2.7 million words of correspondence from 1417 to 1681 (Nurmi 1998).

It is intended for use in historical sociolinguistics, and each of the letters is encoded for sender, recipient, region, form of address, etc., using a COCOA-like encoding scheme derived from that used for the Helsinki Corpus. One paper in the volume (Nevalainen 1996a) investigates social stratification in Tudor and early Stuart English by an examination of the distributions of *ye* v. *you, be* v. *are, the which* v. *which*, and *who* v. *(the) which*. These show differences with regard to social rank at the beginning of the period, but a convergence towards the end, with a tendency for the intermediate ranks to adopt the new forms first. Nevalainen also looks at gender differences in a manner not dissimilar from Burrows's study on Jane Austen, but the interest here is in the predominance of language changes introduced by women (Nevalainen 1996b). The parallels with many other sociolinguistic studies, whether synchronic or diachronic, are obvious. Similar procedures can be used to examine child language, political speeches, legal documents, regional variations, interview transcripts, and the like. Stubbs (1996) devotes a whole chapter to the examination of words 'which are central to contemporary British culture' (1996: 157). One area he addresses is that of employment or work. He notes that *work* occurs in a large number of compound nouns (1996: 177) and that *working* occurs in fixed phrases. The BNC sampler includes *working class, working together, working order. Job* also occurs in many fixed phrases and tends to have negative connotations (1996: 178). *Labour* also has negative connotations – Stubbs speculates on whether the British Labour Party is aware of this. In the BNC sampler many of the instances of *labour* are in the *Labour Party* or the party simply referred to as *Labour. Career* is strongly positive and *employment* often indicates legal use.

Although finding examples is useful in itself, interest has grown in the measurement of the significance of examples. Some of the techniques discussed in Chapter 7 also apply here, but a number of other measures are used for lexical work. The type/token ratio is the most common and the most simple to calculate. It measures the range of vocabulary in a text. Type is used for the number of different words or vocabulary items. Tokens are the instances of each type. For example, if the word *and* occurred 100 times, it would score 1 as a type and 100 as a token. The type/token ratio is simply the number of types divided by the number of tokens. It is always a number between 0 and 1. Type/token ratios close to 1 indicate a wide spread of vocabulary. Those close to 0 indicate a small range of vocabulary as, for example, might be found in child language. Unless further linguistic analysis has been carried out on the text, each different form of a word will be treated as a type, and for inflected languages this can mean many forms of the same word. The type/token ratio can be used for comparative purposes but it is dependent on text length, since the rate at which new words are introduced in a text decreases throughout the text. It can therefore only be used to compare texts of approximately the same length.

Computers have made it possible to study lexical collocations or words which frequently occur close to each other. For this kind of analysis, one word is chosen as the node or keyword and a program then scans the concordance entries for that word and collects up all the words which occur within a certain distance of the word. This distance is called the span; it might be up to ten words, although a span of five is fairly common. Sometimes common words are omitted from the span so that the analysis can concentrate on content words. Jones and Sinclair (1974), in a paper summarizing work reported in more detail in 1970, describe an exploratory collocation analysis performed on a corpus of spoken English where they first examine the 'lexical patterning' of common words (*the, a, and, of, in, to, I, you, it*). They also then investigate further what words might be most suitable for collocation analysis and concentrate their study on some frequently occurring nouns and verbs. The concept of time occurs frequently throughout the text and they create a diagram showing the relationships and distances between 'time' words and their immediate collocates (1974: 41).

Berry-Rogghe (1973) discusses the relevance of collocations in lexical studies with reference to an investigation of the collocates of *house*, from which she is able to derive some notion of the semantic field of *house*. This study was carried out on a relatively small amount of literary text and this may have affected the results. For example, the only three occurrences of *decorate* in these texts are as a collocate of *house*. However, Berry-Rogghe describes her methodology in some detail and the method she used for calculating the significance of collocates has been adopted by various other projects and is also implemented in the TACT program. Her program counts the total number of occurrences of the node, and the total number of occurrences of each collocate of the node within a certain span. It then attempts to indicate the probability of these collocates occurring if the words were distributed randomly throughout the text, and can thus estimate the expected number of collocates. It then compares the expected number with the observed number and generates a 'z-score', which indicates the significance of the collocate.

The first table she presents shows the collocates of *house* based on a span of three words and in descending order of frequency. First is *the*, which co-occurs thirty-five times with *house*, but the total number of occurrences of *the* is 2,368. *The* is followed by *this, a, of, I, in, it, my, is, have*, and *to*, before the first significant collocate *sold* where six of the seven occurrences are within three words of house. Four words further on is *commons*, where all four occurrences collocate with *house*, obviously from the phrase *House of Commons*. When reordered by z-score, the list begins *sold*, *commons*, *decorate*, *this*, *empty*, *buying*, *painting*, *opposite*. In a later paper and working with a larger corpus, Berry-Rogghe uses this technique to investigate phrasal verbs, by looking at the significance of immediate left-hand collocates of *in* (Berry-Rogghe 1974). The list begins with *interested*, *versed*, *believe*, *found*, *live*. Right-hand collocates of *in* begin with *spring*, *spite*, *short*, *reality*, *afternoon*, *fact*, and *daytime*, showing idioms and also time-related topics.

Olsen and Harvey (1988) use Berry-Rogghe's formula in a study comparing French Canadian political texts from 1805 to 1835 with French revolutionary material from the *Journal de la Société de 1789*. They note that the word *droits* occurs frequently in both samples, but it associates with very different words. In 1789 the most frequent collocate is in the phrase *droits naturels*, but this does not occur at all in the French Canadian text. Similarly the most frequent collocate *droits et privilèges* in the French Canadian texts does not occur in 1789 (1988: 458–9). They also examine the collocates of *patrie*, which occurs less frequently than they expected, and of *pays*, which is the most frequently occurring content word in the French Canadian texts where *lois*, *intérêts* feature highly in the collocates (1988: 459–61). They are also able to contrast the use of *peuple* in the French Canadian texts where it represents 'the democratic element of parliamentary government' (1988: 462) with its use in the French material where it is almost synonymous with the nation, correlating highly with nation, and power (1988: 463).

Two other statistical techniques are often used to examine collocates. Clear (1993) provides an explanation of both techniques with useful examples. He notes the importance of being able to find collocates when they are only collocates, relating this to the traditional information retrieval problems of precision and recall. Mutual information measures the strength of the association between two words, but it can also place low frequency items close to the top. To explain it, Clear uses the example of *kith* and *kin* where a corpus contains ten occurrences of *kin*, and five of *kith* all of which follow *kin*. This obviously indicates high mutual information (1993: 278), but it is also non-directional. The occurrence of *kith* is more likely to indicate *kin* than vice versa. The t-score is better for finding frequently occurring items. It measures 'not the strength of association between two items, but the confidence with which we can claim that there is some association' (1993: 281). Mutual information is good for indicating idioms, but t-score gives a better overall picture. At the beginning of a larger survey of the use of statistics in lexical analysis, Church *et al.* (1991) introduce mutual information and t-score in a study of the associations of *strong* and *powerful* in AP Newswire texts. Oakes (1998) introduces a number of other methods for measuring collocations, some of which are only for the mathematically minded. See also Church *et al.* (1994).

For the non-mathematical or those who are suspicious of statistics, even simple counts of collocates can begin to show useful results, especially for comparative purposes. Haskel (1971) reports on an exploratory study using the Brown Corpus where she compared samples taken from press reportage and government documents with fiction. She was interested in the literal or figurative use of words and found that the figurative use occurs more often in the informative prose than in the imaginative prose. In fiction *cut* collocated with *open, belly, concussion,* and *boy.* In press reportage it collocated with *inflate, modest, expenses,* and *estimate. Dead* collocated with *fight, mourned,* and *wounded* in fiction but with issues and republicanism in the press. A similar pattern was shown by *top,* which collocated with *steeple, head, stairs,* and *wall* in fiction and *officials, personnel,* and *executive* in the informative samples (Haskel 1971: 167).

Biber's (1988) investigation of variation in language attempts to identify a range of features which characterize written and spoken language. He believes that many discriminators are needed to identify different text types and he set out to 'systematically describe the linguistic characteristics of the range of genres in English, whether typically spoken, typically written, or other' (1988: 55). The study was constructed so that 'any individual genre can be located within an "oral" and "literate" space, specifying both the nature and the extent of the differences and similarities between that genre and the range of other genres in English'. The London–Lund Corpus was used for the spoken material, and Biber chose the LOB Corpus over the Brown Corpus because he did not want to compare American with British English. He examined fifteen written genres from LOB, six spoken genres from London–Lund and, for comparison, two types of letters which are from American sources. The study is based on sixty-seven linguistic features which he used in earlier research, although he admits that the choice of some of these was to some extent determined by what his tagging program could handle. For each feature he first calculated a rate of occurrence per 1,000, with mean, minimum, and maximum values. He then applied a multivariate technique called factor analysis to these counts, arriving at seven factors or dimensions which have both positive and negative loadings for some of the variables. (See Alt 1990 for an introduction to multivariate analysis and also the discussion in Chapter 7 below.) Dimension 1 has high negative loadings for nouns, word length, prepositional phrases, type/ token ratio, adverbials, and agentless passives. Its positive loadings are more complex, but this enabled Biber to deduce that dimension 1 represents 'high informational density and exact informational content versus affective, interactional and generalized content' (Biber 1988: 107). He describes this as 'informational versus involved production'. Dimension 2 shows 'narrative versus non-narrative concerns', and dimension 3 is 'explicit versus situation-dependent reference' (1988: 110). Dimension 4 is 'overt expression of persuasion' (1988: 111), and dimension 5 is 'abstract v. non-abstract information' (1988: 112–13). Dimension 6 is 'on-line informational elaboration' (1988: 114). He decided not to pursue dimension 7 as the loadings on it were weak.

Biber then examined the genres which associate with each of these dimensions. For dimension 4, professional letters and editorials are at one end with high degrees of persuasion, but broadcasts, which merely report events, are at the other. Speech and writing overlap in some of the dimensions, for example fiction aligns with speech on dimension 5 'abstract versus non-abstract information'. An examination of the samples within each genre revealed some differences in academic prose. This was shown in the use of narrative (dimension 2), with humanities having a high score and technology/engineering a low score (1988: 193), but some samples of the humanities, for example philosophy, have a low score for narrative. Also on dimension 4, academic prose in politics, education, and law is persuasive, whereas empirical disciplines (e.g. social sciences) use the persuasive form less (1988: 194). Dimension 5 (abstract or technical information) draws out the distinction between the sciences, which favour the agentless passive, and the active voice used more often in the humanities (1988: 194).

In a paper published in the same year as Biber's book, Oostdijk (1988) discusses some of the problems she sees in using corpora in studies of variation. While she acknowledges the value of corpora, she has problems with the genre definitions used by Biber and his colleague Finegan in their earlier work. They do not question the validity of the genres in the Brown and LOB corpora which were initially identified by the group of scholars convened to plan the Brown Corpus. Genre is a very difficult topic, especially for general-purpose material, but few if any of the corpus builders have looked to the library community where there is training and expertise in classification and the organization of knowledge. Oostdijk also discusses Biber's selection of linguistic features. These are based on earlier research. Obviously one has to start somewhere, but, as Biber himself pointed out in his study of corpus design, this work is iterative. Revision and modification may well be necessary after some work has been carried out. Nevertheless Biber's study has helped to illuminate some features of spoken and written text and has clearly shown that a multi-dimensional approach can yield useful results.

Although simple searches for sequences of letters can be reasonably effective for some applications, the need for more advanced analysis is obvious. A text in which the words are encoded as their lemmas (dictionary headings) could yield more interesting information for research applications. The lemmas would then be subject to concordance-type analysis. Adding the lemmas by hand might be possible for a small application, but a computer can also provide help with this operation. Lemmatization is especially useful for inflected languages where there can be many forms of one lemma. For languages which have less inflection, researchers began to investigate how part of speech encoding could be added to a text. This is normally called word class tagging. Much of the work so far in this area has concentrated on corpora for natural language processing, but there is no reason why it should not be used for literary analysis, especially when coupled with some manual checking and correction. In corpus linguistics adding word class tags and other kinds of information to a corpus is called corpus annotation. Leech (1993) provides an excellent overview, noting that the annotations should be easy to extract or remove from the corpus, and that the annotation scheme should be clearly explained.

The Brown Corpus was the first corpus to be tagged for parts of speech. The tagging process was carried out by two graduate students (Greene and Rubin) supervised by Kučera and Francis. This was a semi-automatic process (Leech 1997; W. N. Francis 1980). A computer program was able to tag about 77 per cent of the corpus successfully by working with a lexicon, a list of word endings, and a set of rules (Garside 1997: 105). The computer could attempt to strip endings from words, look the resulting stems up in the lexicon, and then apply rules indicating what sequences of tags can occur. The dictionary contained 2,860 words, of which 61 per cent had a unique tag, and the ending list consisted of 446 strings. A program called TAGGIT then attempted to choose the correct tag by inspecting the surrounding words and applying a series of rules. A researcher went over all the results to choose the correct tag where the computer program had offered several tags and to correct erroneous tagging. The Brown system used seventy-seven tags. Some computer-based tools can also assist with the checking by searching the entire corpus for similar instances. The tagging of the Brown Corpus was significant, not only because it was the first and laid down a methodological groundwork for word class tagging but because it provided an accurate tagged corpus which could be used as a reference by other tagging systems.

Many taggers now exist. The use of a tagger is reported by Cobuild in many of their publications including the introduction to the second edition of the Cobuild dictionary (*Collins Cobuild* 1995). Biber (1988) describes his tagger in some detail in an appendix. Church *et al.* (1991) also report the use of their own tagger in their study of collocations in the AP Newswire texts. Leech and his group at Lancaster have been working on tagging and annotation systems for corpora for many years and a more detailed examination of their CLAWS system can show what is involved in developing a tagging system for English. The Lancaster group has continued to publish details of CLAWS, its successes and problem areas as it has developed. CLAWS was used to tag the 100 million words of the British National Corpus.

The first version of CLAWS (CLAWS1) was written between 1981 and 1983 in order to tag the LOB Corpus. Garside (1987) describes the tagging process in some detail. A program first prepared the text for tagging by converting it to a vertical format with one word per line accompanied by a reference locator for the word. Punctuation was also treated as a kind of word so that the CLAWS could use this to detect the end of a sequence of tags. Certain other tasks were performed by the pre-editing stage. Contracted forms such as *he'll* were separated into two units. Capitalized forms which are not at the beginning of a sentence were retained because these might be proper nouns which are difficult for any tagger, but other capitals at the beginning of a sentence were converted to lower case. With CLAWS1 a human editor inspected the corpus for any further problems, such as abbreviations and arithmetic formulae, and all of these were stored so that future versions of the program could detect them automatically. The tagging itself was carried out by two programs. WORDTAG assigned one or more tags to each word and CHAINPROBS attempted to choose the most likely tag.

CLAWS begins by using WORDTAG to examine each word in turn. It first checks for any genitives *'s* or *s'* and then looks the word up in a lexicon. The lexicon for CLAWS1 contained some 7,200 forms and the nucleus of it was constructed by linguists. The lexicon is treated as a dynamic object, with new information continually being added to it or existing information being refined. It may have several possible tags for one word, and these are stored in order of decreasing likelihood with the rare ones marked as such. Approximately 65–70 per cent of words are found in the lexicon.

WORDTAG then deals with various forms which are made up mostly of numerals. The next step is to look at hyphenated words and attempt to identify prefixes (*hyper-*, *mis-*, *out-*, etc.) (Garside 1987: 38). The part of the word after the hyphen is looked up in the lexicon and then in a list of suffixes list if necessary. If this part-word is found, various rules are then applied according to the tags assigned to the part-word. If the word is not hyphenated, the next stage looks for initial capitals and attempts to remove suffixes such as *-ish* and *-ian*, and will then assign the proper noun tag. A more complex series of steps deals with the analysis of suffixes. The suffix list for CLAWS1 contained 720 word endings of up to five letters. The program can thus, for example, identify words ending in *-ness* as a noun. Garside discusses some problem suffixes, notably *-able* (adjective), *-ble* (noun or verb), and *-le* (noun). The program looks for these in this order and exceptions such as *cable* and *enable* are in the lexicon. The suffix *-s* is dealt with in a different way. It is removed from the word and the resulting form is looked up in the lexicon and in the suffix list. But for these words the only possible cases are the third person singular of the verb or a plural noun. The example given by Garside is *kinds*, where the lexicon gives noun or adjective, but the *-s* form can only be the noun. Any words that have no tagging assigned to them at the end of all these processes are given a tag of noun, verb, or adjective.

When the text has been processed by WORDTAG, every word has one or more tags associated with it. Garside notes (1987: 39) that about 35 per cent will have more than one tag. The CHAINPROBS program attempts to select the most likely tag by inspecting the surrounding words. It does this by using the likelihood or probability of occurrences of pairs of tags: these initial probabilities were derived from the Brown Corpus tags. The Lancaster group began by using the rules in the Brown TAGGIT program, but Marshall (1987: 43) notes some of the difficulties encountered because the TAGGIT rules only work where words in the surrounding context of the word being considered have unambiguous tags. Marshall then goes on to describe in detail how CHAINPROBS was developed. It was based on an analysis of co-occurring tags in the Brown Corpus from which a matrix of probabilities of any one tag being next to any other tag was built. These probabilities can be applied to the words, and from them some indication of the strength of the preference for a tag can be derived. Marshall gives an example sentence where the word *involved* in 'this task involved a very great deal of detailed work for the committee' is assigned the tags [VBD]90/ VBN/10 JJ@/0 which indicates that the probability of it being a past-tense verb is 90 per cent and the probability of it being a past participle is 10 per cent. The probability of it being an adjective (JJ which is also marked @ for rare) is 0. CHAINPROBS investigates all possible sequences of tags for each sentence and uses the probabilities to offer the most likely analysis. The development of CHAINPROBS continued on a trial basis with the output being inspected by humans and refinements being made to adjust for errors. CLAWS has developed in this way over many years and the statistical models embedded in it can be refined as it draws on more texts which are already tagged.

Idioms or multi-word terms are a particular problem for taggers. The first version of CLAWS included a program called IDIOMTAG, which ran after WORDTAG and looked for a list of some 150 phrases (Garside 1987: 40), notably those beginning with *as* where the word following *as* has been tagged as a possible adjective resulting in a phrase like *as strong as*. An initial investigation of these forms led the Lancaster team to develop something which they have called a 'ditto-tag', which marks a sequence of words which has a special meaning and a meaning which is different from the one derived when the words within the sequence are treated separately. Blackwell (1987) describes the development of IDIOMTAG and discusses several problem areas. Difficulties occurred in cases where an adverb is embedded in the idiom sequence, for example *so as not to*, which the first version of IDIOMTAG did not recognize as being similar to *so as to*.

Nevertheless, CLAWS1 successfully tagged 96–97 per cent of the LOB Corpus. The tagging was checked and completed by linguists. The first refinement to CLAWS was an attempt to eliminate the pre-editing stage, but the lexicon has also been refined and developed. N. Smith (1997) reports that various versions of the lexicon contained 15,000–23,000 entries in the early 1990s. Eliminating human operations with the text became particularly important when the tagging of the 100 million-word British National Corpus began. While it is possible for humans to check and correct 1 million words, this could not be done for 100 million words. CLAWS4 is described in Garside (1997), where he elaborates on the statistical models which estimate the sequence of tags using what is called a 'hidden Markov model' (1997: 105). For the BNC, CLAWS was able to make use of the SGML tagging to identify foreign words which might have accented characters, and also fractions and abbreviations. But CLAWS also needed to recognize opening and closing SGML tags and assign them a tag of NULL. Some of the SGML needed to be filed and then returned to the text, and all capitalization had to be retained. The lexicon lookup stage for the BNC tagging is very close to that used for the LOB (Garside 1997: 112–13), except that the default tag now also includes adverbs. Much of the recent development of CLAWS has concentrated on the 'ditto-tags'. A new rule-based template tagger has been developed to deal with these, but it has been designed in a general-purpose way to deal with other pattern and rule matching needs (Fligelstone, Pacey, and Rayson 1997).

The spoken part of the BNC presented a new challenge for CLAWS. The program not only had to recognize the SGML tags representing, for example, laughs and pauses in the spoken material but also to deal with the ill-formed data which often occurs in speech. Garside (1995) outlines the modifications designed to deal with spoken text. These include additions to the lexicon for 'words' such as *grrr, blah, okey-dokey*, and other slang and taboo words, additions to the set of contractions including *d'ya, gotta*, special treatment for some truncated words and interventions of *er* and *erm*, and various types of repetition. The BNC part of speech tagging is implemented by a <w> tag for each word as is shown in

<w PPIS1>I <w VV0>hold <w AT1>a <w JJ>great <w NN1>enthusiasm <w IF>for <w JJ>exotic <w NN1>foliage <w NN2>plants <w CC>and <w VH0>have <w VVN>started <w TO>to <w VVI>expand <w APPGE>my <w NN1>collection<c YSTP>.

(BNC Sampler C9c S0022)

Much debate has developed over what should go in a part of speech tag set. The original Brown Corpus tag set had seventy-seven tags. This set was extended to 133 tags for CLAWS1 and 166 for CLAWS2 (Garside 1987: 30). However the larger the number of tags, the more difficult it is for either computers or humans to distinguish between them. The BNC was originally tagged with the CLAWS5 tag set of sixty-one tags plus punctuation. The sampler where the tagging has been refined and hand-checked uses CLAWS7 with 135 tags plus twelve punctuation tags. Leech has argued on several occasions that there is no 'God's truth' about tagging (Leech 1993: 275, 1997: 6). No single annotation scheme can claim authority. Schemes should attempt to be theory-neutral and the importance of speed, accuracy, and consistency demand simple schemes. Individual users may then extend the scheme if they wish. He also notes that software systems sometimes work better with artificial tags, giving the example of the word *one* in English, which can be tagged as ONE or can be made into three tags which require much human disambiguation (Leech 1993: 280). Like many others, the CLAWS tag set has been designed so that it can be decomposed by a computer program. As can be seen from the example above, tags beginning with N are nouns, those beginning with V are verbs, and adjective tags begin with JJ. The errors in the initial tagging of the LOB Corpus are discussed by Johansson (1985), where he also comes to the conclusion that sometimes ambiguity is intended by the author and that in many cases there is no clear distinction between tags.

CLAWS is also relatively successful with literary material and is certainly very much better than the EYEBALL system used by Ross (1973), which has twenty parts of speech and also attempts to carry out some clause analysis. Ross (1981) reports that he used this system to analyse Blake, Keats, and Coleridge, and also Conrad's *Heart of Darkness* where the program helped to illuminate Conrad's use of prepositional phrases (1981: 99). EYEBALL worked by first looking up forms in a dictionary and then applying rules which are described in some detail in Ross (1973), but it needed much error correction. Milic's (1967) work on Swift predated computer assistance with word class tagging and it was carried out on hand-entered codes.

The ICE project has adopted a rather different approach in its tag set (Greenbaum and Yibin 1996). Its tag set was originally based on the set developed by the TOSCA research group in Nijmegen, but has now been developed in different directions. It includes nineteen word classes. One or more features may be associated with each word class and these are included as part of the tag, making a total of 262 combinations. The tagging is carried out at this level to make it easier for a subsequent syntactic analysis program. An automated annotation assistant helps the human annotator select the most appropriate tag from those generated by TOSCA's tagger. ICE is also being tagged by a program called AUTOSYS, which uses three tag sets: LOB, ICE, and the skeleton version of ICE (without the features) (Fang 1996a).

The need for consistency across projects has led Sampson to call for what he describes as a 'Linnaean taxonomy' of language (Sampson 1993). Too many groups are constructing analysed corpora without much agreement about what the annotations mean. But whether it would be possible to get various groups to agree on such a taxonomy is doubtful. Perhaps the easiest parts of it would be the many features which Sampson notes have been ignored in linguistics, namely punctuation, dates, addresses, and numbers, all of which occur very frequently in natural language and need to be considered by any language processing program. Beyond very simple tags there appears to be much inconsistency and more tendency towards the 'gradiency' noted by Johansson (1985). A comparison of the tagging systems in the Brown and LOB corpora was carried out by Belmore (1992) with the intention of arriving at a better classification system, but much more research is needed in this area.

Some attempts have also been made to compare human and machine annotation. Källgren (1996) reports on a number of experiments carried out in the process of annotating a corpus of Swedish which follows the compilation principles of the Brown and LOB corpora. She argues that the results from working with an inflected language such as Swedish can help not only researchers working on other inflected languages but also those working on English. Experiments were carried out using several taggers, one of which can be trained on untagged text. It does this by making its choice of tag based on what it has found so far. The results of tagging 50,000 words with this system were compared with manual disambiguation of the same text, which was first processed through a dictionary and given some post-processing before humans made the final choices for ambiguous tags. Källgren was then able to compare the results of the fully automatic system with the human tagging and to examine the types of inconsistency that occurred. The most frequent errors occurred in function words, but the humans and the machine made rather different types of error. Only two errors occurred in the top ten for both humans and machine. Prepositions and verbal particles caused problems for both, as did determiners and pronouns. A detailed examination of the errors identified many proper nouns, but, as Källgren notes, mixing proper and common nouns does not affect syntactic analysis (1996: 193). She also indicates that occurrences of proper nouns in a training set can cause many extra tags to appear in the lexicon, all leading to more confusion on the part of the lexicon-driven tagger. Källgren concluded her analysis by agreeing with Garside that some words should take alternative tags, simply denoting that their interpretation is open to doubt.

The difficulties of syntactic analysis and other parsing programs are much greater than the problems encountered in word class tagging. A short summary can be found in Leech (1997). Work has proceeded by building 'tree-banks' of parsed text which can be used to train a parsing program, and these often contain simple models called 'skeleton parsing'. The complex tagging system used for TOSCA and subsequently modified for ICE was devised so that a parsing program, could use it. The TOSCA parser offers multiple analyses and thus requires a good deal of manual effort and intervention. It was used for the British component of ICE, (Greenbaum 1996b: 8), but the ICE team found that it needed too much manual intervention and Fang (1996b) describes their efforts to improve on it. See van Halteren (1997) for more discussion of syntactic analysis.

As part of his plan to create a taxonomy of language, Sampson has created the SUSANNE corpus, which is documented thoroughly in Sampson (1995) as well as being available in electronic form. SUSANNE consists of approximately 130,000 words taken from the Brown Corpus and annotated with various kinds of linguistic tagging. Sampson chose to work with these samples because they had previously been subjected to manual grammatical annotation by Ellegård (1978). Sampson revised and extended Ellegård's work, and his tagging includes word classes, surface grammar, and the logical or functional grammar. The depth and complexity of this analysis can be seen for surface grammar where Sampson devotes a chapter of just over 200 pages with 544 itemized points, most of which are illustrated by examples from the corpus. In his introduction Sampson acknowledges several limitations, most notably the lack of head–modifier relationships (1995: 31). SUSANNE is in many ways a monumental work, but it illustrates all too well the complexities of this kind of analysis and should serve to warn anyone who is interested in parsing of the problems in store.

Because of the needs of natural language processing and the potential commercial applications, much of the large-scale effort in linguistic analysis has been concentrated on modern prose material and on spoken text. The examples described here have been almost exclusively from English, but work is in hand to develop similar tools and systems for other major languages. The European Union Project EAGLES laid the groundwork for defining standards for language engineering, covering text corpora, computational lexicons, grammar formalisms, and spoken language (EAGLES n.d.). See especially the EAGLES paper on the morphosyntactic annotation of corpora (Leech 1996).

However, a good deal of success has been reported for morphological analysis of material which is more likely to interest humanities scholars, particularly for inflected languages such as Latin and Greek. These languages are fairly regular in nature and it is possible to build a lexicon that contains irregular forms as well as many non-inflected words. Bozzi and Cappelli (1987) discuss the structure of a lexical database for Latin which is used for morphological analysis. The program assumes what they call an 'operative' rather than a linguistic stem which makes it easier to perform searches (1987: 30). For example the operative stem of *amo* is *am*, which is designated as a verb from which it is possible to analyse all the forms of the verb. Their system uses a basic dictionary of 57,000 entries, each of which is associated with codes to aid the analysis program, for example to check that the segmentation process has broken the word into components that are compatible with each other (Bozzi and Cappelli 1991). They also use a table of suffixes, a table of endings, and a table of postfixes such as *-vis*, and *-cumque*. The lemmatization program attempts to identify the base form of the word, using rules which it derives from the dictionary.

Crane's (1991) analyser for Classical Greek forms one of the core components of the Perseus Project, but it was developed earlier as part of an intelligent retrieval system for the TLG. It builds on earlier work by Packard, and first attempts to strip endings from words (Packard 1976). Unlike Packard's system, Crane's program can also handle diacritics, which he claims increases accuracy by about 25 per cent (Crane 1991: 244). Crane also extended the system to handle various Greek dialects. In Attic Greek alone there are approximately 2,000 inflections and, after various experiments where the number of endings grew enormously and began to interact with each other in a 'messy' way, he reorganized his system to generate the endings automatically by applying a series of rules. All the information is stored in a database which has been subject to revision over time. By October 1990, Crane's program had analysed over 3 million words of Greek, using a database of over 40,000 stems, 13,000 inflections, and 2,500 irregular forms.

Work is ongoing to annotate the Helsinki Corpus (Pintzuk and Taylor 1997). The Penn–Helsinki Parsed Corpus of Middle English (PPCME) has now been released. It contains some 510,000 words mostly taken from the Helsinki Corpus and annotated for syntactic structure (Penn–Helsinki Parsed Corpus n.d). Other collections of humanities material could be made available with some linguistic annotation to aid analysis. The annotation needs to be well documented and the implementation of it organized in such a way that other scholars can ignore it if they want to. The method of encoding the analysis implemented for the BNC might serve as a model with tag names appropriate to the nature of the material. Storing the tags in the corpus makes more sense than generating them on the fly. It saves computing time and also makes it possible for corrections to be made where necessary.

Adding value of this kind to a text can eliminate many of the ambiguities apparent in searching for strings, but it can also introduce many more problems and ambiguities. From the perspective of the user of a very large monitor corpus, Sinclair (1992) argues that analysis should be restricted to what the machine can do without human checking (1992: 282–3). For large corpora which are constantly being updated this approach makes some sense, but questions remain on what to do about the words which the tagger cannot deal with. The solution proposed by Sinclair is more study of the texts and analysis of collocations to feed into the tagger, and some method of bypassing doubtful decisions. Much depends on the nature of the material and the applications for which it will be used. It is worth investing the time to correct errors in a small corpus which is going to be studied in detail for different purposes, provided that the compiler of the corpus can find a way of dealing with very difficult forms. For the individual humanities scholar, linguistic annotation can become a very time-consuming task. The detailed descriptions of some of the programs in this chapter give some idea of what is involved. They are interesting in themselves, but projects of this kind are not to be embarked on lightly with the expectation of rapid results. Progress is still being made by trial and error, and the most fruitful results seem to be derived from statistical analysis based on probabilities and from programs which can learn from material that has already been encoded with analysis.

Although the value of these linguistic tools and language corpora is very clear, a number of pitfalls are apparent. It is all to easy to count things without much apparent purpose and to find answers for which no clear questions have been posed. It is easy to draw conclusions without enough reference to the nature of material in the corpus. Ball (1994) discusses several pitfalls, illustrating each with examples. She notes the particular problem of finding and then counting null instances, particularly for *that*. Biber describes his pattern for finding zero complementizers, but Ball found several instances in the LOB Corpus that this pattern would not find. She does not recommend excluding missing instances as Biber does. Ball also criticizes the units by which some frequencies are measured. More often than not this is a rate per number of words, or sometimes per number of sentences if sentences are encoded, but in some cases clauses are more appropriate. However, clauses cannot easily be identified automatically. They are thus not marked in corpora and researchers tend to base their work on units such as words and sentences which can be identified automatically. Johansson (1994) also draws attention to the pitfalls in corpus work. He advises corpus compilers to be systematic and to provide good documentation. Researchers should start from the problem and then select an appropriate corpus, and evaluate the results in the light of the limitations of that corpus. Nonetheless, the value of corpus work for many linguistic applications has finally been recognized and many of the tools originally designed for literary applications are suitable for simple but effective linguistic analysis. Conversely, new tools developed in corpus linguistics are gradually beginning to feed into better techniques for literary analysis.

7 | Stylometry and Attribution Studies

We have already seen how effective computer-based tools can be for finding and then counting features within a text. In this chapter we will examine how quantitative analyses based on counts can be used, particularly for authorship attribution and related problems. Such stylometric analyses can serve two main purposes, both of which would otherwise be very difficult to tackle in any systematic way. First, they can build an overall picture of a collection of material from the occurrences of certain features. Secondly, they can provide concrete evidence to support or refute a hypothesis about the material. Comparative studies based on quantitative and statistical analyses make it possible to determine whether the usage of some feature or set of features is significant and have provided much new evidence in some well-known cases of disputed authorship. Holmes (1994) provides a useful summary of authorship attribution with an emphasis on statistical tools. See also Holmes (1998), which traces the development of stylometry in the humanities.

Authorship studies are one area where computer-based work has attracted a good deal of popular interest. Claims that 'the computer says that author X wrote text Y' occur regularly in the press and elsewhere, but usually without too much indication of how or why these claims are being made. The quantitative methods used in authorship studies are in some cases similar to those discussed in Chapter 5. Methodological issues are obviously crucial for these studies. What to count, how to measure the counts, and what kinds of statistical analysis to carry out must all be determined by the researcher, who must of course then also interpret the results and place them within the wider landscape of traditional scholarship on the question being studied.

Whether or not linguistic habits are measurable in this way is itself debatable, but various projects have shown that it is possible to characterize an author or a set of texts by linguistic fingerprints. Clearly, if

these features are to be used for comparative purposes or as discriminators they need to be consistent in material of known authorship. They
need to be examined to see whether they change over time or how much
effect genre or text type has on their usages. Furthermore, authors can
deliberately change their habits and so tests for consistency over a
period of time are often needed. For comparative work a suitable set
of control texts must be chosen. Here more is almost certainly better,
but some studies have been limited by the availability of electronic text.
As in other computer-based studies, methodological issues are crucial,
but there is no clearly defined and commonly accepted way to proceed.
So much depends on the nature of the material, the scope of the project,
and the inclinations of the researcher.

Stylometric work has attracted more than its share of criticism from
other scholars. Some are genuinely sceptical. Others seem to find
empirical work alien to the literary scholar's way of working and have
thus sought to find ways to discredit it. As in some of the aspects of
computer-based literary research, there are three possible areas where
stylometry can lay itself open to criticism, all of which can easily be
addressed. First, the researcher may not situate the argument or basis
for the analysis within traditional scholarship on the topic. This scholarship can help to establish a hypothesis which can be supported or
disproved by stylometry. Without such a clearly defined purpose, the
study can be open to the criticism that it does not have a specific
objective. Secondly, there is the danger of measuring and counting
features either for the sake of it or because the features are easy to
count. This danger has become more apparent with the use of computers because of the relative ease or difficulty of identifying certain
features automatically. Counting the number of letters per word, or
number of words per sentence, or individual instances of word forms is
easy, and too many projects have tended to concentrate on these. What
is counted must obviously be related to the nature of the problem, and
the results discussed and interpreted in relation to the problem. Thirdly,
poor choice of comparative material or control texts can lead to conclusions which are suspect and would never be reached if more appropriate material had been used. Now that more electronic text is available
and it is easier to enter text with OCR, there is less excuse for poorly
chosen control text.

Numerical studies of text predate computers by some considerable
time and an examination of early studies is important for an understanding of later methodologies. Williams (1970) gives a short history
beginning with Augustus de Morgan, Professor of Mathematics in
the University of London. In an 1851 letter to the Revd W. Heald at

Cambridge, de Morgan proposed counting word lengths in the Pauline epistles because he had a gut feeling that the Epistle to the Hebrews was composed of longer words than the epistles which begin with the Greek word *Paul*. Williams then goes on to discuss T. C. Mendenhall, who had acquired a copy of de Morgan's letter in the 1880s. Mendenhall set about some practical experiments on word lengths. He prepared a number of graphs where he plotted the number of letters per word against the number of words of this length. In his earlier publication (Mendenhall 1887), he was able to show a peak word length of three letters in all the authors he studied except John Stuart Mill, who peaked at two-letter words. In this publication he also looked at sample size and, for comparative purposes, one sample of Latin which shows a peak at two-letter words. Mendenhall published a second paper which tackled the Shakespearian authorship question (Mendenhall 1901). In this paper, he was able to show that Shakespeare's peak word length is four letters, a feature shared with Marlowe but with no other author he examined.

Williams notes that Mendenhall's results were all published in the form of graphs rather than as raw data. Counting the number of one-letter, two-letter, three-letter etc. words by hand is likely to be not only dull but also prone to error. Mendenhall employed two women to carry out much of his counting, and they used what must have been the first ever word-counting machine, which is described as follows:

The operation of counting was greatly facilitated by the construction of a simple counting machine by which a registration of a word of any given number of letters was made by touching a button marked with that number. One of the counters, with book in hand, called off 'five', 'two', 'three', etc., as rapidly as possible, counting the letters of each word carefully and taking the words in their consecutive order, the other registering, as called, by pressing the proper buttons. (Mendenhall 1901: 102)

But even the monotony of this method must have introduced some errors. Williams goes on to discuss several other numerical studies. He was interested in methodology and, for the non-mathematical, his book is helpful because of the insightful comments on much of this work. He did not use a computer and thus was not conditioned by the kinds of searches and counts that can easily be done by a computer. He discusses parts of speech on the same terms as other features such as word length and sentence length, whereas much computer-based attribution work avoids parts of speech because the tools to identify parts of speech are not so readily available.

Ellegård's work on the *Junius Letters* is notable for his contribution to methodology and also because it was one of the earliest studies to use a computer (Ellegård 1962a, 1962b). The *Junius Letters* appeared in the *Public Advertiser* from 1769 to 1772. Ellegård notes that the authorship of the *Junius Letters* has remained 'one of the minor mysteries of English literary history' (1962a: 7). Of the various candidates for authorship, Sir Philip Francis was favoured by many, but other candidates have also been proposed. Ellegård set out to make a systematic investigation of this authorship question by looking at the *Junius Letters*, works by Francis, and works by other contemporaries. He invented what he calls 'Junian plus-expressions', and 'Junian minus-expressions' where plus-expressions are words and phrases favoured by Junius in comparison with his contemporaries. He calculated a distinctiveness ratio by dividing the frequency rate in Junius by the frequency in a million word sample of fifty-nine contemporary writers. The distinctiveness ratio gives a number greater than 1 if the word is favoured by Junius (a plus-word) and less than 1 if it is a minus-word. He compiled lists beginning with words with the highest distinctiveness ratio, but was forced to accept that many of his words and phrases were infrequent and thus subject to chance fluctuations. He chose to get round this difficulty by grouping sets of word together, and from these groups he could show that the *Junius Letters* are closer to the works of Francis than to those of the other writers.

More tests were carried out using sets of synonyms, for example *until* and *till*, where Junius preferred *until* in 78 per cent of cases. However, these tests were less conclusive, although some did also point to Francis. One of the problems with Ellegård's approach was that his choice of words was to some extent subjective, something which he himself admits. Picking out words by simply reading texts inevitably leads to some lack of consistency since it is not possible to get an overview of the kind that can be provided by concordance programs. Ellegård was able to use a computer for some of his calculations, but his work was carried out before computers were powerful enough to perform the word counts. He thus had to rely on his own judgement and hand counts to select words and phrases for study. These eventually totalled 458, but his comments on this trial-and-error method of selecting words are interesting. 'I often found that expressions I believed to be characteristically Junian were just characteristic of Junius' age, or of the type of literature that the letters represented' (Ellegård 1962b: 114). The use of computers avoids such trial-and-error methods to get an overall picture of vocabulary from which significant words and phrases can be selected. Ellegård concludes that 'the linguistic evidence is amply sufficient by itself to warrant the conclusion that Philip Francis and Junius were one and the same' (1962b: 118), but he also adds this to a mass of other non-linguistic evidence. For the linguistic analysis in particular, he notes that several of the characteristically Junian words and phrases occur also in high proportions in Francis's more formal works. Ellegård's major contribution to the methodology was the 'plus' and 'minus' words.

The early 1960s saw one other very influential authorship study, the work carried out by Mosteller and Wallace on the *Federalist Papers* (Mosteller and Wallace 1964). These papers present a classic scenario for an authorship study: they are a series of eighty-five essays published in 1787–8 in an attempt to persuade the citizens of New York to ratify the American Constitution. All were published under the name 'Publius', but the papers were written by Hamilton, Madison, and Jay. The authorship of twelve papers was disputed, but it was known from external evidence that these twelve papers were written either by Hamilton or by Madison. Thus there were only two candidates for authorship (not many, as in the case of the *Junius Letters*) and there was plenty of material on the same subject matter written by these two candidates. Mosteller and Wallace were principally interested in the statistical methods, and their book is rather difficult for the non-mathematical reader. I. S. Francis (1966) gives a good explanation of the background to the problem and Holmes and Forsyth (1995) also summarize the historical question at the beginning of their paper.

Mosteller and an earlier collaborator began by investigating sentence length in the 1940s, but after much hand counting they established that both Hamilton and Madison had mean (average) sentence lengths of approximately thirty-five words. Neither was there much difference in the spread or range of lengths. Disheartened, they abandoned the investigation, but Mosteller returned to it almost twenty years later in collaboration with Wallace. They began to investigate vocabulary usage in samples of Hamilton and Madison (both *Federalist* material and other works) and found this more fruitful. Their main investigation was based on the usage of thirty 'marker words' which they arrived at by examining samples of Hamilton and Madison. Some of these words were more or less synonymous. For example Hamilton's rate per 1,000 for the word *while* is 0.26 whereas the rate for Madison is almost 0. The word *upon* is favoured by Hamilton at 2.93 per 1,000, whereas its rate in Madison is 0.16. Overall the tests pointed to Madison as the author of the disputed papers, with the evidence for no. 55 being fairly weak. In a summary of the conclusions reached by Mosteller and Wallace, I. S. Francis (1966: 76) notes that for the thirty words used in the main study, there would have to be changes to between fifty and 100 words in each paper to make them appear Hamiltonian.

The *Federalist Papers* have become a kind of 'classic' in authorship studies. The historical background is well documented and the amount of text is not too large for student projects and not too small for statistical analyses. Work on the *Federalist Papers* has made two major contributions to the methodology. One is the investigation and comparison of synonyms. The second is the general context of the problem with only two candidates for authorship and plenty of comparative material by them on the same subject matter and in the same genre. Since it seems to be generally accepted that this authorship problem has been 'solved', the *Federalist Papers* have begun to be used by other researchers as a test for new methodologies (Merriam 1989; Holmes and Forsyth 1995; Tweedie, Singh, and Holmes 1996a).

These early projects have thus laid the groundwork for what to count. Mendenhall found something of interest in word length, but, as Williams argues, word length is in some way related to the context. The writer does not have much control over word length. It is certainly related to part of speech, but very few researchers in authorship studies have attempted to apply any of the part of speech tagging programs discussed in Chapter 6. Another approach is to investigate sentence length, on the rather obvious grounds that all authors construct sentences and that sentences are therefore something which they share in common and which might form a basis for comparison. A graph showing sentence length plotted against the number of sentences of each length has a similar curve to a word length graph. It has a peak at the lower end of the sentence length scale and then a very long tail leading to sentences of possibly up to 400 words and beyond. The tabulation of sentence length data showing the number of sentences with one, two, three, four, etc. words can thus be cumbersome, and it is fairly common to group the totals in fives, showing the number of sentences with 1–5, 6–10 words, etc. Of course, for any study of sentence length, the question of what a sentence is arises. Unless they are very sophisticated, computer programs are very likely to identify a sentence as something between two full stops, or possibly between full stops and other punctuation such as question marks or exclamation marks. If abbreviations have not been encoded separately, these will be identified as sentence delimiters. The researcher must also decide whether colons and semi-colons indicate new sentences for the purpose of the analysis.

Drawing on work pioneered by Wake (1948), sentence length has been much used by Morton and his collaborators in their investigations of Greek prose (Morton and Levison 1966; Morton and Winspear 1971; Morton 1978). In the case of Greek, the definition of a sentence can be less clear because the punctuation has been added by modern editors.

Morton (1978: 99) counters this argument by saying that in the sciences many features cannot be classified exactly. He argues that his definition of a sentence (a group of words marked by full stop, colon or interrogative mark by a modern editor) is 'generally used and widely recognised'. The real question is whether the number of exceptions to this definition is large enough to skew the results. Marriott's (1979) definition of a sentence in his study of sentence length in the *Historia Augusta* (*HA*) is criticized by Sansone (1990) for similar reasons. Marriott claimed that his analysis of the *HA* strongly supported the thesis of single authorship, rather than its having six authors as is indicated in the manuscripts. Sansone argues that the texts used by Marriott were not all edited by the same person and must therefore have variation in the punctuation. This would be easy enough to show with a computer-based study, but Sansone contents himself by highlighting a few sentences selected by serendipitous means.

Frischer *et al.* (1996), in a very detailed and thorough investigation of several Latin prose historians and biographers, show that sentence length (what they call 'number of words per strong stop' (1996: 111)), should not be used as a discriminator because the range of mean lengths of the sentences of the six *HA* authors is much the same as the range of mean lengths of those of the other authors studied. In particular they criticize Marriott for his choice of control texts, arguing that they are not the same genre as the *HA*. Binongo's (1994) study of the Philippine author Nick Joaquin, who writes in English, shows that the same author can use very different sentence lengths in different works. He took two collections of Joaquin's short stories: one has very long and rambling sentences, but the other consists of very short sentences. Binongo looked at the thirty-six most frequent words and was able to show that these two collections are in fact similar. He then compared these samples with samples from four other authors and the method still discriminated Joaquin.

Word frequencies, particularly for common words, have been shown to be better discriminators. Common words are relatively independent of subject matter and they also occur frequently enough for it to be possible to make useful comparisons on fairly small amounts of text. Most of the *Federalist* marker words identified by Mosteller and Wallace are common words. Ellegård had more difficulty with the *Junius Letters* because he did not particularly focus on common words. Many of Morton's studies of Greek texts have concentrated on particles and other very common words in Greek. He notes how scholars 'neglect the frequent words in a text' (Morton 1978: 26) and claims that scholars do not have a complete view of Greek texts because they often ignore the very common words which make up most of the text. Of course the view rather depends on the nature of the research being carried out on the texts, but the value of studying common words as discriminators is emphasized by this statement, which also supports Burrows's (1987) view.

If the investigation is to concentrate on common words, which words should they be? How many words should be counted and how should the results be tabulated? Raw counts cannot be used for comparisons unless the texts are the same length. It is normal to reduce the counts to a rate per 1,000 words or to percentages, but in any case, the numbers are small. For example, in English texts the most frequently used word has an occurrence of around 4 per cent, or 40 per 1,000 words; the comparable figure for Greek is around 5 per cent. Concentrating the investigation on one or two words makes it easier to carry out comparisons without getting into more complex statistical methods. However, it then becomes all too easy to concentrate on the one or two words which support the hypothesis that the researcher is trying to prove and to ignore others. This has been the tendency in some of Morton's work, for example on the Pauline epistles. In his 1963 lecture at the University of Saskatchewan, Morton (1965) showed that the proportion of occurrences of the Greek word *kai* (meaning 'and', but with a rather stronger meaning than 'and' in English) is less in Romans, 1 and 2 Corinthians, and Galatians, and that Hebrews stands out on its own. See also Morton and McLeman (1966). The positions of these words in sentences might also be important, especially again for Greek, where many common words act as particles and occur close to the beginning of sentences. Morton also tabulates counts by showing the number of sentences with 0, 1, 2, 3, etc. occurrences of the word he is interested in, but the purpose of this does not seem entirely clear. It is so obviously dependent on sentence length.

A more thorough study would make use of many common words, also separating out homographs and dividing the words into groups according to their function. Kenny's *The Aristotelian Ethics* provides one model which is worth examining in detail (Kenny 1978). The problem tackled by Kenny was not one of authorship but rather to examine the three books which appear in both the *Nicomachean* and the *Eudemian Ethics* to try to ascertain to which set of treatises these three books originally belonged. Kenny adopted some of Morton's methodology, but he extended it by studying a total of thirty-six particles, nineteen prepositions, and various pronouns, adverbs, and demonstratives, and the definite article, covering in all 60 per cent of the vocabulary (Kenny 1977). His book includes three chapters on the vocabulary analyses as part of a larger study which investigates the historical and philosophical background to the question. Kenny used a concordance to help him disambiguate homographic forms and to divide the words into the appropriate categories. In most cases he was able to show that, contrary to earlier scholarship on this topic, the three books resemble the *Eudemian* rather than the *Nicomachean Ethics*. Once this overall picture had been established, Kenny then began to look at sections within the three books to see whether any part of them was more 'Nicomachean'. He divided them into seventeen sections of 1,000 words and then grouped sets of his marker words together, because otherwise the expected number of occurrences in a sample of 1,000 words was low. The groups were selected following Ellegård on the basis of a distinctiveness ratio showing Nicomachean and Eudemian favourites. The results showed that all seventeen samples resembled the *Eudemian* more than the *Nicomachean Ethics*.

Even when common words are to be studied there are still some elements of choice about what to look at. Particles, prepositions, and the like have the advantage of not having many inflectional forms, but they can often have several different meanings and a thorough study would need to separate all the meanings, using a concordance as a tool. Of course, to test the validity of the methodology for an authorship study, enough material of known authorship needs to be examined. Burrows (1992a), in a paper which has been widely cited, attempted to show that an authorship study can be carried out based on the fifty most common words. He set himself two tasks. In the first he assumed that he was presented with four tables of frequency counts of raw scores for the fifty most common words taken from four texts labelled A, B, C, and D. He was to examine the data and to comment especially on Text A. On the basis of his previous work he could see that the counts were taken from novels because of the high incidence of some personal pronouns and the verb *said*. After standardizing the counts so that like was compared with like, he was able to show a clear distinction between Text A and Text B, and also between Text A and Text C. The distinction between Text A and Text D was much less clear. He was also able to deduce that Text A might have more dialogue than Text B. His method correctly identified the relationship between the texts, which were by Henry James and Jane Austen. Text A was the 1877 version of *The American*, Text B was *The Portrait of a Lady*, Text C was *Mansfield Park*, and Text D was the 1907 revision of *The American* (Burrows 1992a: 96). In a second experiment discussed in the same paper, Burrows assumed that he now knew that Text A was either by Henry James or by Jane Austen and the problem was then to discover which was the true author. In this experiment he worked only on the narrative sections and compared Text A with three Austen and two James novels. At this stage he also expanded contractions and separated homographs, the latter affecting eleven of the fifty words. Since the control texts were not all the same length he selected twelve samples from each of the two authors and first established whether the common words could function as discriminators within those samples before examining the remainder of the texts. He was able to show how close the Austen novels are to each other but to also to situate Text A closer to the James samples.

Many of the studies we have examined so far operated with samples of text. Measurements derived from one or more samples can be used to make predictions or estimations of the likely occurrence of the features in the 'population', that is, the entire set of whatever is being studied. If something is being sampled, there are two obvious questions to be answered: how to choose the samples, and how big the samples should be. In the case of textual data, defining the population may not be easy. It might be all the works of one author, or it might be all the works in one particular genre or period, or it might be, as Morton tried to establish, everything in Greek prose. The researcher has to choose what makes most sense for the particular project and try to justify the choice as much as possible. Now that much more text is available in electronic form, less work is being carried out on samples, but when texts of different lengths are being compared, the counts must be standardized. Samples are also useful to help determine whether some feature can actually act as a discriminator. If the feature does not occur consistently within samples from the same text or author, it cannot be expected to function as a discriminator.

Two basic methods of sampling are generally recognized. One is random sampling where random number tables are used to select either a starting point or a subset of an already determined set of text segments. True random sampling is indeed that, since it is not influenced by any external factor, but, on its own, random sampling is more appropriate when very little is known about the population. This is very unlikely to be the case for text-based work. Also, for text samples, random sampling has the disadvantage of possibly not giving complete coverage. It would be possible, if, for example, an author wrote both political documents and novels and both are to be used, for a true random sampling procedure to generate only samples from one genre. Stratified sampling therefore makes more sense. Stratified sampling assumes that a good deal is already known about the population to be studied. It makes it possible to take samples from different types of material on the basis of what is already known about that material.

Once texts, or sections of text, have been chosen by stratified sampling, it is possible to use random sampling methods to determine the exact starting point or sections to use.

The size of samples is also a matter for discussion and depends to some extent on what is being studied. Intuitively we know that large samples might be required in order to get some reasonable data on features that occur only rarely, but how large is large? Ellegård was hampered because many of the words he investigated did not occur very often. He finally came up with the suggestion that a sample should be expected to contain at least ten occurrences of the feature being studied (Ellegård 1962a: 14), a procedure also adopted by Kenny when he grouped words in his study of 1,000-word segments within the disputed material. Ellegård was much concerned about sample sizes, but, because of his concentration on less frequent words, he was not able to come up with any real theoretical basis for this other than what he could derive by inspecting his samples. Morton has tended to base his samples on the number of sentences and to assume that a minimum sample of 100 sentences is appropriate because sentence length is periodic (Morton and Levison 1966: 148).

The size and choice of samples has been the subject of much discussion in corpus linguistics, and researchers in attribution studies could draw more on the work carried out by corpus linguists where there have been more investigations of the size and representativeness of text samples. A corpus, which is intended to be 'representative' of the language, most usually consists of samples taken from different types of text. Although the primary uses of a corpus might be rather different from those for a literary electronic text, the procedures used by corpus compilers can help to shed light on the size of samples. Johansson and Hofland (1989: 2–5) describe the sampling procedures for the LOB Corpus. Having first decided on the genres to include, the corpus compilers took three sources (bibliographies or catalogues for books, newspapers and periodicals, and government documents) and selected titles by random from these sources. They then used a random sampling method to select a start page for each 2,000-word sample. The samples are not exactly 2,000 words; they end at the end of the sentence in which the two-thousandth word occurs. Biber (1993) discusses a range of issues concerned with corpus design. He backs up his discussion with some worked examples drawn from the LOB Corpus and the Lund Corpus of Spoken English. His work on sample size is especially interesting because it takes pains to distinguish two kinds of feature. The first kind can be plotted on a straight-line graph since the number of occurrences increases directly in proportion to the length of the text;

the second kind produces what he calls a 'curvilinear' graph, since there is no direct proportional relationship between the frequency of occurrence of the feature and the text length. The rate of introduction of new words is the most obvious curvilinear feature.

Samples taken from the beginning or ending of a text are less likely to be representative of the whole. Morton tends to operate on the first 100 or 200 sentences of a Greek text without offering much explanation, except possibly that some of the texts he is examining are rather short. It would be preferable to use a random starting place, perhaps by using random number tables. Although it would be perfectly possible to select sentences at random rather than a continuous sequence of text, this is rarely, if ever, done. Muller (1973) operates on every twentieth word for some of his vocabulary studies, but with text the occurrence of one word is not independent of its neighbours and this method may only be appropriate for some kinds of analysis. Opinions on the choice and size of samples therefore vary considerably, but one of the advantages of computer-based work is that it is very easy to redo the analysis with different samples either of different size or taken from different parts of a text.

These quantitative studies rely on statistical analyses to show whether the results are significant or not. Some of these statistical studies may appear rather daunting to the humanities scholar, but it is not difficult for the non-mathematical person to learn enough statistics to carry out simple analyses. There are many computer programs which can carry out a variety of statistical analyses. What is important is for the scholar to understand what statistics are valid for the data being studied and how to interpret the results. Kenny (1982) is an excellent introduction to the basic tools. This book assumes no previous knowledge and starts at a very simple level of counting words. Thomson (1973–5) also addresses the needs of the humanities scholar, concentrating mostly on hypothesis testing. His later paper (Thomson 1989) explains clearly how to assess these kinds of studies, using earlier publications by Morton and M. W. A. Smith as examples. Oakes (1998) is rather more advanced and, although it does include some literary problems, is primarily intended for computational linguists. Stevenson (1989) also offers some words of caution on the use of statistics for data drawn from literature, particularly in hypothesis-testing where she draws a good parallel between a hypothesis that a fertilizer might produce better tomatoes (something that can be tested exactly) and the kinds of literary hypothesis which rely on unproven opinions.

In simple terms statistics are used for two purposes. One is to create a description of the data and the other is to make predictions. Predictions usually rely on probabilities, and it is conventionally accepted that a

5 per cent probability (a 1 in 20 likelihood of an outcome happening by chance) indicates something significant. A 1 per cent probability (a 1 in 100 likelihood of this outcome happening by chance) indicates something highly significant. Many of Morton's analyses use a chi-square test which yields a probability value. The chi-square is simple, although rather cumbersome, to calculate, but it only operates on one feature or variable and can thus be 'misused' by highlighting one feature whose probability is significant. Two texts or variables can be compared by correlations which are conventionally represented as a number between 0 and 1 showing the strength of the correlation between them. See, for example, the correlations between various books of the New Testament based on the twenty most common words and analysed by Kenny (1986). Given that authors all use more or less the same set of common words, correlations based on word frequencies can always yield values close to 1 and may not necessarily indicate anything of significance. Kenny considers a correlation of 0.88 to be low, but he does find more similarity between Luke and Acts (1986: 72–5) than between John and Revelation (1986: 76–9).

Rather than relying on one or two features or variables, many recent studies have used what are called multivariate techniques. The purpose of multivariate analysis is to investigate the relationships between many different objects based on many different variables. Alt (1990) is a very good general introduction and Biber (1988) explains the technique of factor analysis in relation to some text samples and the features within them. Some multivariate techniques operate by reducing the many different variables to a small number of underlying factors which are loaded positively or negatively with some of the variables in the study. The first factor or dimension has the highest amount of information and, depending on the nature of the data, most variables can be represented in a small number of factors, sometimes even only two. It is possible then to examine the relationships between the objects or the variables by plotting them on a diagram showing spatial relationships. In practice, the important information can be found on the first two dimensions, enabling the results to be presented in two-dimensional rather than multi-dimensional form. Frischer et al. (1996) also use multivariate techniques in their study of word types in some Latin prose. They present one view of their results in a cluster analysis diagram (a dendrogram, or tree diagram) which shows the relationships between the texts (1996: 133). In it those texts which are closest to each other combine to form a single cluster at a certain level of similarity which is measured as a percentage. This cluster combines with other texts at a lower similarity threshold until all the texts form one cluster (the top or root of the tree).

See also the discussion of multivariate techniques in connection with the analysis of manuscript traditions in Chapter 8.

From the foregoing it can be seen that there are no hard-and-fast rules on how to go about an attribution study, except perhaps that more is better. This means more text and more tests. So much depends on the nature of the project, and possibly also on the availability of reliable electronic texts. The following two case studies carried out by humanities scholars might help to shed more light on methodological topics. All use several tests and discuss the validity of the tests in the light of the material being studied as well as the results.

In a fairly short paper Estelle Irizarry examines an important question surrounding the first published novel in Latin American literature, *The Misfortunes of Alonso Ramírez* (Irizarry 1991). This work was written by Carlos de Sigüenza y Góngora who, as Irizarry says, 'clearly states that he transcribed the story that the illiterate Puerto Rican adventurer Ramirez told him' (1991: 175). However, many scholars have thought that Ramirez was invented by Sigüenza. Irizarry set out to 'ascertain whether the personality of the Puerto Rican sailor was sufficiently strong and unique to leave its mark on the learned Sigüenza's written version of his story to differentiate the novel from other narrative works authored by Sigüenza alone' (1991: 175). Irizarry based her analysis on three narrative texts written by Sigüenza within three years of *Misfortunes*, regularizing the spelling, and carrying out some tests on complete texts and others on samples of 4,000 words where the test was dependent on text length or required manual analysis. She was also able to use another corpus of Spanish for reference. She began by looking at type/token ratio on both lemmatized and unlemmatized texts, the latter on the grounds that the high number of inflected forms in Spanish contributes to variety. *Misfortunes* shows shorter sentences, but there was no significant differences in word length. Significant differences were found in the words at the beginning of sentences, with *Misfortunes* favouring gerunds and conjugated verbs. Irizarry then compiled a list of plus- and minus-words by looking not only at single words but also at some morphological and syntactic constructions, all of which had to occur at least five times in one sample of 4,000 words. She found that some words and expressions which occurred frequently in the narrative texts do not occur in *Misfortunes* at all. Irizarry concluded on the basis of these various tests that Ramirez probably was a real person and goes on to discuss the literary and historical implications of this. This study included several tests, some of which required hand counts because they relied on features which cannot be detected by computer programs. Irizarry would be much less happy to base her conclusions on the result of only one test.

Dixon and Mannion (1993) present the methodology and the results of a study of eleven periodical essays attributed posthumously to Goldsmith and compared them with authentic Goldsmith material and material by four other authors. This study was the result of a collaboration between a humanities scholar and a mathematician. The mathematics are explained in some detail complete with formulae, but the formulae are preceded by a simple explanation of the purpose of that particular analysis. The article is readable by the non-mathematician who has some understanding of the basic principles of multivariate analysis as outlined above. This paper is interesting because of the detailed justification of the choice of essays being studied and the control texts, and because of the comprehensive set of tests undertaken. Dixon and Mannion rejected several of Ellegård's tests because of the variety in Goldsmith's material, and also because of possible compositorial changes to the texts (for example *while* and *whilst*). They examined a total of twenty-two features, some of which required handcoding of the analysis and were thus carried out on samples of 1,000 words (for word-based tests) and sequences of fifty sentences for sentence-based tests. They applied several multivariate tests, finding among other things that the principal components method did not reduce the data to a small enough number of dimensions. They needed fifteen components to represent 90 per cent of the data and so they adopted a different method to reduce the problem to one dimension. They carried out a cluster analysis using several different clustering methods, all of which showed the genuine Goldsmith samples close together. However, one of the two samples from two of the control authors was also close to Goldsmith, leading them to conclude that 'stylistic evidence alone will not always satisfactorily distinguish these three Anglo-Irish [Hugh Kelly, Arthur Murphy, and Goldsmith] from one another' (1993: 17). Only one of the disputed essays was close to the Goldsmith samples, but this was also the one which has most strongly been attributed to Goldsmith because of other evidence. Dixon and Mannion discuss the other ten essays in some detail in the light of the results of the analyses and in relation to external evidence. Their conclusion is that 'the ten remaining essays cannot claim to be more than "possibly by Goldsmith", though some of them are more distinctly possible than others' (1993: 17).

Needless to say, the Pauline epistles have attracted a good deal of attention from those interested in computer-based analyses. Scholars have long debated whether only four of the letters (Romans, Galatians, and 1 and 2 Corinthians) were written by Paul, rather than the entire fourteen. Of the remaining ten letters, Hebrews is generally considered to be the least Pauline in nature. The Paulines were the subject of de

Morgan's 1851 letter, and also of Morton's earlier work which popularized computer-based authorship studies. Morton (1978: 167) discusses Wake's earlier analyses of sentence lengths in the Paulines, following this with some of his own analyses. He examined sentence length within individual letters and across the corpus, and was able to show that Romans, Galatians, and 1 and 2 Corinthians are close together and that Hebrews is anomalous. His 1966 study with McLeman focused on the Greek word *kai*, which he had established was consistent in the other Greek authors he studied as well as being independent of genre (Morton and McLeman 1966). The proportion of *kai* showed a group of Romans, 1 and 2 Corinthians, and Galatians, with possibly Philemon, but there were some differences between some of the samples, especially in Romans. Hebrews was very different.

Mealand (1992) discusses the Paulines in the context of his wide-ranging essay on the value of computer-based studies, noting again how much the computer can help in giving an overall picture. Neumann's doctoral dissertation is most useful for the history and many references to previous work that is offers (Neumann 1990). Greenwood (1992), in what he acknowledges is a 'primitive' analysis based on the ten most common words in the Paulines and treating each chapter separately, also places Romans, Galatians, and 1 and 2 Corinthians close together and most Hebrews chapters some way out, with the remaining letters in the middle. In a second paper he first examines the fifty words which occur more than 100 times overall in the corpus, and then carries out a multivariate analysis which again produces some support for 'Morton's proposition' (Greenwood 1993: 218).

Ledger (1995) also applies multivariate methods based on 1000-word samples. He examines all of the New Testament to begin with in order to situate the problem within a wider context. On the basis of letters at the beginning of words (nineteen in total where the most infrequent are grouped together), the nine most frequent letters at the ends of words, and the type/token ratio, he is able to place Romans and 1 Corinthians close together and separate Hebrews from this cluster, but he also establishes that Ephesians, Colossians, 1 Thessalonians, and 1 and 2 Timothy are 'in many cases closer to *Heb*[rews]' (1995: 95). An examination of the most important discriminators revealed the type/token ratio and words ending in the letter sigma. Further investigation of the latter showed that this was to some extent due to content, but not entirely. Ledger also concluded that his method had been able to make some discrimination and that if Hebrews was to be assigned to a different author, his evidence was that these five other letters might also follow and that their authenticity 'must remain doubtful'. It is rather a pity that these many studies of the Pauline epistles have been carried out independently. A cumulative approach to the results presented in them would be extremely useful not only for the Pauline question but also as a further validation of the methodologies.

There have been very many attempts to use stylometric tools to tackle Shakespearian authorship questions, and here it is only possible to highlight one or two. A useful discussion of the validity of some methods for the study of authorship and chronology of the canon is in Wells and Taylor (1987: 76–109). They warn of the dangers of drawing too many conclusions from computer-based analysis of internal evidence, especially when this evidence is not supported by external evidence. But they do go on to carry out a simple analysis of the frequency of ten function words and find that it supports the view that there are thirty-one core plays and reveals some differences in the disputed works. They also suggest that progress could be made by a combined approach of professional Shakespearians and professional statisticians working with computers and concordances which are able to make these studies more reliable and more practical. Horton (1987) experimented with a number of methods in his investigation of *The Two Noble Kinsmen* and *Henry VIII*. He was concerned both with what features to study and what statistical measures to apply to those features. Concentrating on a set of function words he was able to examine the two plays scene by scene. Horton admits that his results for *The Two Noble Kinsmen* might be more satisfying to the reader 'who accepts the traditional division' (1987: 308) than the results for *Henry VIII*, but his work is extremely useful from a methodological point of view since it is an assessment of the effectiveness of these tools. *Pericles* has been tackled by various scholars and various techniques, but see especially M. W. A. Smith (1987, 1988, 1989) and Jackson (1991). All follow somewhat similar methodological patterns, focusing on common words, and possibly some collocations, and with some discussion of the control texts being used. Surprisingly few attempt to get the kind of overall picture that is possible with computer assistance, and the discussion of control texts tends to concentrate on one or two other plays.

In his 'sociolinguistic' study, Hope (1994) is dismissive of computational stylometry, which he appears to think is about 'average length of word', and the frequency of words at the beginning of sentences (1994: 8). His study is based on auxiliary *do* including missing occurrences, on relatives including missing occurrences, and a smaller analysis of *thee* and *you*. Admittedly, computer-based tools cannot directly count missing forms, but these situations can, as Burrows notes when he also comments on missing *thats* in Sabol's study of narration in *The Good*

Soldier (Sabol 1989), be checked using concordances of words which precede or follow missing forms (Burrows 1992b: 184). Hope must have been hampered by the need to carry out all the counting by hand, and he had to reduce the number of samples with which he could work. The whole study would have been more comprehensive if it had been carried out with some assistance from computers, but the results are presented in a series of diagrams which are very effective in conveying their message. Very few of the computer-based studies really make use of the computer's obvious ability to present results visually.

We can conclude this overview of quantitative approaches by an examination of two new methodologies which began to be adopted during the 1990s. Of these, the most promising appears to be neural networks. Tweedie, Singh, and Holmes (1996b) provide an introduction to the methodology and also review some previous work, noting that stylometry is essentially pattern recognition and that neural networks 'have the ability to recognize the underlying organization of data, which is of vital importance for any pattern recognition problem' (1996b: 250). The structure of a neural network is fairly complex, but basically it consists of a set of processing elements which take input from other elements or from data, and then apply a weighted processing function to that input and send the resulting output to other elements. The elements are related to each other in layers (called a 'multi-layer percep-tron') and hidden layers between the input and output layers also perform some computation. Each of the elements in the network can be a stylistic discriminator. The network must be trained on some data in order to tune the weights used in the processing. In effect this means that the network can 'learn' something about the habits of a known author in this training phase. It can then attempt to classify doubtful text on the basis of what it has learned. Although different in some respects, these procedures are rather similar to those being used in linguistic analysis and language understanding, where the computer 'learns' from text which has already been tagged with linguistic analysis and uses what it has learned for tagging new text.

Matthews and Merriam (1993) apply the method to the Shakespeare and Fletcher question using training data taken from earlier work by Merriam and from Horton (1987), and report considerable success. In a further paper they look at Shakespeare and Marlowe, also with some success (Merriam and Matthews 1994). Although they acknowledge that this work is still at an early stage of experimentation with the methodology, they report that they are encouraged. These initial experi-ments were conducted with few words, and it would be interesting to explore the technical aspects of working with a larger and more varied training set. Tweedie, Singh, and Holmes (1996a) use the *Federalist Papers* as a test of neural networks and report that the network was able to classify all twelve disputed papers as Madisonian, when eleven of the marker words chosen by Mosteller and Wallace were used in the training set. They were also able to look at the joint papers (nos. 18–20) and draw conclusions which are in line with those reached by Mosteller and Wallace. Neural networks seem therefore to be promising, but they require good mathematical and computing skills.

The second relatively new technique is called cusums (cumulative sum charts), sometimes also spelled 'qsum'. The method was originally devised by Morton, and is explained in Farringdon (1996). Cusums are intended to compare two features, one of which is length of sentences. The other might be the number of two- or three-letter words within each sentence, or the number of words with initial vowels in each sentence. The cumulative sum is a kind of progressive deviation of values from the average. Many of the examples given by Farringdon operate on the first twenty-five sentences of a given text. It is easy then to compute the average sentence length and to draw a chart showing the cumulative deviations from this average across the twenty-five sentences. The line on the chart will always return to a deviation of zero on the last sentence. The second feature is then presented in a similar fashion as the number of occurrences per sentence, and the line representing its cumulative sum is superimposed on the chart of the sentence length. It is then claimed that similar patterns for each line indicate uniform authorship. If the experiment is repeated with some sentences from a different author inserted in the middle, the pattern of the two lines on the chart will diverge.

There appear to be several problems associated with this technique. The scaling on the charts is crucial and changes to this can cause the lines to coincide or to diverge. It therefore becomes very tempting to choose a scaling which makes the chart appear to prove or disprove something. Farringdon (1996: 22–3) discusses the problem of anomalies in the text, for example long sentences and lists which cause what she calls 'blips' on the chart. The recommendation is to ignore these types of sentences, which again seems rather arbitrary. If many more sentences were being analysed, such anomalies would not be so noticeable overall and would be better included. Others have criticized the cusum technique (Canter 1992; Hardcastle 1993; Hilton and Holmes 1993; Sanford *et al.* 1994; de Haan and Schils 1994). They have shown that it does not effectively detect consistency in written or spoken material, and that there is no real statistical validation of the technique. These criticisms are firmly countered in Farringdon (1996), but there is a good deal of unease in any case about authorship studies based on samples of only a few sentences.

When authorship attribution techniques are applied to forensic matters, the unease becomes much greater, especially when the techniques are produced as expert evidence in courts of law. Much of this expert evidence centres round statements given by persons accused of certain crimes where there might be some possibility that the statements have been fabricated or altered in some way. It is relatively easy to impress a jury by presenting charts and diagrams, but these procedures are problematic for several reasons. First of all the length of these statements is usually too short for any kind of representative sample of text. In fact of all the methodologies we have examined only the cusum test operates on a small amount of text. Secondly, if the statement has been transcribed by a police officer it may not be a verbatim transcription, but may be reworded slightly into more of a written rather than a spoken language. Thirdly, there are big questions about what comparative material to use. Often short letters written by the accused, or possibly also diaries if they exist are taken as control texts. But neither of these represent the same kind of material as a statement, which is usually taken down in writing by another person from material spoken by the accused. Holmes (1998: 114) gives a very good overview of the use of the cusum test as a forensic technique, describing its application and reception in various court cases. For other forensic applications see also Bailey's (1979) attribution study of the Patti Hearst material, the study of the Evans statements described in Svartvik (1968), and Don Foster's work with the Unabomber manifesto (Crain 1998).

Like some of the techniques examined in earlier chapters, it is best to treat a computer-based attribution study as a part of a broader research project and to ensure that the attribution work is placed within a larger context. The more successful projects have used a variety of different tests, although with some tendency to concentrate on common words. Some statistics are necessary to carry out a truly empirical project, but it is not difficult for the humanities scholar to learn enough statistics and to use standard statistical software. Most researchers seem now to favour multivariate techniques which provide a larger overall picture. In very few cases have these projects produced what is generally accepted to be conclusive evidence, but in many more they have added to what is already known, building up the evidence for or against a specific author. It is a pity that these techniques have attracted so much popular attention. They may well be better appreciated if they were confined to academic research circles.

8 | Textual Criticism and Electronic Editions

Much confusion seems to surround the topic of electronic editions. Some people take it to mean the preparation of electronic texts. Others assume that it is about putting electronic texts on the Internet, perhaps with some annotations and also multimedia enhancements. Others again take it to mean digital images of manuscript or other sources. Others prefer to discuss the theoretical implications of electronic textuality (Sutherland 1997). Those scholars with a more traditional bent assume that electronic editing is about typesetting and using computers to help with the preparation of material which will be distributed in print form. This chapter examines various tools and techniques for the preparation and publication of scholarly editions, moving from tools to assist with the production of traditional printed scholarly editions to models for publishing electronic material in image and text form. It will try to cut through various theories of editing to assess what can and cannot effectively be done. It will also briefly discuss the Internet as a means of publishing editions.

Ott (1992) outlines eight steps for the production of a critical edition: collection of witnesses, collation, evaluation of results of collation—to make a genealogy and select variants for publication, constitution of copy text, compilation of apparatuses, preparation of indexes, preparation of printer's copy, and publication. This set of procedures has traditionally been followed for Classical and other older material, the aim being to produce a printed volume containing the text established by the editor, together with introductory material and various apparatuses, notes, and commentary, possibly also with indexes of various kinds. As we shall see, computers can provide invaluable help at all of these stages, but for some functions the time taken to prepare the material for computer processing can outweigh the benefits for some of the stages, especially in the case of preparing many manuscripts for collation.

124

When computers first began to be used for scholarly editing, the emphasis was very much on collation. It was initially thought that collation was a fairly mechanical process which could be simulated by computer. However, the kinds of comparisons needed for complex text are much more sophisticated than those provided by standard software for comparing computer files. Several problematic issues soon emerged, and four in particular became the subject of many debates. The first concerned the number of manuscripts that could be collated at the same time. Some programs can only handle two, requiring many processes where the number of manuscripts is large. For programs that can collate many manuscripts at once, as indeed in manual methods, one manuscript must be designated as the base text and used as a basis for comparison. Practical questions of how much material can be displayed on a screen or printed on sheets of paper often influenced these decisions. A second and bigger question was how to prevent the collation program losing its place when there was a substantial interpolation in one manuscript. It was soon found that markup was really needed to help the program realign the manuscripts, especially in cases where there were also many variants around the realignment position. Verse text is easier to handle because variants must match the metre and the interpolations are normally whole lines.

A third issue concerned the nature of variants, for example whether a variant consisting of several words is one variant or several. In a manual collation, the editor makes these decisions, but in an automated system there may be an expectation that the collation will produce a complete list of variants without human intervention. The alternative is an interactive or machine-aided system where the user is invited to store comments or edit each variant as it is found. This method can be very effective, but more often than not the collation will need to be carried out several times if there is a problem anywhere. This will be very tedious unless the program is able to recall the user's previous interactions so that they do not have to be repeated by hand each time that the program is run.

Fourthly, it makes sense for variants found by a collation program to be stored in the computer for further analysis, but few of the earlier programs did this. Rather, they concentrated on producing printout that simulated the traditional apparatus. Hockey (1980) summarizes various early collation programs. A further discussion can be found in Gilbert (1973), who also investigated several other programs before producing her own integrated system. In Gilbert (1979), she outlines her system for collating prose texts (medieval Latin philosophy), noting that it is appropriate for the repetitive nature of this material, as well as discussing ways of storing and then accessing the variants.

Of the many collation systems that have been written, two stand out because of their sophistication and functionality. TuStep (Tübingen System of Text Processing Programs) is a suite of programs developed since the 1960s at the University of Tübingen under the direction of Wilhelm Ott (Ott 1999). Collation is only one component of TuStep, which has been used for the preparation of many critical editions. TuStep is a completely modular system and integrated set of programs, driven by user commands and a data description language. The programs are run in the appropriate sequence and TuStep is designed so that the editor can intervene at any stage and make changes to the intermediate files before running the next program in the sequence. Ott argues strongly in favour of batch rather than interactive processing because it is so much easier to redo work. He also sees collation as just one program in the bigger system and he uses the collation component of TuStep for other purposes besides the collation of manuscripts. Among the many editions prepared with the aid of TuStep is Gabler's *Ulysses*. The preparation of this edition is described in detail in Gabler (1980). In this edition, the clear reading text on right-hand pages was generated automatically from the 'synoptic display' on left-hand pages (Ott 1988: 102) and the markup in the synoptic display was also generated by computer from the variant files. It is easy to see how, in an electronic version, the user could switch between the clear reading text and the synoptic display at the click of a button.

Robinson's Collate program is a powerful interactive collation program running on Macintosh computers. The first version of Collate was written when Robinson was preparing an edition of two Old Norse poems which exist in forty-four manuscripts (Robinson 1989a). Robinson devised a Macintosh font to transcribe the characters of these manuscripts, and he found it easier to enter new manuscripts by editing the closest one that was already in electronic form rather than entering all the text again. The collation operated with normalized forms, which were looked up in an electronic dictionary of all the words. Robinson found the construction of the dictionary time-consuming (1989a: 100), but a word list and other concordance tools can be used to assist with this process. Lists derived from this dictionary form an excellent source for an investigation into the spelling habits of scribes. The dictionary also helps to maintain consistency and to give the editor an overall picture on which to base individual decisions.

Robinson also discusses his use of the master text which 'simply provides a series of pegs on which the manuscript variants may hang' (Robinson 1989a: 102). He focuses on identifying where the manuscripts are different from each other, not how they differ from a master. But

Collate could do more than find situations where words are identical and are thus a perfect match or are not identical and are thus not a match. He was able to identify scribal variants and also cases where words are distinct in scribal form but identical in sense. In essence his procedures rely on the editor examining the results and building up a file of sense variants, that is, a process of visiting and revisiting the material making use of what has already been found in it. This version of Collate identified 56,944 readings in the forty-four manuscripts and Robinson queried only eight of these variants.

After achieving this level of success with the collation of his Old Norse material, Robinson then set about rewriting Collate so that it could function as a general-purpose collation program. The resulting program, also called Collate, has been widely used for a variety of different projects. In Robinson (1994) he describes the background to Collate including the many lessons learned from the first version. Using the incipit from Chaucer's Wife of Bath's Prologue as an example, he first discusses the problems of identifying variants automatically, for example what to do about spelling variants and whether variants are one word or several. He then outlines what he considers to be the main principles of computer collation. The ability to handle multiple manuscripts at the same time enables the editor to get an overview of the spellings of a word across all manuscripts. Tools to help the editor define and store regularized spellings help to identify variation between texts. The collation is also interactive, enabling the scholar to intervene at any time to control the definition of individual variants. The program should also keep a record of the scholar's interventions and choices so that the collation can be rerun without the scholar having to redo all the interventions manually. A graphical user interface and a series of pull-down menus and windows make clear what is going on at any stage.

Collate recognizes several kinds of markup. It requires what are called block markers which mark pieces of text that are to be collated with each other. The piece of text identified as block 1 <1> is collated against block 1 in every other text. The blocks may be very large, but it makes sense to keep them to a reasonable size. Collate also recognizes COCOA-like markup for blocks and it can use these to identify variants, for example by folio number and line number. Other markup for features such as italic or ornamental capitals can also be collated. Collate provides many options for display or storage of the result of the collation. These include display in the traditional apparatus format, or reordering in different ways, or tagging for input to other programs.

The scholar drives Collate by first setting up a 'prepare' file which provides information about the format of the text. The scholar can suspend the collation at any time when it is running, or move it about, or restart it from a different position in the text. It is also possible to suppress all agreements with the master text or to change to a different master, or to handle punctuation separately. All in all, this is a very sophisticated program designed by a humanities scholar who has a good understanding of the issues. Robinson chose to develop Collate for Macintosh computers and no IBM PC version is available.

But the textual critic needs to do more than identify variants. Conclusions have to be drawn from analysing variants, and if there are large numbers of variants, this task can be a major undertaking requiring counts and tabulations by variant and by manuscript. An electronic database of variants can help here. Robinson attempted to analyse the 'sea of variants' produced by Collate using relational database technology (Robinson 1989b). Although he used an earlier mainframe program, Microsoft Access could be used to carry out work of this kind. A relational database consists of a series of interrelated tables with rows and columns. The main table used here included a row for each variant manuscript in which the variant appears and the type of variant. Further tables gave keys to the manuscript names and also described the variant in more detail. From this database it is very easy to extract, for example, all the variants which occur only in certain manuscripts, or the readings which are unique to a particular manuscript, or the number of readings a given manuscript has in common with other manuscripts. It is also possible to generate profiles of readings and witnesses as, for example, was also done by Ott for some samples from the New Testament (Ott 1973a).

However, although a relational database makes it possible to extract much information from the many variants, with this very large number of variants it can only be used rather clumsily to derive groupings of manuscripts. Robinson discusses how he managed to extract some groupings by starting from his own knowledge of possible groupings of the manuscripts and by external evidence (Robinson 1989b: 178). But a relational database is not designed to derive groupings or clusters from the data within it. It is intended to answer questions of the type 'show me all of the objects which satisfy these criteria', or 'count all the objects which satisfy these criteria'. It would be adequate to investigate the relationships between a small number of manuscripts, but for his problem Robinson knew that he would have to turn to other statistical and mathematical models.

By placing a message on the Humanist electronic discussion list in July 1991 (Robinson 1991), Robinson teamed up with an evolutionary biologist, Robert O'Hara, to apply what is called cladistic analysis to the same manuscript tradition (Robinson and O'Hara 1996). They describe cladistic analysis as 'trees of history', tracing the development of such trees in systematic biology and noting the similarity with historical linguistics and the 'tree of human languages' (1996: 117). Put simply, cladistic analysis software takes a collection of data and attempts to produce the tree or trees of descent or history for which the fewest changes are required, basing this on comparisons between the descendants. Cladistics is also able to handle the kinds of problems which occur with lost manuscripts and errors which occur in a certain order.

Robinson and O'Hara used the PAUP (Phylogenetic Analysis Using Parsimony) program to analyse a table containing all the agreements and disagreements in the manuscripts. Working only with this data, PAUP created a family tree, which was very similar to the one which Robinson had painstakingly created by hand using external evidence of the manuscript tradition and with the assistance of the database described above. In their discussion of this method, Robinson and O'Hara indicate that they believe the result would have been even closer if additional information such as sequences of readings had also been fed to PAUP. But they also note that the method is less successful if there is a substantial amount of contamination in the manuscript tradition, because the method assumes that there is much more vertical transmission than horizontal transmission. They add that these programs tend to produce trees that divide into two branches and no more. Robinson claims that this analysis might have saved him six months' work. A similar cladistics study of the manuscripts of St Augustine's *Quaestiones in Heptateuchum* carried out in the late 1980s is reported by Lee (1989).

Mathematical models can be used to study manuscript relationships, which are not based on stemmata. In the late 1960s John Griffith published two papers in which he argued that family trees are not necessarily the best way of representing manuscript traditions, especially where there are what, also following the analogy of biology, he called 'mutants', that is, readings which do not fit into the tree model (Griffith 1968; 1969). Griffith was thus interested in investigating how manuscripts group or cluster together without the expectation that some manuscripts are derived from others. He did not use a computer in the work described in these two papers, arguing that 'the best computer for the job is located between the ears of the investigator' (1968: 114). With pencil and paper he tabulated the agreements and disagreements, first in samples of the manuscripts of Juvenal, and later in two samples from the Gospels. He was then able to map the relationships between the manuscripts on a straight line which he calls a spectrum line. He could then compare two samples from the same text by placing the lines one above the other.

However, Griffith became dissatisfied with the straight line model because the manuscripts at the end of the line appeared close together when in fact they were far from each other as well as being far from the others. He then turned to computer models in order to investigate a multidimensional approach (Griffith 1979). Using a multivariate technique, he revisited the samples of Juvenal and the Gospels and also tested samples from Horace and from Aeschylus. The results are presented in the form of diagrams, which show the relationships between the manuscripts in three-dimensional space. See Griffith (1984) for an example. Even with the fairly primitive graphical tools available to him at that time, it is easy to see the manuscript groups in these diagrams. This kind of approach makes most sense when it makes use of already existing knowledge of the manuscript tradition, as indeed Griffith did. If it is known that some sections of a manuscript are closer to one manuscript and other sections are closer to a different one, the procedure can be tested with different samples whose boundaries fit the known divisions. If the analysis were carried out on the whole manuscript, the results would be looser because of the averaging of the results. Like many other computer-based tools, the technique can thus serve to confirm and quantify what is already suspected from other evidence or hand analysis. Griffith used only significant variants in his analyses, but he also discusses the relative importance of variants and whether some weighting could be applied to very significant variants.

Galloway (1979) reports an experiment with cluster analysis and a set of variants from the manuscripts of *Lai de l'ombre*, comparing the results of her analyses with stemmata produced from the same set of variants by Bédier and by Quentin. The Clustan program, which she used, provides various methods of cluster analysis. Galloway notes the problems with single linkage clustering, where chaining can occur, and with complete linkage, where it is difficult to arrive at groupings. But she was able to produce dendrograms that are very similar to the trees in the original Bédier and Quentin analyses. Like Griffith, she was concerned that these mathematical methods make no provision for the editor's subjective judgements or for external knowledge of the data. The methods are more suitable for survey data or other analyses carried out by social scientists. Nevertheless, this is a fruitful area of enquiry to assist with the study of Classical and medieval manuscript traditions. A very clear survey of multivariate techniques as applied to manuscript traditions can be found in Pierce (1988) where he discusses not only what to measure but how to measure.

Text analysis tools such as concordances can be invaluable aids in the preparation of editions. They enable the editor to see at a glance when a reading occurs elsewhere in the text and thus help to make decisions between variants. By bringing together all instances of the same word or sequences of words, they can also provide material for annotations and commentaries. The editor is provided with an overall picture and is thus not tempted to describe or comment on a form as being unusual when it occurs in several other places. TuStep integrates these text analysis functions, but many editors have used other concordance programs.

It is not surprising that editors have for long viewed the computer as a useful tool for typesetting complex editions. The possibility of errors creeping in to a carefully edited text at the typesetting stage, and often the requirement to include non-standard characters, has encouraged editors either to submit electronic copy to their publisher or to prepare their own camera-ready copy. Tools range from desktop publishing software to high-end typesetting systems and from elementary and sometimes amateur graphic design to productions of the highest scholarly standards.

Making up pages with a critical apparatus is particularly difficult, because the make-up of the text lines and apparatus must proceed in parallel. It is not known in advance how much space the apparatus will take up, since there may be several variants for one reading and the normal format is to place these one after the other on the same line, not to put them on separate lines. Line numbers must also be assigned to each lemma in the apparatus, but except for through line numbering in verse texts where the lineation is fixed, line numbers cannot be assigned until the text has been formatted for typesetting. The TuStep programs are the most sophisticated humanities typesetting system known to me. Ott (1988) describes the functions of the programs as part of the larger text analysis and preparation suite. The first version was available in 1969, but by 1974 TuStep was able to make up pages with footnotes, running heads, and up to nine levels of critical apparatus (1988: 90). The whole is run as a batch process for ease of making changes. Ott (1979) argues that it is not possible to make up these complex pages by manual methods and he stresses the value of an automated batch system that can be rerun easily if changes need to be made. TuStep also generates a second file matching the page and line numbers of the typeset text. This second file can then be used as a source for generating indexes and other supplementary material, which must be keyed to page numbers. This last feature is extremely useful. It is all too easy to submit electronic copy to a publishing house where the text is then reformatted to fit the design of the book. In this process, for prose texts in particular, the lineation is changed to fit the chosen line length and all assigned line numbers then also change. Ott also notes that the modular design of TuStep makes it easy for editions or other material to be published in instalments and then to merge all the instalments together with updated annotation to produce a final comprehensive work once the editor has reached the end of the series.

But more and more editors are attracted to the idea of distributing and publishing editions electronically. There are a variety of reasons for this. Printed scholarly editions are expensive and the cost model for printing requires a certain number of books to be produced up front. It has been thought that electronic editions might be cheaper to produce, but, as we shall see, the amount of labour needed to produce a printed edition may not decrease for an electronic one. It still entails all the scholarly processes which are required for a print edition with the added complications of keeping up with new technology. But much more discussion has concentrated on the power and flexibility of the electronic medium. The editor is freed from the constraints of the shape and format of the printed book. This makes it possible to include much more material and also to avoid privileging one view or version of the text. In fact it makes it possible to include every version or manuscript both in transcription and as a digital image. But the apparently infinite capacities of computers can lead to very ambitious projects which may not in the end have as much scholarly value. It is very tempting to provide as much source material as possible, but this can be at the expense of adding the critical analysis which makes the edition useful. The possibility of making changes over and over again to electronic information can also slow a project down, particularly if the changes have ramifications throughout the material. Rather too many so-called 'editions' have been appearing on the Internet which consist of little more than digital images of the source material and perhaps a transcription.

Much recent discussion has centred on the idea of presenting many versions of the text electronically and allowing the user to navigate through this material as a kind of hypertext. See, for example, the essays by Bornstein and McGann in Finneran (1996). Several of these projects have taken to calling themselves an 'archive' rather than an edition, simply because they present a lot of source material to the user but much less in the way of editorial annotations or navigation tools. The user can be left to wander round at will, sometimes not knowing how or why a particular page has been reached. The onus is on the reader of the edition, the user, to determine what is useful and to choose what route to take through the material. This has been hailed as empowerment of the reader, but more often than not it can lead to confusion: the reader knows what to do with a book, but is much less sure about what to do with electronic information unless it is something very obviously searchable such as a reference work. Furthermore, with a collection of electronic materials, it is less easy to get some sense of what the whole is, unless the initial screens provide a list of contents. In an insightful paper, Lavagnino (1996) discusses the problems of hypertextual reading for editions. Besides the usual discussion of the limitations of the current generation of computer screens, he also notes that these hyper- textual editions are not really usable in the way that printed editions are because they provide so few scholarly tools and apparatus (1996: 114).

But the major difference between a printed and an electronic edition is that a fairly standard and well-documented model has developed for a printed edition, but no such thing exists for an electronic edition. Most experiments lack a framework or structure within which the reader can operate. There has been much discussion and speculation about what an electronic edition should look like and what it should be able to do. However, in only a few cases has this speculation been realized in a concrete product which scholars can use and which can serve as a starting point for further research.

The Web and the HTML markup language provide one option, which is easy to implement but rather too simple. One interesting example of a Web-based edition is the *Charrette* project at Princeton (Uitti 1994). Here the initial screen provides an overview of the site and from there the user can go to the edition where eight manuscripts have been transcribed. There is a link to a page describing the transcription codes, which also shows what the characters look like in the manuscripts. The user chooses one manuscript and then selects the folio to be examined. This leads to the transcription with links to the image and to the other manuscripts. For example, by starting with manuscript G, the user can inspect the transcription of a folio of G and then go to see the transcription of the other manuscripts at the same point, or to inspect an image of the manuscript. The images have been annotated very simply, giving the name of the manuscript and the folio number and every fifth line number. Although SGML has been used for the archival form of this material, the links are implemented neatly in HTML.

For their *Lyrical Ballads* project, Ronald Tetreault and Bruce Graver have implemented another approach using HTML and frames. This material is again derived from an SGML version, but the use of frames

133

makes it possible to see the transcription and page images side by side (Graver and Tetreault 1998; Tetreault and Graver 1998). But in these HTML-based editions, searching is very weak and can only be carried out with the browser's Find in Page option.

The Internet Shakespeare Editions under the general editorship of Michael Best address a rather different question (Best 1999). The aim is to 'to make available scholarly editions of high quality in a format native to the medium of the Internet'. This project therefore does not plan to put on to the Internet existing versions of Shakespeare, but to re-edit his works in a manner that can only exist on the Internet. The texts are being produced in text only format, also in HTML, and in SGML with digitized graphics where appropriate. Best discusses annotation in relation to the intended audience which he says is 'the scholar', but he envisages two levels of annotation, with the second containing more detail and possibly links to external sites. The whole will be accompanied by critical materials (articles, indexes, etc.) and there will be a critical introduction to each text. A special issue of the electronic journal *Early Modern Literary Studies* is devoted to this project and Best's Afterword in this collection discusses the many challenges he faces (Best 1998).

In December 1997, the Committee on Scholarly Editions of the Modern Language Association of America published *Guidelines for Electronic Scholarly Editions* (Modern Language Association of America 1997). These guidelines are based on the already existing guidelines for printed editions with the goal 'to enhance the usability and reliability of scholarly editions by making full use of the capabilities of the computer' (1997: introduction). The introduction also notes that the guidelines are 'phrased in terms of desiderata rather than requirements, since hardware and software capabilities are changing so rapidly; and some desirable features are not yet technically or economically feasible'. These guidelines make a serious attempt to move into the electronic arena the range of principles deemed important for printed editions, the overarching requirement being the scholarly quality of the edition. The textual essay which outlines the principles and rationale on which the edition is built is perhaps even more important in the electronic medium, because, with the increased flexibility, the user is less likely to know what to expect. The guidelines discuss the possibility of replacing the apparatus by full-text transcriptions and including collation software to generate variants and filter different kinds of variants. They also stress the need for standardization of the character set, encoding and documentation of the source documents, recommending the use of the Text Encoding Initiative where possible. In particular TEI headers should provide adequate metadata for each source file.

There is some discussion of digitized facsimiles, but the recommendation is that these should be in addition to transcriptions with links between the transcription and the image at line, and possibly word, level (1997: section I.D.1). Linking between images and transcriptions at the page level is obviously very easy, but creating links at the word level is much more complex. Inserting these links by hand is far too time-consuming and so attention has turned to attempting to do this automatically by applying image analysis tools to the digital image to identify the location of each word on the image (Zweig 1998). This is in effect a kind of OCR but with the aid of an already existing transcription. The advantages of retaining the original lineation in the transcription are obvious here.

The MLA guidelines also envisage a central 'archive' accessible over the network. Scholars will access the material together with a range of analytic tools for retrieval of words, preferably in lemmatized form, and for collation, as well as links to external dictionaries for assistance with morphological analysis etc. The guidelines make some mention of hypertext, but as a way of linking to other material in the edition rather than duplicating the material. For example where the textual essay discusses examples, a link could be provided to actual examples in the edition (Modern Language Association 1997: introduction). Hypertext is also mentioned in the context of linking to annotation and also possibly for the display of parallel texts. Hypertext is not touted as the solution to all editorial problems, and the guidelines recommend that the edition should include 'a rationale of the kinds of hypertext links (two-way, one-way) used as well as the categories of information that they are used to connect' as well as including on the links 'information to indicate their scholarly purpose and to facilitate searching by category (e.g., source)' (1997: section II.B.2.a). Clearly something much more sophisticated than HTML linking is envisaged here.

No software yet exists for some of the functions outlined in these guidelines, but they do represent a level of thinking which is crucial to the development of better software. The guidelines focus on principles and on scholarly requirements and distance themselves from technical topics. They encourage the scholar to first decide what he or she wants to do then to investigate how to do it. Shillingsburg's (1996) principles concentrate much more on the nature and specification of an 'archive', which he envisages is stored somewhere on the network. Reflecting perhaps his interest in editing modern texts rather than the classical perspective of the MLA guidelines, Shillingsburg's first specification for the archive is that the electronic edition should be multimedia (1996: 33). He also envisages an environment where users can add commentary to the archive, and where they print and quote from it, as well as various options for linking. But some of these functions are discussed in the context of current software rather than as a detailed set of desiderata and the reader is left with the impression of somewhat vague specifications. Shillingsburg does, however, finish by outlining a 'user-friendly' navigation system which allows, for example, retracing a session's use of the archive, and pinpointing where the user is within the archive to avoid the feeling of being lost. See also Faulhaber (1991) and Hockey (1996) for further discussion of features that might exist in this new editorial environment.

Two projects have seriously attempted to realize some of these goals in a working system. The first of these, the Model Editions Partnership (MEP), set, as its main objective, the construction and evaluation of a number of models for electronic documentary editions (Chesnutt 1999). Funded by the National Historical Publications and Records Commission in the United States, the MEP brought together seven documentary editing projects and three co-ordinators led by David Chesnutt to develop a foundation for the next generation of historical editions. The project set out to address questions of intellectual access to electronic representations of source documents and to create samples illustrating various methods of approach. These historical documents are usually short and mostly take the form of letters, but they also include diaries, newspaper cuttings, memoranda, and the like. The MEP based its work on the use of a TEI-based SGML markup scheme to put what Chesnutt calls 'the intellectual frameworks' or the 'glue' around the material. Essentially, SGML defines the pegs or structures within which the editorial work sits and which guide the user around the documents (Chesnutt 1997).

In the first stages of the project, the three co-ordinators visited all seven projects to discuss their methods of work and to elicit ideas for the electronic editions. With the exception of Chesnutt's own project, *The Papers of Henry Laurens*, the projects made fairly limited use of computers. All were using word processors. Some had relational databases to control their source material and one or two had experimented with creating Web sites. But all were focused on preparing printed volumes. They were interested to see the possibilities for electronic editions, but knew little about what was involved in creating these editions and what these editions might look like. Chesnutt had previously over a long period developed various computer systems for the Laurens papers, including typesetting and a program to assist with the preparation of the detailed conceptual indexes contained in these volumes (Chesnutt 1983). In the initial visits the co-ordinators also showed the project staff some mock-ups of electronic editions and invited them to 'dream' about what they would like to do.

The outcomes were incorporated in a prospectus for electronic historical editions (Chesnutt 1996). Like the MLA guidelines, the MEP prospectus places great emphasis on maintaining current scholarly excellence. It strives to build on these standards of excellence to make many more things possible in electronic editions than can be done in print. It notes the possibility of changing editorial practice on the basis of experience and therefore promotes an open architecture. Electronic editions can easily be updated after publication and also published in different forms, all deriving automatically from one archival copy. A simple mock-up example showed the projects how easy it is to move from a clear text to a complex diplomatic transcription at the click of a mouse. Variants, some of which have considerable historical importance, can be embedded in the text so that readers can view them or suppress them as they wish. But a major advantage of the electronic medium for this kind of material is the ability to offer more than one organizing principle. In a printed work, only one linear sequence is possible and usually this is chronological. It is easy to extract from an electronic edition all the letters written to one person, or all that mention a certain person or place or topic, or all documents which are taken from newspapers.

Annotations can be linked to several places. In printed volumes a biographical note is created the first time that a person is mentioned and then any further references to that person even in later volumes, cross-refer to that note. In an electronic edition a link can be made to the full annotation from every occurrence. Electronic editions also make it possible to build cumulative indexes, which are too expensive to produce in print. The MEP also discussed illustrations particularly in relation to maps, which help explicate, for example, the journeys of Susan B. Anthony or the military campaigns of Nathanael Greene. The MEP prospectus also discusses in detail how good markup can facilitate this and how common methods can ultimately lead to shared material and links to standard reference works.

Three models for electronic editions are proposed in the MEP prospectus and samples of all three were implemented. An image edition presents the original documentation with supplementary material and search tools. One of the MEP models, the Margaret Sanger papers, is based around images of Sanger's pamphlet *The Woman Rebel*. It also includes a searchable chronology and short biographies of some of the key people, as well as details of the source and current location of the documents, and a historical essay discussing the context for the documents. All are linked within a conceptual framework so that the user can work with the edition, either by starting with the historical essay, or going to a list of documents, or using the chronology as an entry point. The MEP model for the Stanton–Anthony papers is a combined edition that includes transcriptions as well as images of some documents. This model also has links to maps of the period showing the places mentioned in the documents.

The samples from the First Federal Congress and the Ratification of the Constitution are examples of what the MEP calls 'live text editions'. They give transcriptions of the documents with full text retrieval. The user is presented with a list of documents and can browse this list or search for keywords. Annotations are accessed via hypertext links. The MEP has also experimented with what it calls 'transition editions', that is, page images of material which already exists in print form. The idea here is to make this material available quickly and more cheaply with the expectation that transcriptions can be created later by OCR. The conceptual indexes from the original volumes are used to access the page images so that the user has the same means of access as is provided in the printed version. The MEP samples were built using INSO Corporation's DynaText software which is an SGML-based program for creating and using electronic books with annotations, links, etc. The editions are delivered over the Internet using DynaWeb, another INSO product that interacts with the DynaText book, sending user queries to the book and converting the results to HTML for display on the Web. The limitations of HTML-based Web technology are very apparent in DynaWeb. The program appears rather 'clunky' and it would be far better if the user could interact directly with the markup rather than via HTML. This will only be possible when XML becomes the markup language of the Web. But, in spite of this, the MEP models have advanced our thinking and represent a practical understanding of what is possible. Because they use SGML, they can easily be migrated to new software later.

Robinson's *Wife of Bath's Prologue* is another working model for an electronic edition. It also uses the DynaText program, but it avoids the problems of the Web since it is delivered to the user on CD-ROM (Robinson 1996). This CD-ROM represents the first publication in a massive undertaking where Robinson and his collaborators plan to publish transcriptions and digital images of all the pre-1500 manuscripts of Chaucer's *Canterbury Tales* together with a set of scholarly tools to analyse and manipulate this material. The earlier editors, Manly and Rickert, worked with some 60,000 cards and Robinson surmises that they 'were simply overwhelmed by the immense amount of evidence they gathered' (1996: Introduction, p. 11). It is inconceivable now to think about handling that amount of data without a computer, but to complete the entire *Canterbury Tales* will still be an enormous task. *The Wife of Bath's Prologue* CD-ROM contains fifty-eight manuscripts and early printed editions of this text. This represents 1,200 pages, or three megabytes of transcriptions, but added to this are transcriptions of the glosses, descriptions of the witnesses, and spelling databases in which words are organized by lemma and by grammatical category, as well as regularized and unregularized collations generated by Robinson's Collate program. The CD-ROM contains about 10 million items of information. The whole is encoded in SGML which, as in the MEP, puts the intellectual frameworks around the material and makes navigation possible. Robinson used the SGML markup to generate the 1.9 million hypertext links automatically.

The CD-ROM opens with two windows, a table of contents on the left and the text on the right. The base text for the collation is in the right-hand window, and clicking on any word in the text opens another window containing a regularized collation of that word giving a list of variants of the word and the witnesses which have each variant. A double click at this point brings up the unregularized collation. A click on a sigil opens another window with the text of that witness at that point. At the beginning of the transcription of each page is a camera icon, which takes the user to a digital image of the page. The images are digitized in black and white, but they are adequate for the user to inspect the variant and also to investigate doubtful readings. The user may thus move around from the transcription of a witness to a collation to an image at will. A new window is opened at each stage and so it is very easy to end up with many open windows. Comparisons between witnesses or between transcription and image can easily be made by positioning the windows side by side. Once a witness has been opened, the user needs to remember which one it is. The title bar of windows containing images gives the name of the witness, but for transcriptions and other windows, there is only a generic title. However, the usability of the windows is much better than what is provided in current Web technology.

The initial left-hand window is a table of contents of the entire CD-ROM. Any of the witnesses can be opened from here and used as a starting point for the collations. The table of contents entry for each witness also leads to notes to the transcription, a description of the witness, images of the witness, and a spelling database for that witness. The spelling database for each witness gives all the headwords with their part of speech and links to their different spellings. There is also a spelling database for all the witnesses, which gives the total number of occurrences of every spelling of every headword and links to the places where each spelling occurs. Finally the CD-ROM contains papers giving an overview of editing the *Canterbury Tales* by Norman Blake, a discussion of the transcription guidelines by Peter Robinson and Elizabeth Solopova, Stephen Partridge's discussion of the manuscript glosses, and a detailed list of sigils and a bibliography. A 'find' box for simple searches is provided on most windows and the book menu leads to a set of more sophisticated searches which use the SGML markup.

The production of this CD-ROM remains a remarkable achievement, but it raises a number of questions, some of which Robinson himself has addressed. What should appear the first time that the user opens up the CD-ROM? Whatever appears first will send signals to the user indicating what the CD-ROM is about, what kind of user is being addressed by it, and also the scope of the material on the CD-ROM. The table of contents window on the left is helpful, but the version of the text which appears is the 'Base Text for Collation', which Robinson explains as 'a very lightly edited representation of the Hengwrt manuscript' (1996: Introduction, p. 14). Perhaps more information could be provided about this. The manipulation of variant readings is one activity which lends itself very well to computer processing, but there can be a tendency to provide information which is easy to generate automatically. Robinson is less guilty of this than some projects, but the tendency to inclusiveness can still overwhelm the user. The computer processing also tends to reduce everything to the same plane or level. It does not privilege important material and the user is thus expected to know what is important in this database.

The book-like model of DynaText provides a framework within which to operate, but after a while it becomes constricting and it would be good to have other routes into the material. But on the other hand, the user becomes used to a particular format. If the next CD-ROM in the series, *The General Prologue*, has a different user interface, users who are already familiar with *The Wife of Bath's Prologue* will be irritated if they have to learn something new, especially if they want to continue using both. But perhaps a bigger issue is that the CD-ROM presents rather than analyses the material. In a paper on the *Canterbury Tales* presented at a conference in Rome in May 1998, Robinson concentrates on analysis rather than presentation (Robinson 1998). After a discussion of the analysis tools provided by Collate, he presents the results of the PAUP analysis of some 16,000 sets of variants in *The General Prologue*. This, he argues, is only a starting point. A database analysis helps to illuminate the PAUP cladogram (tree diagram) and to investigate variants that appear at a particular point in the tradition. Would it be more appropriate to include tools such as these on the next CD-ROM and, if so, will users learn to grasp their full potential? That remains to be seen, but what is clear is that the more powerful the systems are, the more potential there is for asking interesting questions and thus the more demand that it should be possible to ask those questions. Undoubtedly this is a ground-breaking and well-documented project, but its influence beyond the immediate area of tools for electronic editions remains to be seen. For further information see the collections of papers in Blake and Robinson (1993, 1997).

We have touched on images earlier in the discussion of the MEP and the *Canterbury Tales* project, but it is appropriate to finish this chapter with an examination of archives or editions where images are the central focus. The Rossetti and the Blake Archives at the University of Virginia are two well-known examples (McGann 1997a; Eaves, Essick, and Viscomi 1999). With Blake, in particular, the image representation of the material is very important since it conveys much more than can be found in printed editions. Both these projects and a number of other planned enterprises (Yeats, Dickinson, etc.) follow the editorial theories promoted most notably by Jerome McGann (1983, 1993). In his critique published in 1983, McGann drew attention to the differences between editing Classical and medieval texts with a long manuscript transmission and editing modern texts. The editor of modern texts has much information available about the texts and is concerned with different versions produced by the author and not with seeking a single ideal text. In McGann (1993) the idea of 'bibliographical codes' as opposed to 'linguistic codes' is expounded, particularly in relation to Morris, Blake, Dickinson, and Rossetti. The physical appearance of the text is important and this must be provided to the reader in some form, for which digital images appear to be an obvious solution. McGann has set out the principles for his Rossetti Archive, and it will be interesting to see how many of these can be realized in practice as the archive develops and is published (McGann 1996, 1997b). In his 1996 paper he shows how some of his original ideas can be implemented with a Web browser as well as being brave enough to publish some of his SGML markup. In the later paper he begins to discuss some tools for working with images, including annotating images and morphing, which he prefers to call 'deformations' and which he claims help to reveal some of the patterns in the Rossetti images. Some of the other papers in Finneran (1996) also discuss images and the physical representations of textual sources.

Although images obviously enable the reader to see the original in some detail, the inability to search images makes the study of the physical appearance of material more difficult. The TEI has been criticized for its inability to encode the physical description of a text. Lancashire (1996a: 123) notes that 'TEI tends to see text as structured by authors' and laments its lack of assistance with encoding any bibliographic features. His guidelines for encoding Renaissance Electronic Texts (RET) also attempt to address this problem with tags for bibliographic divisions and structures, but not for descriptions of images.

The Blake Archive consists of digital images and transcriptions of a number of Blake's works. Each text is referred to as an electronic edition and it consists of a searchable transcription delivered to the end user via DynaWeb. Various tools are provided for the images, for example to help the user get some sense of size and to link annotations to images, something which is very clumsy on the Web, although easy to implement in most standalone hypertext systems. The Blake team has taken great care in digitizing the images (Kirschenbaum 1998), but links between the images and the text are at the level of the page or image, not of lines or words. The major issue with images is how to search them. Software tools to inspect images of the quality of works of art are a long way off and so the searching must depend on keyword terms. The Blake team have prepared their own set of terms based on their knowledge of the material, and these are presented to the user as a series of check boxes in a flat structure. From this the user gets an immediate sense of the kinds of items which have been indexed for the images, but the list grows fast with the addition of new works to the archive.

An alternative approach might be to use an already existing set of conceptual index terms. The Getty Art and Architecture Thesaurus is a hierarchical indexing system suitable for works of art (Getty Vocabulary Program 1999). ICONCLASS, developed at the universities of Utrecht and Leiden, is also intended to serve as a set of indexing terms for iconographic information (ICONCLASS Research and Development Group 1999). It is also hierarchical, with ten major categories. With the existence of these different systems, one begins to wonder about the possibility of a generic set of index terms mounted on the network that could be used by projects which are indexing images for searching. Such an index will help when users want to work with more than one collection of material. Further speculation is beyond the scope of this book, but this is an area to which more attention should be paid. Nor is this the place to discuss the technical details of imaging. An excellent introduction can be found in Besser and Trant (1995), which also has a useful introductory bibliography.

Image editions are still rather new. Their enthusiasts have written much more about the possibilities opened up by them than about their reception by users. Access seems to be the key issue here. Being able to see representations of the original Blake material in colour makes a very big difference, especially for teaching and for non-Blake scholars. The Blake Archive is also searchable, but the lack of searchability of many image-based projects is beginning to cause some concern, especially for scholarly applications. Flanders (1997) also notes the apparent lack of depth in these editions and the requirement for scholarly apparatus of various kinds. Lavagnino (1996) comments on the lack of scholarly tools in many hypertext editions where the material is merely presented without much in the way of search tools. The MLA guidelines focus on transcriptions of the text with the provision for linking to images taking second place. Many of these issues relate to the intended audience. Scholars want to work with fine detail and to be able to search their material in many ways. Those who work with one or two manuscripts want to see the original manuscripts for themselves to be sure that no distortion has occurred in the digitization process. Access to the digital image may help them later, but it is not a substitute for the original. Images perhaps have more potential for a broader audience, for groups of people who are not likely to have the opportunity to see the originals. The MEP image edition of the Margaret Sanger papers shows how images can be placed in the context of surrounding annotation and supplementary material that really helps users understand what the images are about. Lack of contextual information is a serious problem with many Internet resources: collections of images without much context may be visited once, but are much less likely to be revisited and seriously used.

Multimedia can add even more bells and whistles to electronic editions. Given the large file sizes required for audio and video, there is less experience of how this might turn out in practice. Short examples can illustrate the point, but experiments need to be conducted to find out how users react, for example, to the inclusion of readings of poetry, including long poems, or to lengthy film clips. The possibilities of moving around these at will is obviously attractive, but so far there is little experience of what happens when they are linked to a text, which people tend to assimilate in a different way. This begins to bring computing and electronic resources more into the realm of television. The two are likely to converge at some point in the future, but experiments need to be conducted on user needs in order to ensure that this convergence functions as effectively as it can. People tend to operate with short pieces of information on computer screens. Will they be willing to use this medium to listen to longer items or watch complete film clips? All this is some time in the future, but even with present systems it is all too easy to become seduced by the possibility of multimedia and thus for the edition to place too much emphasis on what Gatrell (1996) calls 'gimmickry'. There is a place for multimedia to enhance the material, but it should not detract from it.

The network can vastly facilitate collaborative editing projects. Even at a simple level where all the members of an editing team have access to the same electronic file system and tools, much repetitive work can be reduced or eliminated, and checking for inconsistencies can be aided by computer programs. It is also possible to envisage network-based editions where digital images and transcriptions of one or more texts are available on the Internet, and annotations and commentary can be added by several scholars working in different places, or even be made available for anybody to insert annotations. Such a project was outlined by the Electronic Peirce Consortium where it was planned to mount some of Peirce's manuscripts with tools for multiple annotation carried out remotely by different scholars (Neuman *et al.* 1992).

This assessment of electronic editions has covered a very wide range of topics from using computers to assist with the traditional kind of editing to new forms of publishing that are only possible electronically. Many choices need to be made at the start of a project. The two most important considerations are the intended audience, and the size and scale of the project. A small project intended for classroom delivery might achieve its objectives best by creating a Web site and using simple Web-based tools. At the other end of the scale a massive project like the *Canterbury Tales* or the planned *American Documentary Heritage* of historical editions needs the kind of intellectual frameworks provided by SGML in order to scale up to the projected end-product. Yet the question of audience opens up options that are not possible in a print publication. The very nature of a book (size, typeface, and number of footnotes and annotations) sends signals about the audience for which it is intended. See, for example, Small (1991) for a discussion of annotation and audience. With careful planning and markup it should be possible to create an electronic publication which can be used by several different types of audience by including different levels of annotation from the simple to the scholarly. This might be a route towards the economic viability of electronic editions, but it requires careful design of the different levels of encoding.

SGML also has the advantage of not being tied to any particular computer system, and thus ensures longevity of the material as well as intelligent searching. But there is no software yet that delivers the functionality laid out in the MLA guidelines, nor indeed any that satisfies the various presentational requirements of the modern approaches to editing. It seems reasonably clear that images work best when they are accompanied by appropriate contextual material, but more experiments need to be carried out to determine what that material should look like. The MEP is one of very few projects that has set as its major objective, not the creation of an edition in itself, but an advancement of our understanding of how to build electronic editions. More projects of this kind and a synthesis of the results would serve the growing community of electronic editors very well indeed.

9 | Dictionaries and Lexical Databases

With the advent of the *Oxford English Dictionary* on the Internet and on CD-ROM as well as of many smaller dictionaries on CD-ROM, electronic dictionaries are now common reference tools. They make it possible to look up words very quickly, to compare usages, and to examine quotations and definitions very easily. But much more can be done with computer-based tools and dictionaries. Computers are now widely used in the preparation of dictionaries. There are many advantages in maintaining and updating a dictionary in electronic form, most obviously that printed versions can be typeset directly from the electronic copy. But more than that, electronic dictionaries are beginning to be used by computers in retrieval systems. The computer looks up a search term in the dictionary and can derive more information about that word and its collocates and various forms, and it can refine the search request using that information. This raises questions as to whether the same dictionary or lexical database can be used for many purposes by both humans and computers, and if so, what that database might look like. Here we trace the development of the uses of computers and dictionaries, and assess various types of resources. See also Meijs (1992) for a useful overview.

Well before the possibilities of delivering dictionaries in electronic form became apparent, the compilers of historical dictionaries began to realize the benefits of using computers in their work. In the simplest case the computer can act as an enormous filing system, which has one very big advantage over card and paper files; it can be searched not just by headword but in many different ways. Even a file of electronic quotations ('slips') can yield many benefits. It can provide a picture of the overall source of quotations, the authors and types of material in quotations, and gaps and omissions in the coverage of sources. For a historical dictionary, a search by date can help to assess coverage by period. An electronic collection of slips can also allow the editor of the dictionary to examine the corpus of slips to see whether any other slips include the same word or follow a similar pattern to the word whose entry is currently being compiled. The papers in Zampolli and Cappelli (1984) examine the possibilities and limits of the computer in lexicography, and these topics are further developed in Cignoni and Peters (1991).

One possible approach to compiling a dictionary is to create concordances of a corpus of all the relevant source material and examine these for interesting usages for each entry. This approach was the original source of some large-scale collections of text now in common use. The Trésor de a Langue Française (TLF) and the ARTFL material was originally compiled for the preparation of a new French dictionary (Gorcy 1984). A corpus such as this one soon becomes very large. It can provide useful examples of rare words, but produces far too many citations for common words. More complex programs are needed to sort through all of these. The requirement for working with collocations or linguistic analysis of the corpus was all too apparent and the TLF team were using some collocation tools by the beginning of the 1980s.

A more manageable project and one of the first corpus-based dictionary projects is the *Dictionary of Old English* based in Toronto. From the outset this was intended to be compiled from concordances, and a planning meeting held in March 1969 laid the groundwork (Cameron, Frank, and Leyerle 1970). A further meeting in 1970 established procedures for defining the corpus of texts and yielded the first significant product from this project, a detailed list of all the texts in the corpus with associated identification codes, and a plan for creating electronic versions of those texts (Frank and Cameron 1973). The entire corpus is approximately 3 million words, which is a manageable size for making and then examining concordances for every word. The most frequent word occurs about 15,000 times and it was possible for an editor to read through these occurrences in order to select useful ones for the dictionary. Concordance programs may not necessarily produce useful citations for a dictionary (de Tollenaere 1973). Often the context is cut off at a certain number of words or the program relies on recognizing certain punctuation marks to identify the ends of sentences. To avoid these difficulties, the Old English Corpus was encoded with quotation units embedded in it. The editors of the *Dictionary of Old English* thus have a concordance of all their material accessible to them as they are working and they are able to use this in a computer-based system for creating and editing entries. But to work with these effectively the editors also need tools to bring together all variant spellings and all forms of the same lemma.

The benefits of using a corpus in lexicography are immediately apparent, even if it is only from selected texts. Lexicographers can have access to concordances of a variety of texts for use as reference tools. Howlett (1984) draws attention to the value of concordances of selected texts for his work on the *Dictionary of Medieval Latin from British Sources*. One can also imagine the use, for example, of the TLG for creating or updating a Greek dictionary. Fillmore and Atkins (1994) provide an interesting view of the value of corpora in lexicography in their study of the word *risk*, where they contrast dictionary and corpus evidence. They examined the descriptive framework for *risk* in ten current one-volume dictionaries, also taking care to allow for the possible differences between British and American English. They discovered a number of differences in the treatment of *risk* in these dictionaries, mainly omissions, lack of clarity, particularly in *take a risk* and *run a risk*, and incompatibilities. They concluded from this examination that it would not be possible to combine these ten entries into a single unit without rejecting some elements (1994: 362). They then turned to examining 2,213 concordance entries for *risk*, taken from two corpora, one of which was the Cobuild corpus and the other was provided by the American Publishing House for the Blind. From this they built a set of semantic frames for *risk* which were multidimensional in approach, and then contrasted these with the dictionary evidence. Dictionaries are of course constrained by time and space, but Fillmore and Atkins concluded that corpus evidence could lead to a new kind of dictionary which can only exist in electronic form.

The *Collins Cobuild English Language Dictionary* was the first significant completed example of corpus lexicography in English (*Collins Cobuild* 1987). The lexicographers worked mostly with a concordance of about 7.3 million words (Krishnamurthy 1987: 63), but for forms which occurred less than fifty times in this corpus, reference was made to a concordance of a larger corpus of 20 million words. The context lines were 100 characters in length, but for some words such as conjunctions, longer and left-sorted contexts were provided but from a smaller corpus. Cobuild dealt with the problem of too many concordance entries for common words by using a sampling program that took every 'nth' entry. Krishnamurthy also describes the process of working with the concordance lines in some detail. First the concordances for all the forms of a word were assembled. Then the different meanings of a word were marked. A right-sorted concordance and a more general inspection of collocates were very helpful in determining the lexical patterning of a word. Examples were selected directly from the concordances, although in some cases very long sentences were shortened.

The lexicographers then created hand-encoded slips which were subsequently entered into a database which was used for on-line editing of the text, carried out with reference to concordances of the larger corpus. It may also have been possible to automate some of the slip-creation process, but this would still require much judgement and hand editing on the part of the lexicographers. The *Cobuild Dictionary* is intended for learners of English, and Fox (1987) discusses the role of examples for this kind of dictionary. The corpus provides natural, authentic, and interesting examples, but there are questions about how some of these can be put into context when the example sentences are short or directly relate to the preceding sentence.

A second edition of the *Cobuild Dictionary* was published in 1995 (*Collins Cobuild* 1995). The second edition is much more than a light revision of the first edition. It contains many new words and the information was also checked against the Bank of English, which by then had reached 200 million words, including 15 million words of spoken text. In the introduction to this edition, the editor-in-chief John Sinclair gives a very clear overview of the value of corpus data for lexicography. Besides tools for the inspection of collocations and lexical patterning, the corpus has provided frequency information. Using this the editors were able to highlight very frequent words with a system of diamonds in the margin of the text. Sinclair gives an example of concordance entries for *play* and *light* showing also word class tags. In the example for *play*, these tags were used to display all forms of the verb, but not the noun (1995: p. xii). Longman now use the BNC as a major source for their dictionaries. Among other things, the frequency information from the tagged corpus is used to put the most frequent meaning first (Summers 1996).

The value of computers in organizing and managing material and in helping to maintain consistency is very obvious, but historical dictionary projects face more difficulties than many other electronic text projects, and it is as well to be aware of these at the outset. One immediate problem is the many different character sets and symbols which might be needed for a historical dictionary. But perhaps the most difficult problem is simply the length of time that the project is expected to take. Over its lifetime, which may be at least half a century, the project will need to adapt to new computer systems many times over. The early pioneers learned the perils of this the hard way and sometimes lost almost a year moving from one software system to another. Bratley (1984) identifies several problems from the computer scientists' viewpoint, the first being that 'computer scientists tend to think in weeks … but lexicographers plan in decades' (1984: 83). SGML may be the best solution here, but the current state of SGML-based software is such that an SGML-based historical dictionary project could not function effectively without a full-time programmer. Bratley also notes that dictionaries can be very big databases, but the editors of historical dictionaries may not necessarily be aware of the problems of scaling up when they start with a small amount of material. Again computer scientists are aware of the issues involving large databases, and applications from commercial use may well address exactly the same computational problems. Writing in the same volume, Farr (1984) notes the same problems but from the point of view of the funding agency, and he stresses the need to be clear on methodological questions.

Moving from a manual system to a computer-based system or updating a computer system provides an opportunity for a dictionary project to revisit and redesign its objectives. The computer-based system offers many more possibilities than a manual one, but the project manager needs to decide which are important to themselves and their users, and how to implement these effectively in a way that will also outlast several computer systems in the future. If the project has already published some fascicles, it may also want to maintain some consistency with existing material and to be able to merge new material with existing and already published entries. Matthews and Rahtz (1986) discuss the value of a database for the *Lexicon of Greek Personal Names,* a research project which began in 1972 in Oxford. They were forced to refine many of their judgements and make decisions at the time when the database was being designed and created, but the time taken for this was amply repaid later. Fascicles of the lexicon can be typeset directly from the database, and the consistency imposed by the database eliminated much proof-reading and correction at the proof stage (Matthews 1998).

The *New Oxford English Dictionary* is the best known and almost certainly the largest dictionary project which has transferred from a manual to an electronic system. The project began in 1984 when Oxford University Press (OUP) decided to move to an electronic system and at the same time to merge the existing supplements with the main dictionary. OUP recognized that this would be a landmark project and that it would require careful planning, implementation, and management. This was a truly enormous project. The estimated size of the text was 350 million characters with the new printed version expected to fill 63,000 columns of text (Weiner 1985a: 247). But even in 1985 the project planners recognized the value of an electronic dictionary database, possibly also enhanced with images, maps, video, and the like, for both lexicographers and the public.

The *OED* was the first significant academic project to use structured markup. The markup system was SGML-like, but it does not conform to a DTD. Entries in the dictionary were examined in detail and a list of some thirty basic features was first drawn up (Weiner 1985b: 4–5). It was important to identify a set of tags which could be encoded by keyboard operators at this time and so the number of thirty was eventually reduced to a more manageable set. Manually tagging the entire text (around 50 million words) would have been impossible, but the typography of other features was retained with the expectation that some of these could be identified later by a program. OUP also conducted a survey of potential users (both academic and commercial) to try to identify what kinds of questions might be answered by an electronic dictionary. The results of this survey are presented in detail in Benbow *et al.* (1990). They are not particularly conclusive and reflect the interests of the different communities surveyed. These included the academic world (linguistics, computer sciences, history of the language), professions (librarianship, law, accountancy, medicine), and other occupations (journalism, advertising, and commerce) (1990: 156). One of the problems of a survey like this is user expectation. The potential of an electronic dictionary was hinted at in some of the specific questions, but many of the respondents had little practical experience of working with electronic dictionaries. The survey did not directly address the possibility of the dictionary being used by computer systems.

OUP partnered IBM and the University of Waterloo in Ontario, Canada to develop the dictionary. The Waterloo group worked on the encoding scheme and were also interested in the dictionary as a testbed for the design of database systems. The Pat program, now renamed the Open Text search engine and used by several digital library projects, was originally developed at Waterloo to search the tagged dictionary. IBM gave equipment and lent staff who designed a workstation to assist the lexicographers in Oxford. A program was devised to merge the supplements with the main dictionary, as far as was possible. This entailed updating some of the existing entries as well as inserting new ones. Every entry then had to be revised by a team of lexicographers. The project was completed on time and the new printed version (second edition) of the dictionary published in 1989. Tompa (1992) describes the markup structure for the *OED* and the retrieval system developed at the University of Waterloo. The markup tags are very short, for example <E> for entry, <HL> for headword lemma, and <EQ> for earliest quote. They thus clutter the text less and take up less space than tags consisting of complete words, but it takes a little longer to remember what they all signify when reading an entry.

The electronic version of the second edition is available on CD-ROM (Oxford University Press 1994), as well as over the Internet at some institutions. On the CD-ROM version, a search for a headword in a box to the top left of the screen brings up first a word list of forms in another window at the bottom left. A click on any word in the word list brings up the dictionary entry in a larger window to the right of the screen. The displays are well designed and make good use of the added computer screen dimension of colour, which the user can also control. The quotations are presented in date order in an easy-to-read format where each quotation starts on a new line. The initial word lookup box also gives access to phrases, variant forms, phonetics, Greek, a date filter, and a part of speech filter. Choosing the date filter or part of speech filter first restricts the search to the chosen date range or part of speech. My experimental word search for *beck* produced four noun forms and one verb form. The first noun form, for *beck* meaning a stream, is attested first in the spelling *becc* in the fourteenth century.

In the electronic version, the entire text of the dictionary can be searched, not just the headwords. A search of this kind first generates either one line of text including the search term, or the headword whose entry includes the search term. A click on either of these options opens another window showing the complete entry where the search term was found. The entry display can also provide a map showing the structure of the entry, a feature which is very useful for common words. A search of the entire text of the dictionary produced 335 occurrences of *beck*, including several where *Beck* was found because of quotations from Beck's *Drapers' Dictionary*. The search menu also permits searches of etymologies, definitions, and quotations. When an etymology search is requested, the bottom left window brings up a list of all the languages used for etymologies. The user can jump into this list by starting to type the term, thus ensuring that the correct language is placed in the search box. A second box is for cited forms used to explain the derivation of the headword, and a third makes it possible to search any of the text in the etymology field. A search produced twenty-five occurrences of etymologies from Albanian as a language, but fourteen of these included Albanian in the text of the field. Quotations can be searched by date, author, title, or text. *Shakes.* appears in a staggering 33,303 quotations, but it is very advisable to use the quick scan through the list of author names to determine the form of the spellings and abbreviations of authors' names. From this I noted one *Shak.* The first version of the *OED* has several spellings of Shakespeare and the merging of them into one was not perfect. Results can be stored and then output as text, but without the structural markup. For more advanced users the *OED* on

CD-ROM provides a query language which is not difficult to learn. This makes it possible to combine many kinds of searches. Queries can be saved for future use.

The user interface to the Internet version of the *OED* can be designed by the institution where it is hosted. The Web interface at the University of Alberta permits searching by headword and also within the definitions, etymology, quotations, and by date (including the earliest entry) as well as all the text. The ability to search by fields other than headword makes the *OED* a possible resource for the history and usage of the English language, and thus of social, political, literary, scientific, and other cultural aspects. The second part of the user survey was intended to prompt research of this kind with questions like 'Are quotations of the period...that mention the place/institution/person...?' where a possible example is 'date 1500–1600' and 'place Mozambique', or 'List the vernacular English names for the plants of the order *compositae*' (Benbow *et al.* 1990: 200). One can request, for example, all the words of Arabic etymology that entered the language before 1600. But what one finds is all the words for which the compilers of the *OED* have found a quotation dating to before 1600. It is as well to be aware of these limitations. It is all to easy to regard the *OED* as the source of information rather than a representative source, albeit an authoritative medium. However, it can be a useful supplement to other work, as Fischer (1997) shows with his use of the *OED* on CD-ROM to supplement the Helsinki Corpus in a historical study of the verbs *to wed* and *to marry*.

Work is now in proceeding on the third version of the *OED* using a computerized system for editing. Weiner (1994) describes in some detail the specifications for a workstation for editing scholarly dictionaries. The workstation is linked to a networked version of the dictionary material so that all the lexicographers have access to the same material. He notes how much repetitive and labour-intensive work is required and how suitable computers are for handling many of these processes. In a computerized system the slips are kept in electronic form with tags indicating the components of the quotation and with links to a bibliographic file giving full details of the source of the quotation. Corpora such as the BNC and other electronic dictionaries are used to excerpt quotations from the corpus if better ones are found there. Reference to all these materials is made as an entry is being compiled. It is thus very easy to locate other instances of the word throughout all the quotations and other entries whether they are complete or in draft form.

A template can be used for constructing each entry in order to maintain the consistency that is needed for further computer processing. Revision and updates are thus easy to carry out and the computer can keep track of what has been done. Printed copy is made directly using the structured markup tags. Weiner also notes the possibility of sending e-mail directly from his workstation to ask a person working on the reading programme elsewhere in the world to check some information or provide more quotations. He illustrates his article with the processes involved in editing a series of 'new' words beginning *skli-*. These processes on their own make a good specification for a lexicographical workstation and Oxford University Press had already implemented some of them by 1994. Few dictionary projects have the resources that are available at Oxford, but it is easy to see how a scaled-down version of this model could work well for a smaller dictionary project. Bratley and Lusignan (1976) and Venezky (1987) describe potential lexicographical workstations, both in connection with the *Dictionary of Old English*. Although designed for older hardware, both their systems plan a desktop workstation linked to a local networked editing and photocomposing system with access to the corpus and material which has already been edited. Bratley (1984) updates his system to include wide area networking, but the principles remain the same and would be just as suitable today.

Computers make it possible to study early dictionaries in their own right. Kibbee (1992) discusses a range of possible applications for electronic representations of a group of sixteenth-century French–English dictionaries. The first part of his paper is a rather lengthy inventory of features found in these dictionaries. He argues that even an examination of these features tells us something about the compilers of the dictionaries and the nature of the audience for which they were intended. For example, the ultimate source for most of the vocabulary is Latin from history, literature, and philosophy. Kibbee also discusses the organizing principles in the dictionaries, whether they are ordered by subject matter, or alphabetically, or by part of speech (1992: 41–2). He then goes on to describe how various categories of scholars might use the dictionary database, for example historians of linguistics and lexicography, historians of language, and literary scholars who might be interested in the source of literary examples. The dictionaries provide a wealth of information for historians of culture (1992: 64) where again the snapshot of quotations and the authors' comments give their viewpoint on the world around them. Lancashire (1992) shows how early Renaissance dictionaries can contribute to a Renaissance knowledgebase.

The Middle English Compendium (MEC) at the University of Michigan is an example of another kind of project that is likely to become more common in the future (McSparran 1999). It is based on the electronic *Middle English Dictionary* now under completion at Michigan. The dictionary has been reorganized into a vast searchable database. The MEC also includes a searchable 'HyperBibliography' of Middle English containing all the Middle English materials which are cited in the *Middle English Dictionary*. A click on an item found in the bibliography takes the user to more information about the manuscripts etc. A corpus of Middle English prose and verse texts is also being developed by the team and forms the third component of the Compendium. All are encoded in SGML from which links can be generated automatically. It is thus possible to move around the Compendium at will from the bibliography to the corpus to the dictionary and back. The uses of this kind of tool are obvious and the MEC provides a model for other similar collections of material.

The Perseus Project now incorporates a dictionary as well as other text analysis tools. Perseus is a digital library of materials relating to Classical Greece (Crane n.d.). The user can view texts in the original or in translation as well as a wealth of ancillary material including maps, plans of archaeological sites, photographs, vases, sculptures, coins, and the like. Every word in the Greek texts is linked to the corresponding entry in an electronic version of the Liddell and Scott Greek lexicon, both in the intermediate lexicon, which Perseus first used, and also in the large lexicon. When a user text clicks on a word in a Greek text, a second window opens giving the headword for the word, the part of speech for this particular form, an indication of how many times that form occurs in that author and in the entire Perseus corpus, and a link to the entry in the lexicon. The full text of the lexicon entry is displayed in the lexicon window. Every quotation in the entry is linked to the text from which it is taken. The user can move directly to the full text by clicking on the citation reference, for example *Hom. Od.* 10.197 goes to *Odyssey*, book 10, line 197. The links are organized so that in fact several lines of the text are displayed both before and after the actual line referenced by the link. It is thus easy to see how the word is used in a larger context. Perseus is now experimenting with some of the collocation tools discussed in Chapter 6, and the lexicon window also displays words that commonly co-occur with the headword all linked to their own entries in the lexicon. Perseus has also implemented a similar system for Latin using the Lewis and Short Latin dictionary. The dictionaries can be entered via a menu for text tools and lexica. From this menu a user can type in an English word and get the Greek or Latin equivalents, of which there may be many. This search inspects the dictionary entries from Liddell and Scott and Lewis and Short, and so the term must be in the entries in these dictionaries.

Perseus provides a wealth of information, but on closer inspection it is easy to see that the links have been generated automatically. A search for 'glory' in the English-to-Latin search tool yields '28 words whose definitions contain "glory"'. These include *bellicus* 'warlike', where 'glory' appears in the translation of *laus bellicus* 'military glory', and *infra* 'below', in *infra Pallantis laudes jacebunt*, 'they will not come up to the glory of Pallas'. The search does not yet distinguish the word as a definition or translation of the headword from its appearance in quotations for other headwords. A search for *part* in the English-to-Latin search tool produced 896 words because *part* occurs in many of the definitions. The definition of *abdomen* contains 'the fat lower part of the belly, the paunch, abdomen', but many of the 896 words are included because *part* is also found when it is in the form *part.* as an abbreviation for participle. Nevertheless the potential for building bilingual dictionaries is obvious, and further software development can 'parse' the dictionary entries more effectively.

The dictionaries in Perseus and the Middle English Compendium are primarily intended to help people work with the text. The possibility of dictionaries helping computer programs work with text was recognized some time ago. Many experiments have been conducted to attempt to determine how useful such a dictionary might be and what it should look like in electronic form. If the dictionary is structured appropriately, a retrieval or analysis program could derive linguistic and other information about a word or phrase from it, and make use of that information to carry out more sophisticated queries or more advanced analyses. Getting computers to understand natural language is of course a major and very important research area. In order to do this, the computer needs to be able to make reference to a vast resource of lexical and linguistic information in a somewhat similar way to what goes on unconsciously in our own minds as we assimilate language. Such a system needs to work with not only a complex set of rules for understanding the language but also a base of lexical information from which it can derive information to drive the rules. Researchers began to turn their attention to how this vast resource of lexical and linguistic information might be built and began to wonder if traditional printed dictionaries could be a starting point. These would need to be restructured in the computer, but dictionary entries contain a wealth of explicit information and much implicit information which might be derivable by computer programs. See Wilks, Slator, and Guthrie (1996) for some historical background and a discussion of many key issues.

A number of experiments have been carried out using the *Longman Dictionary of Contemporary English* (*LDOCE*) (Boguraev and Briscoe

1989). *LDOCE* is a learners' dictionary where the definitions are made up of a limited vocabulary of some 2,200 words. Semantic information about the headword can be obtained by analysing the definitions and it was thought that this limited vocabulary might avoid some of the problems of circularity in this process (1989: 16). But it also makes the definitions somewhat longer. The procedure adopted by Vossen, Meijs, and de Broeder (1989) for analysing the definitions was first to assign part of speech coding to the 2,200 words and then apply this throughout the definitions. The part of speech coding was assigned manually, but a computer program could then use it to build up some patterns for the definitions.

The machine-readable version of *LDOCE* includes some information which is not in the printed edition, but can of course be used by analysis programs. These include 'subject' and 'box' codes giving some semantic notions. The example given by Boguraev and Briscoe is *sandwich*, which has a box code indicating an 'abstract or human subject', and that it is a 'solid' object (1989: 14). Its subject code indicates that it is food. From an analysis of the definitions and the box and subject codes, and by using collocations, an attempt can be made to build up a kind of semantic network for each word. Wilks *et al.* (1989) derive a network of words which have a close relationship to *marriage*. This is presented as a diagram containing some sixty words with directional arrows showing the relationships between them. They then asked a small group of human subjects to rate the extent to which all pairs from a set of twenty words are related (1989: 207). The conclusion reached is that the human judgements supported the relations derived by computer-processing. Few details are given about this experiment, and presenting subjects with words which are already presumed to be related may well influence their judgement. The diagram is useful to show the relationships, but the information must be restructured and reorganized in order to make it useful for further computer processing. And, of course, this process must be carried out for every word. Barnbrook (1993) also reports on a fairly inconclusive experiment which attempted to extract semantic information from the definitions in the *Cobuild Dictionary*.

The papers in Boguraev and Briscoe (1989) show that it is possible to extract partial semantic information from *LDOCE*, and that this is easiest for concrete nouns, adjectives, and verbs that do not have many nuances of meaning. Combining information from several dictionaries might make a better lexical database. Byrd (1989) reports on an experiment to map the senses, first, from the *New Collins Thesaurus* and *Roget's II: The New Thesaurus* and to identify where the synonym lists overlap. A second experiment with *Webster's Seventh* and *LDOCE* was less successful, possibly due to the differences between British and American English, although Byrd does not mention this. However, he was sufficiently encouraged by his experiments to carry on with automatic mapping procedures. Ide and Véronis (1994) also tested the possibility of merging dictionaries by looking at sense hierarchies in terms for cooking pots in five English (four British and one American) dictionaries. A hypernym can easily be extracted from a definition such as 'ladle: a long-handled spoon' or 'spoon: a metal, wooden or plastic utensil'. They built hierarchies based on a manual analysis of the entries, but found many inconsistencies and circularities. For example, 'tool: an implement such as a hammer'; 'implement: a piece of equipment, tool or utensil'; 'utensil: an implement, tool or container'. Even a saucepan is described as a 'pot' in two of the dictionaries and a 'pan' in the other three. Merging the dictionaries produced some better results, but cooking pots are concrete objects with well-defined uses and must therefore represent some of the simplest terms to deal with in this way. It is doubtful whether many other words could be treated in the same way. The work by Fillmore and Atkins noted above shows the inconsistencies in the definitions of *risk*. Atkins and Levin (1991) found similar problems with an attempt to merge the entries for *whistle* and *whistler* from only two dictionaries. They concluded that this process would work very much better if a larger template or framework for a linguistic database was available.

Various models have been proposed for the design of a lexical database. These obviously depend to some extent on the nature of the project and the uses that will be made of it. An existing dictionary provides some of the information, but a design based only on this is likely to preclude extensions into other applications and structures as envisaged by Atkins and Levin. Tompa and Raymond (1991) analyse the entries in the *OED* and discuss possible models for storing this information. They conclude that their current approach using SGML-like markup is probably the best, but that it cannot handle well for processing what they call 'amorphous components', that is, discursive text, illustrations, tables, cross-references, and implicit information (1991: 265). Since this appears to include all the quotations which make up the bulk of the text in the *OED*, their model might not seem very effective. Tompa and Raymond feel uneasy that the only way to deal with these components is by string searching. However, other users, particularly from the humanities, may feel that this is what they want to do and that the compartmentalizing of material into fixed boxes does not fit too well with humanities modes of research. Ide, Le Maitre, and Véronis (1994) propose an alternative model based on feature structures where information can be nested, and where redundant information can be eliminated, but this model also appears to be based on what they have found in existing print dictionaries, rather than on a machine-tractable framework of linguistic structures.

The group at the Istituto Linguistica Computazionale (ILC) in Pisa have been developing a machine-readable dictionary and lexicon of Italian since the 1970s. Zampolli (1984) reports that at that time the Italian Machine Dictionary, as it was then called, contained three sets of information. The first was a file of 120,000 lemmas containing various categories of data: morphosyntactic labels for parts of speech, gender, etc., an indication of foreign words since these would not be likely to fit into the processing system for Italian, homograph codes which distinguish between lexical and grammatical homographs, a brief definition to help distinguish lexical homographs, pointers to help construct multiword forms, usage, whether archaic, popular, or literary, and a code for the type of morphological inflection. A second file contained approximately 1 million inflected forms generated automatically by a program with category and usage data. A third file contained the definitions for the all the nouns, adjectives, and verbs. The definitions are described by the type of definition (relational, synonymical etc.), the definition itself is also given in restructured form, and an indication of taxonomy, usage, technical sublanguage, etc. is also included (1984: 247–8). Zampolli goes on to suggest many uses and improvements for this dictionary. These include uses by programs for morphological analysis, parsing, natural language processing, and use by humans in translating and generally examining lexical entries. At that time his group was also beginning to analyse the definitions in order to regroup the lemmas into semantic structures. Zampolli also outlines his plans to develop the dictionary into a general-purpose multi-functional repository of lexical and linguistic information for Italian. See also Zampolli (1987) for a further discussion of these issues.

Interest in the structure and uses of machine dictionaries and computational lexicons led Zampolli and Donald Walker to organize a landmark workshop at Grosseto in 1986. This workshop laid the groundwork for much more research on computational lexicons (Walker, Calzolari, and Zampolli 1995). At that meeting Calzolari, now Director of Research at ILC, discussed a range of issues for the organization of an automated lexicon (Calzolari 1995). These were based on her years of work with the Italian dictionary. She emphasized the need for a logical organization of the data rather than a technical one. This is a multidimensional problem where issues of software and hardware, conceptual structure, lexical structure and relations between words, psycholinguistic approaches to model the mental lexicon, and different users and uses all must be considered (1995: 337). She concludes that much of what traditional lexicographers have done is of value for computational lexicons and that a machine-readable dictionary should be viewed as a resource from which a machine can acquire knowledge. Many structures are hierarchical but not all, and there must be links across the hierarchies. A new kind of lexicography is needed. See also Calzolari (1994), which includes a table summarizing possible uses of lexical resources. Ooi (1998) also provides an overview of some models for automated lexica.

One obvious application of a lexical database is as a kind of thesaurus embedded in a retrieval system. The Italian dictionary has now been restructured into semantic hierarchies giving various relationships (synonyms, hyponyms, hypernyms, antonyms, etc.). The user of a retrieval system can then derive from the dictionary not only all the morphological forms of a word, but its synonyms and superordinates. Calzolari (1988) gives an example of a hierarchical tree for animals where distinctions into groups fit well at the lower levels but where some loops and interrelationships are necessary at the higher levels. This structure could be used in a search for animals to yield all types of animals and possibly also related information. She mentions a similar example for vehicles where a subfield of horse-drawn vehicles may also be extracted. Other uses included specialized texts, for example legal material, where some words have a particular meaning. In an important paper drawing together developments in computational linguistics and literary and linguistic computing, Calzolari and Zampolli (1991) show how the machine dictionary of Italian can be used to trace the relationships of the word *libro* 'book' (1991: 284–6). They then investigate the hyponyms of *attrezzo* 'tool' and derive from the dictionary information about what a tool is used for, what it is used in, what its shape might be, and what it is made of. They also look at nouns denoting objects, verbs and adjectives associated with people and with colours, and at agents of (that is, nouns as the subject of) 'selling'.

One potential very large application for linguistic databases is in retrieval systems in digital libraries (Klavans 1994), but such systems have not yet been implemented for general use. The possibilities are obvious, especially for journal collections where full text searches can only operate on the words in the text not on the concepts being discussed. Calzolari and Picchi (1994) present an overview of the lexical database and their textual database retrieval program DBT. Using the example of *andare* 'to go', they show how the lexical database is used first to generate all the morphological forms before a query is submitted. A second example shows a search for hyponyms of *abitante* 'inhabitant', where it would then be possible to examine concordance entries for collocates in order to further refine a semantic search. It is possible to imagine how this might be embedded in a retrieval system for journal articles. For some subject areas the database could be refined to deal only with that subject.

However, although printed dictionaries can be exploited to extract useful information, they provide only a partial representation. Printed dictionaries are created to document the language and for humans to use. They provide many instances of unusual usages, but the common usages are less well covered in relation to their overall use in the language. It is also assumed that the human user of the dictionary knows many words, especially those which make up the definitions. In contrast a computer program which is processing a text must look up every single word in the dictionary every time that the word occurs in the text. Printed dictionaries are particularly poor for common words which are exactly the words for which the computer program needs most information. Calzolari and Zampolli (1991) discuss some of the deficiencies in machine-readable dictionaries and examine the possibilities of extracting more information from corpora. They note that neither the verb *leggere* 'to read' nor the verbs *scrivere* 'to write' and *publicare* 'to publish' are associated with *libro* 'book' in their machine dictionary. Presumably these are so obvious that the lexicographers did not think to include them. In their corpus they found 3,222 occurrences of *libro* and the collocates of *libro* included *leggere* (187 occurrences), *scrivere* (196 occurrences), and *publicare* (107 occurrences) (1991: 298). They go on to support Atkins's view that corpus evidence suggests a very different organizational structure for words than the one that is found in printed dictionaries. Calzolari (1991) also examines verbs for separation and division in the machine dictionary and is able to link corpus evidence of the usage of these words reasonably well to the structure in the dictionary. She concludes this paper by proposing a linguistic workstation integrating a lexical database both monolingual and bilingual, text databases, and a reference corpus with a morphological analysis program, a parser, and a semantic disambiguator (1991: 204–5). Used together these resources can form the basis of a linguistic knowledge base. The expectation is that this knowledge base would be used by computer programs, but the collection of material is not much different from what Weiner envisaged for the lexicographer's workstation for the compilation of a dictionary to be used primarily by humans. Given the size and scope of these projects, it makes sense to design the structure and content of the resources to meet the needs of both humans and of computer programs.

This short history of the development of machine dictionaries and lexical databases helps us to understand the size and scope of these projects and their possibilities. If a resource modelled on the Italian dictionary were accessible to a Web search engine, it would greatly improve the precision of Web searches. The search engine would be able to 'understand' natural language requests and to offer only relevant information, perhaps at different levels of relationship to the search term. Some Web search engines are beginning to attempt to provide more 'intelligent' searching but not yet to the extent that is possible with the Italian system. For the individual user in the humanities, these systems may seem a long way off, but it is possible to speculate on what kinds of research might be facilitated by electronic linguistic resources available for consultation over the Internet, and especially if these resources also included a historical dimension. The use of the Greek and Latin dictionaries in Perseus is beginning to show what might be possible, but these do not yet have the restructured semantic information.

However, it is certainly not beyond the reach of the individual humanities scholar to construct a lexical database of a small number of texts or of material derived from an endangered language. Based on his work designing software for field linguists at the Summer Institute for Linguistics (SIL), Simons (1998) summarizes the requirements for linguistic data and an environment for processing this data in the context of the 'ordinary working linguist' (OWL). He outlines 'five essential characteristics of linguistic data which any successful software for the OWL must account for' (1998: 11). The multilingual nature of linguistic data is important, and he views Unicode as a significant development. More interesting for the present discussion are his views on the nature of linguistic data, which he sees as sequential, hierarchical, multidimensional, and highly integrated. SGML can be used to represent this data, but Simons and his team are developing an object-oriented computing environment for linguistic research called CELLAR. In an object-oriented system, the object is described by a set of attributes which can either be single values, complex objects, or pointers to material stored elsewhere. CELLAR forms the underlying component of SIL's LinguaLinks system which provides a general-purpose set of tools originally intended for field linguists, but which might also be applicable for other projects (SIL International 1999). LinguaLinks includes a PC-based lexical database system.

Much of the research on the structure of machine dictionaries took place in the 1980s and early 1990s. These dictionaries came to be viewed as a dynamic repository of lexical and linguistic information which is constantly being updated. The attention of many computational linguists has now turned to corpora, with the expectation that these will yield much of the information that cannot be derived from dictionaries or is not in them at all. Statistical methods are being used to analyse very large corpora, for example to extract collocations using the methods described in Chapter 6. For an example of how first mutual information collocations and then multivariate analysis applied to sets of words can be used to extract lexical information from a large corpus see Bindi *et al.* (1989). Programs can then augment the linguistic resources with material extracted from corpora. Corpora can also provide information about common words that is lacking in dictionaries. The discussion of corpus evidence for *risk* carried out by Fillmore and Atkins and described earlier in this chapter is probably more relevant for a computational lexicon than for a printed dictionary. But there will still be a need for printed dictionaries, and so further research is needed to determine how these semantic frames, or at least the key components of them, can be presented in book form. More research is needed to establish whether it is possible to maintain a large repository of linguistic information from which printed dictionaries at various levels from learner to scholarly might be produced and which might also serve as a multipurpose resource for many different analysis programs.

WordNet is a completely different approach to creating semantic structures. It was created by George Miller and his team at the Cognitive Science Laboratory in Princeton as an 'on-line lexical reference system whose design is inspired by current psycholinguistic theories of human lexical memory' (Miller *et al.* n.d.). It includes English nouns, verbs, adjectives, and adverbs which are all organized into groups representing lexical concepts. The groups are organized hierarchically so that a user can traverse up and down a tree of hypernyms and hyponyms. A search for *dog* produces six noun senses and one verb sense of which the first is the animal. The WordNet definition for this sense is 'domestic dog, Canis familiaris—(a member of the genus Canis (probably descended from the common wolf) that has been domesticated by man since prehistoric times; occurs in many breeds; "the dog barked all night")' (Miller *et al.* n.d.). Synonyms of *dog* are *canine, canid*. More interesting is a search for hypernyms of *dog* (a dog 'is a kind of'). This produces a tree going upwards through *canine, carnivore, placental mammal, mammal, vertebrate, chordate, animal, life form,* and *entity*. A search for hyponyms of *dog* ('is a kind of dog') produces *pooch* and *cur* then a long list of breeds of dog divided into categories such as 'toy dog', 'hunting dog', 'working dog', etc. Other relationships include holonyms ('is a part of'), meronyms (parts of), coordinate terms (for *dog*, this yields *canine, bitch, wolf, jackal, wild dog, hyena,* and *fox*) and also *familiarity,* that is how common the word is. For adjectives WordNet also provides antonyms. For verbs, WordNet provides synonyms, hypernyms, troponyms (particular ways to 'x' where 'x' is the verb), what the verb entails doing, and sentence frames. It can be seen even from these simple examples that WordNet provides a much more complete specification of these semantic structures than can be derived from dictionaries. WordNet was created by human lexicographers drawing on a variety of resources (dictionaries and thesauri) in electronic and print form (Beckwith *et al.* 1991). It was originally intended to be used as a resource for research in psycholinguistics, but has now begun to be used in computational linguistics and retrieval systems (Fellbaum 1998). A European project to create WordNets of several European languages (Dutch, Spanish, Italian, French, German, Estonian, Czech) is also now complete (Vossen 1999).

Much research still needs to be done on the structure and contents of lexical and linguistic databases, especially for the semantic component, but the examples discussed in this chapter give some idea of the potential. The link between dictionaries for humans and dictionaries for computers needs to be developed further with more collaboration between traditional lexicographers and computational linguists. One can envisage an electronic dictionary which is structured in such a way that various levels of print dictionaries can be generated from it, but which can also be used as an aid in different analysis programs. More experiments with humanities material will help us understand what are the best ways of building these expensive but very necessary tools.

10 | Where Next?

Readers who have worked their way through all the preceding chapters will have arrived at this final chapter with a picture of many different ways of doing things, of different perspectives, and of different needs and requirements. The challenge now is how to put all of this together. The production of high-quality electronic texts and resources is very labour intensive. It is imperative to find ways of making these resources as broadly multipurpose and reusable as possible. This must be done in the context of different theoretical perspectives in scholarship and in the context of a broadening range of users, from undergraduates to senior professors, in high schools and in the community at large for distance learning and for continuing education.

One can begin to imagine what this new kind of scholarship might look like. It will be centred on the Internet which the user will access via a high-speed line from the office, from home, or from a portable 'wireless' device. There will be digital libraries of primary and secondary material with associated metadata which will indicate to the user not only the bibliographic details of the material but also what features are encoded within it, and the scholarly rationale for this encoding. Users may want to carry out broad searches across a large range of material. These searches will be carried out on the server and will be assisted by linguistic analysis tools for natural languages. They will also use a lexical knowledge base to assist with the semantic component of a search. These knowledge bases will be customizable for specific domains if the scholar so wishes. For more specific research, the user will be able to download texts and work with them on his or her client machine, which will have a set of software tools for manipulation of scholarly texts. The user will also be able to build his or her set of links between pieces of this material and to record why each link has been created and who created it. With even a simple understanding of structured markup, it is not difficult to see that all of these functions and more can be implemented, provided that there is some consensus on the semantic component, that is, on the description and organization of the knowledge within them. The user may also want to communicate with the computer either by speech input or by typing natural language sentences. As we have seen, the tools being developed to assist with the study of scholarly electronic texts will also assist with speech and natural language input.

Many communities are already having, and will continue to have, input to the design of this digital library world. Scholars and teachers in the humanities have the knowledge of the source material and the scholarship surrounding it. They have some understanding of the many applications to which the material will be put, but perhaps they have not previously had to try to articulate the processes involved in these applications at the level of detail required for computer systems. The computer systems will be designed and written by computer scientists who understand how to structure the electronic processes so that they are carried out as efficiently and as fast as possible. The skills of lexicographers and librarians are needed to design and develop the key components of lexical knowledge bases, since both these professions concentrate on the description and organization of knowledge terms. The digital library will be maintained by perhaps a combination of libraries and publishing houses, who will need to develop new procedures for managing electronic information. More than anything this entails a closer involvement with the intellectual and technical content, and an ongoing commitment to maintain and develop the information. This will mean bringing new technical skills into the organization.

This electronic scholarship will make many more kinds of research possible, but it will not mean the death of the book, as some have predicted. Books will be around for a very long time and they will continue to be used for the purposes for which they were designed. It is much easier to read from a book than from a computer screen and it seems unlikely that any new device for communicating with computers will be as easy for reading as books are. It is much easier to get an immediate sense of the size and scope of a book than it is of an electronic resource, and of course books are still more portable than computers. Electronic texts should really be treated as a supplement to books, to use for those functions which are difficult to do with books, for example searching, analysis, and hypertext linking. It is easy to create books or printed material from properly structured electronic text, but the creation of books should be just one of many applications.

The most significant intellectual advances in electronic text technology in the humanities have been in the areas of text encoding and representation, but more than anything this has taught us that text is complex, and that representing text for computer-based analysis requires significant levels of interpretation. SGML/XML and the TEI have begun to provide solutions to the question of a syntax and methodology for representing text and the features within a text, but at present they are not easy for the individual scholar to use. Specialized software tools are needed to create SGML/XML text and the scholar may have to learn these as well as get to grips with all the problems of interpretation in the text.

Creating SGML/XML text will become much easier when these functions are embedded in word processors, but this has not yet happened satisfactorily. WordPerfect's attempt to incorporate SGML, in Version 7, was not a success. It was not well documented and it contained some errors. But more than that, it was implemented as an add-on, so that the SGML functions and the word processing functions operated side by side in the text. They were not integrated with each other, and often appeared to be in conflict. What is needed is a program which looks like a familiar word processor to the user, but creates markup tags instead of word processing functions and uses stylesheets to display or print the text in different formats.

Software tools for analysis lag further behind. Pieces of the future world of scholarship outlined above are operational at some research institutions, but few of these have come to a marketable state or are usable by an individual humanities scholar without support from the developers. The DOS-based desktop text analysis tools TACT and OCP provide better functionality than many other programs, but are now difficult to use for anyone who started computing after the introduction of Windows. There have been some recent text analysis developments for Windows, but the MonoConc and WordSmith programs were designed initially for linguistic analysis. Concordance with its ability to handle COCOA-type references seems most appropriate for literary material. TuStep has very rich functionality but it takes some time to learn how to use it. Desktop tools for analysing SGML/XML-encoded text do not yet exist, but the XML stylesheet language XSL offers some possibilities for rapid new developments.

Software development is now the big challenge facing humanities computing specialists. Complex tools are needed, but these tools must also be easy for the beginner to use. There needs to be a way of starting in a simple way and working up to complex functions without loss of understanding of the process. Involving users in their design, as was done with OCP and TACT, seems essential. The design stage of OCP involved conference presentations, visits to other institutions, and a lengthy consultation process with potential users (Hockey and Marriott 1979). But this was carried out many years ago when computing was mainframe-based, making it much easier to identify users. At that time there were fewer committed users, given the hardware which they had to use. For a new set of programs to gain acceptance, there needs to be widespread consultation at the design stage. The Internet makes it much easier to reach people, but managing an international effort to develop a set of common tools to meet the needs of many people is an enormous task.

Exactly what a new set of software tools might do is still a matter of debate. There is a need to provide concordance and text analysis functions in an SGML/XML environment, but text analysis should really form part of a larger system. The Web is now the centre of most computing, and there is a much bigger need to provide delivery and manipulation tools for humanities electronic texts over the Web. The tools should include text analysis functions, but they should also be able to provide the functionality needed for electronic editions and other electronic publishing activities. Future systems will include delivery of pieces of text and provide a set of tools to manipulate the text, for example lemmatization, word frequencies, concordances, some forms of linguistic analysis, metrical analysis, and all the other applications discussed in this book. The toolset will be organized so that users can 'mix and match' what they need. New users will start with a packaged set of components offering commonly used functions, but more advanced users will be able to break the package into constituent parts and use these modular tools to build up their own packages to suit their own needs. Many of the features outlined in Bradley's (1998) proposed architecture for a new text analysis system could be extended to a more general electronic publishing and delivery system for the humanities.

A project starting now is faced with a huge number of questions on how to go about the work. It is unfortunate that so much effort in computing in the humanities has been put into the creation of resources rather than into research leading towards better creation and delivery of resources. The Model Editions Partnership is one of the few projects which has concentrated on finding out more about how to do it. Its prospectus, discussed in Chapter 8, could provide a model for other application areas. There needs to be more emphasis on documenting the intellectual rationale and the scholarly and computational processes which have been created and tested. Too many projects and funding agencies seek to associate themselves with high-profile Web resources, rather than serious contributions to the intellectual development of electronic text technology.

The apparently infinite capacity of computers has led to much larger projects than have been envisaged in the past. It is tempting to seek to include everything, and in an electronic hypertextual environment the boundaries are not easy to define. Many projects begin with grand objectives but find that the scope of the project has to be scaled down in order to get some part of it into a state which, if not finished, is at least usable by the scholarly community. Thus, it makes sense to begin with smaller pieces which are themselves intellectually coherent and can stand on their own. These can also serve as a testbed, and, with careful design, can be modified later without too much effort. Computers make it possible to include very much more material, but they do not significantly reduce the amount of time needed to research and prepare that material for publication.

There is often a tendency to cut corners in the planning phase because of the need to produce something complete enough for visibility on the Internet in order to get further funding. This may mean revisiting the visible material and redoing some of it later. Long-term projects need to be particularly aware of the problems of technology obsolescence and migration of data to new systems. They should expect to allocate time to the need to transfer to new systems every few years. Poor initial design has been a failing of many projects. This leads to constant patching of computer systems and often to the situation where no one person knows how they work, leading to possible irrecoverable failure of the computer processes. The startup time for a computer-based project can be expected to be longer than for a paper-based project, but this is repaid many times over by the advantages of having an overall picture available all the time.

It is all too easy to prepare ambitious plans with what seem to be ideal world solutions to the computing part of the work. In the real world, practicalities tend to take precedence. It is sensible to choose software for which there is already some expertise in the institution. Otherwise too much time and money will be spent learning how to use the software and getting technical support. It is also sensible to choose well-known and widely used software. Otherwise the supplier may be out of business before the project is finished.

The choice between SGML/XML and another markup scheme can be difficult. Large and well-supported digital library projects can and should take advantage of the longevity and processing power of SGML/XML, but they cannot do this without personnel who have some SGML/XML programming skills to work with the material. Individuals may find SGML/XML more difficult until better software tools are available. With some understanding of the basic principles of SGML, it is not difficult to design a markup scheme which is easier to work with but can be converted automatically to SGML/XML later.

This might be a better approach for an individual scholar or a shorter project.

Humanities scholars often tend to underestimate the amount of computing involved in an electronic project. There is a tendency to think that a part-time student could perhaps plan and organize the computing, or that entering information into the computer is a mechanical process for which few skills are required other than typing. The most successful projects integrate the computing and the humanities research at all levels. The computer systems are designed by computing specialists with a humanities background and working with humanities researchers. A project which does not have a computer programmer is going to waste much time making editorial changes one by one with a word processor. These changes could be carried out much more effectively and accurately by a series of special-purpose computer programs or scripts which a programmer can write very quickly. As the collection of electronic material builds up, programs can be written to check for consistency and coverage, and generally to aid verification. The overall picture provided in this way would be impossible to achieve by any other means and it saves a large amount of time which would otherwise be spent on repetitive work.

A collaborative long-term electronic project needs careful management and organization. A shared network-based environment can greatly facilitate collaborative work when groups of people in different places are working on the same material, but everyone on the project needs to have a good understanding of what is happening. Documentation of every detail is crucial when several people are involved. Without it misunderstandings occur, leading to erroneous results. SGML and XML make it possible to include encoding tags indicating who is responsible for each piece of work and to trace the development of each electronic document. A Web-based document management system such as that developed by the Orlando Project ensures that a document can only be edited by one person at a time and can insert project management information when the new version of the document is returned to the system (Brown *et al.* 1997).

More effort needs to be directed towards the development of guidelines for evaluating computer-based work. Some institutions are beginning to take some steps in this direction, but, as anyone who has reviewed software knows, this is not a particularly easy task. It is very different from evaluating material in print. It takes time to understand all the possibilities in a piece of software. Too many software reviews tend either to reproduce parts of the user manual or publicity material, or to say that the program cannot perform a certain set of functions when, with a little ingenuity, it can be made to do so. A thorough evaluation of computer-based research needs to take account of both the scholarly content of the research and all the technical implementation. At present there are very few people who are able to do all of this. Funding agencies tend to include at least one computing specialist on review panels which are looking at computer-based projects and to expect proposals to include some technical detail on the methodology. Reviewers who have a little computing expertise tend to favour the programs which they know, even if these programs are not particularly suitable for other projects.

The theory and practice of electronic text technology is now being taught in several institutions. At some institutions the teaching is at the undergraduate level where part of a BA degree is in computing in the humanities. Other institutions are planning a master's course which might cover a broader range of material and provide a route for humanities graduates to move into electronic publishing and digital library applications, as well as other aspects of information technology. These are all areas where there is a skills shortage. Humanities graduates who have a combination of critical thinking and practical computing skills are very employable. Summer institutes and schools can bring together a combination of scholars, students, librarians, and computer specialists to learn new techniques and benefit from interaction.

The Internet provides the opportunity for the tools and techniques developed in computing in the humanities to be put at the centre of the scholarly arena. Research in humanities computing will continue to contribute to the methodological aspects of humanities research and, with new and better methodologies, new and better research can be carried out. As we have seen, electronic text technology poses significant intellectual challenges for the humanities, and solutions to these challenges will continue to feed into new and better tools and techniques, and into new research opportunities. The future is very bright, with the possibility of effecting a real transformation in the way that scholars go about their work as new tools are introduced and new questions asked.

References

Allén, S. (1970). 'Vocabulary Data Processing', in H. Benediktsson (ed.), *The Nordic Languages and Modern Linguistics: Proceedings of the International Conference on Nordic and General Linguistics*. Reykjavik: Visindafelag Islendiga, 235–61.

Alt, M. (1990). *Exploring Hyperspace: A Non-Mathematical Explanation of Multivariate Analysis*. London: McGraw-Hill.

Aston, G., and Burnard, L. (1998). *The BNC Handbook: Exploring the British National Corpus with SARA*. Edinburgh: Edinburgh University Press.

Atkins, B. T., and Levin, B. (1991). 'Admitting Impediments', in U. Zernik (ed.), *Lexical Acquisition: Exploiting On-Line Resources to Build a Lexicon*. Hillsdale, NJ: Lawrence Erlbaum, 233–62.

Atkins, S., Clear, J., and Ostler, N. (1992). 'Corpus Design Criteria'. *Literary and Linguistic Computing*, 7: 1–16.

Bailey, R. W. (1979). 'Authorship Attribution in a Forensic Setting', in D. E. Ager, F. E. Knowles, and J. M. Smith (eds.), *Advances in Computer-Aided Literary and Linguistic Research: Proceedings of the Fifth International Symposium on Computers in Literary and Linguistic Research*. Birmingham: Department of Modern Languages, University of Aston in Birmingham, 1–15.

Ball, C. N. (1994). 'Automated Text Analysis: Cautionary Tales'. *Literary and Linguistic Computing*, 9: 293–302.

Ballester, A., and Santamaria, C. (1993). 'Transcription Conventions Used for the Corpus of Spoken Contemporary Spanish'. *Literary and Linguistic Computing*, 8: 283–92.

Barnard, D. T., Burnard, L., Gaspart, J.-P., Price, L. A., Sperberg-McQueen, C. M., and Varile, G. B. (1995). 'Hierarchical Encoding of Text: Technical Problems and SGML Solutions'. *Computers and the Humanities*, 29: 211–31.

——Hayter, R., Karababa, M., Logan, G., and McFadden, J. (1988). 'SGML-Based Markup for Literary Texts: Two Problems and Some Solutions'. *Computers and the Humanities*, 22: 265–76.

Barnbrook, G. (1993). 'The Automatic Analysis of Dictionaries: Parsing Cobuild Explanations', in M. Baker, G. Francis, and E. Tognini-Bonelli (eds.), *Text and Technology: In Honour of John Sinclair*. Amsterdam: John Benjamins, 313–31.

Bauer, L. (1993). *Manual of Information to Accompany the Wellington Corpus of Written New Zealand English*. Wellington: Victoria University of Wellington. <http://www.hit.uib.no/icame/wellman/well.htm>

References

Bauman, S., and Catapano, T. (1999). 'TEI and the Encoding of the Physical Structure of Books'. *Computers and the Humanities*, 33: 113–27.

Beckwith, R., Fellbaum, C., Gross, D., and Miller, G. A. (1991). 'WordNet: A Lexical Database Organized on Psycholinguistic Principles', in U. Zernik (ed.), *Lexical Acquisition: Exploiting On-Line Resources to Build a Lexicon.* Hillsdale, NJ: Lawrence Erlbaum, 211–32.

Belmore, N. (1992). 'Pinpointing Problematic Tagging Decisions', in G. Leitner (ed.), *New Directions in English Language Corpora: Methodology, Results, Software Developments.* Berlin: Mouton de Gruyter, 111–21.

Benbow, T., Carrington, P., Johannesen, G., Tompa, F., and Weiner, E. (1990). 'Report on the *New Oxford English Dictionary* User Survey'. *International Journal of Lexicography*, 3: 155–203.

Berkowitz, L. (1993). 'Ancilla to the Thesaurus Linguae Graecae: The TLG Canon', in J. Solomon (ed.), *Accessing Antiquity: The Computerization of Classical Studies.* Tucson: University of Arizona Press, 34–61.

Berry-Rogghe, G. L. M. (1973). 'The Computation of Collocations and their Relevance in Lexical Studies', in A. J. Aitken, R. Bailey, and N. Hamilton-Smith (eds.), *The Computer and Literary Studies.* Edinburgh: Edinburgh University Press, 103–12.

—— (1974). 'Automatic Identification of Phrasal Verbs', in J. L. Mitchell (ed.), *Computers in the Humanities.* Edinburgh: Edinburgh University Press, 17–26.

Besser, H., and Trant, J. (1995). *Introduction to Imaging.* Santa Monica: The Getty Art History Information Program. Accessed on 5 May 2000. <http://www.getty.edu/gri/standard/introimages/index.html>

Best, M. (January 1998). 'Afterword: Dressing Old Words New'. *Early Modern Literary Studies*, 313. Accessed on 3 February 2000. <http://purl.oclc.org/emls/03-3/bestshak.html>

—— (1999).'The Internet Shakespeare Editions' [Web page]. 15 August 1999. English Department, University of Victoria. Accessed on 9 November 1999. <http://web.uvic.ca/shakespeare/>

Biber, D. (1988). *Variation Across Speech and Writing.* Cambridge: Cambridge University Press.

—— (1993). 'Representativeness in Corpus Design'. *Literary and Linguistic Computing*, 8: 243–57.

Biggs, M., and Huitfeldt, C. (1997). 'Philosophy and Electronic Publishing; Theory and Metatheory in the Development of Text Encoding'. *The Monist*, 80: 348–66.

Bindi, R., Calzolari, N., Monachini, M., and Pirrelli, V. (1989). 'Lexical Knowledge Acquisition from Textual Corpora: A Multivariate Statistic Approach as an Integration to Traditional Methodologies', in *Using Corpora: Proceedings of the Seventh Annual Conference of the UW Centre for the New Oxford English Dictionary, St Catherine's College Oxford, September 29–October 1, 1989.* Waterloo: UW Centre for the New OED, 170–96.

Binongo, J. N. G. (1994). 'Joaquin's *Joaquinesquerie, Joaquinesquerie's* Joaquin: A Statistical Expression of a Filipino Writer's Style'. *Literary and Linguistic Computing*, 9: 267–79.

References

Blackwell, S. (1987). 'Syntax Versus Orthography: Problems in the Automatic Parsing of Idioms', in R. Garside, G. Leech, and G. Sampson (eds.), *The Computational Analysis of English: A Corpus-Based Approach*. London: Longman, 110–19.

Blake, N., and Robinson, P. (eds.) (1993). *The Canterbury Tales Project Occasional Papers Volume I*. Oxford: Office for Humanities Communication.

——— (1997). *The Canterbury Tales Project Occasional Papers Volume II*. King's College London: Office for Humanities Communication.

Boguraev, B., and Briscoe, T. (eds.) (1989). *Computational Lexicography for Natural Language Processing*. London: Longman.

Bolton, W. (1990). 'The Bard in Bits: Electronic Editions of Shakespeare and Programs to Analyze Them'. *Computers and the Humanities*, 24: 275–87.

Bozzi, A., and Cappelli, G. (1987). 'The Latin Lexical Database and Problems of Standardization in the Analysis of Latin Texts', in F. Hausmann *et al.* (eds.), *Data Networks for the Historical Disciplines? Problems and Feasibilities in Standardization and Exchange of Machine Readable Data*. Graz: Leykam, 28–45.

——— (1991). 'Automatic Lemmatization of Latin Texts', in H. Best, E. Mochmann, and M. Thaller (eds.), *Computers in the Humanities and Social Sciences: Achievements of the 1980s, Prospects for the 1990s*. Munich: K. G. Saur, 373–8.

Bradley, J. (1998). 'New TA Software: Some Characteristics and a Proposed Architecture'. December 1998. Accessed on 26 August 1999.
<http://pigeon.cc.kcl.ac.uk/ta-dev/notes/design.htm>

Bratley, P. (1984). 'Computers and Lexicography: Advances and Trends', in A. Zampolli and A. Cappelli (eds.), *The Possibilities and Limits of the Computer in Producing and Publishing Dictionaries. Linguistica Computazionale III*. Pisa: Giardini, 83–96.

—— and Lusignan, S. (1976). 'Information Processing in Dictionary Making: Some Technical Guidelines'. *Computers and the Humanities*, 10: 133–43.

Bray, T., Paoli, J., and Sperberg-McQueen, C. M. (eds.) (1998). 'Extensible Markup Language (XML)'. 10 February 1998. World Wide Web Consortium. Accessed on 16 November 1999.
<http://www.w3.org/TR/1998/REC-xml-19980210>

'British National Corpus' [Web page]. 3 November 1999. Oxford University Computing Services. Accessed on 24 November 1999.
<http://info.ox.ac.uk/bnc/>

Brown, S., Fisher, S., Clements, P., Binhammer, K., Butler, T., Carter, K., Grundy, I., and Hockey, S. (1997). 'SGML and the Orlando Project: Descriptive Markup for an Electronic History of Women's Writing'. *Computers and the Humanities*, 31: 271–84.

Brunner, T. F. (1993). 'Classics and the Computer: The History of a Relationship', in J. Solomon (ed.), *Accessing Antiquity: The Computerization of Classical Studies*. Tucson: University of Arizona Press, 10–33.

Bucher-Gillmayr, S. (1996). 'A Computer-Aided Quest for Allusions to Biblical Texts Within Lyric Poetry'. *Literary and Linguistic Computing*, 11: 1–8.

References

Burnard, L. (1986). 'From Archive to Database', in *Méthodes quantitatives et informatiques dans l'étude des textes*. In honour of C. Muller. Geneva: Slatkine, 145–58.

—— (1988). 'Report of Workshop on Text Encoding Guidelines'. *Literary and Linguistic Computing*, 3: 131–3.

—— (1995). 'What is SGML and How Does it Help?'. *Computers and the Humanities*, 29: 41–50.

—— and Sperberg-McQueen, C. M. (1995). 'TEI Lite: An Introduction to Text Encoding for Interchange, TEI U5'. June 1995. Accessed on 16 November 1999. <http://www-tei.uic.edu/orgs/tei/intros/teiu5.html>

Burr, E. (1996). 'A Computer Corpus of Italian Newspaper Language', in S. Hockey and N. Ide (eds.), *Research in Humanities Computing 4: Selected Papers from the 1992 ALLC–ACH Conference*. Oxford: Oxford University Press, 216–39.

Burrows, J. F. (1987). *Computation into Criticism: A Study of Jane Austen's Novels and an Experiment in Method*. Oxford: Oxford University Press.

—— (1992a). 'Not Unless You Ask Nicely: The Interpretative Nexus Between Analysis and Information'. *Literary and Linguistic Computing*, 7: 91–109.

—— (1992b). 'Computers and the Study of Literature', in C. S. Butler (ed.), *Computers and Written Texts*. Oxford: Blackwell, 167–204.

Burton, D. M. (1981a). 'Automated Concordances and Word Indexes: The Fifties'. *Computers and the Humanities*, 15: 1–14.

—— (1981b). 'Automated Concordances and Word Indexes: The Early Sixties and the Early Centers'. *Computers and the Humanities*, 15: 83–100.

—— (1981c). 'Automated Concordances and Word Indexes: The Process, the Programs, and the Products'. *Computers and the Humanities*, 15: 139–54.

—— (1982). 'Automated Concordances and Word Indexes: Machine Decisions and Editorial Revisions'. *Computers and the Humanities*, 16: 195–218.

Busa, R., SJ ([1965]). 'An Inventory of Fifteen Million Words', in J. B. Bessinger and S. M. Parrish (eds.), *Literary Data Processing Conference Proceedings*. White Plains: IBM, 64–78.

—— (1992). 'Half a Century of Literary Computing: Towards a "New" Philology'. *Literary and Linguistic Computing*, 7: 69–73.

—— (1998). 'Concluding a Life's Safari from Punched Cards to World Wide Web', in L. Burnard, M. Deegan, and H. Short (eds.), *The Digital Demotic: Selected Papers From DRH97, Digital Resources for the Humanities Conference, St Anne's College, Oxford, September 1997*. London: Office for Humanities Communication, 3–11.

Buzzetti, D. (1999). 'Text Representation and Textual Models', in *Conference Proceedings: ACH–ALLC'99 International Humanities Computing Conference June 9–14, 1999*. Charlottesville: University of Virginia, 219–22.

Byrd, R. (1989). 'Discovering Relationships among Word Senses', in *Dictionaries in the Electronic Age: Proceedings of the Fifth Annual Conference of the UW Centre for the New Oxford English Dictionary, St Catherine's College Oxford, September 18–19, 1989*. Waterloo: UW Centre for the New OED, 67–79.

References

Calzolari, N. (1988). 'The Dictionary and the Thesaurus can be Combined', in M. W. Evens (ed.), *Relational Models of the Lexicon: Representing Knowledge in Semantic Networks*. Cambridge: Cambridge University Press, 73–95.

—— (1991). 'Lexical Databases and Textual Corpora: Perspectives of Integration for a Lexical Knowledge Base', in U. Zernik (ed.), *Lexical Acquisition: Exploiting On-Line Resources to Build a Lexicon*. Hillsdale, NJ: Lawrence Erlbaum, 191–208.

—— (1994). 'Issues for Lexicon Building', in A. Zampolli, N. Calzolari, and M. Palmer (eds.), *Current Issues in Computational Linguistics: In Honour of Don Walker. Linguistica Computazionale IX–X*. Pisa: Giardini, 267–81.

—— (1995). 'Structure and Access in an Automated Lexicon and Related Issues', in D. E. Walker, N. Calzolari, and A. Zampolli (eds.), *Automating the Lexicon: Research and Practice in a Multilingual Environment*. Oxford: Clarendon Press, 335–56.

—— and Picchi, E. (1994). 'A Lexical Workstation: From Textual Data to Structured Database', in B. T. S. Atkins and A. Zampolli (eds.), *Computational Approaches to the Lexicon*. Oxford: Clarendon Press, 439–67.

—— and Zampolli, A. (1991). 'Lexical Databases and Textual Corpora: A Trend of Convergence Between Computational Linguistics and Literary and Linguistic Computing', in S. Hockey, N. Ide, and I. Lancashire (eds.), *Research in Humanities Computing 1: Papers from the 1989 ACH–ALLC Conference*. Oxford: Oxford University Press, 272–307.

Cameron, A., Frank, R., and Leyerle, J. (eds.) (1970*). Computers and Old English Concordances*. Toronto: University of Toronto Press.

Canter, D. (1992). 'An Evaluation of the "Cusum" Stylistic Analysis of Confessions'. *Expert Evidence*, 1: 93–9.

Chesnutt, D. (1983). 'Twentieth-Century Technology and Eighteenth-Century Letters: A Case Study of *The Papers of Henry Laurens*', in S. K. Burton and D. D. Short (eds.), *Sixth International Conference on Computers and the Humanities*. Rockville: Computer Science Press, 94–103.

—— (ed.) 30 May 1996. *A Prospectus for Electronic Historical Editions*. Accessed on 21 October 1999.
<http://adh.sc.edu/mepinfo/MEP-Docs/proptoc.htm>

—— (1997). 'The Model Editions Partnership: "Smart Text" and Beyond'. *D-Lib Magazine* July/August 1997. Accessed on 9 November 1999.
<http://www.dlib.org/dlib/july97/07chesnutt.html>

—— (project director) (1999). '*The Model Editions Partnership*' *[Web page]*. University of South Carolina. Accessed on 9 November 1999.
<http://adh.sc.edu/>

—— Hockey, S. M., and Sperberg-McQueen, C. M. (1999). 'Markup Guidelines for Documentary Editions'. 4 July 1999. Accessed on 16 November 1999.
<http://adh.sc.edu/MepGuide.html>

Chisholm, D. (1976). 'Phonological Patterning in German Verse'. *Computers and the Humanities*, 10: 5–20.

Church, K., Gale, W., Hanks, P., and Hindle, D. (1991). 'Using Statistics in Lexical Analysis', in U. Zernik (ed.), *Lexical Acquisition: Exploiting On-Line Resources to Build a Lexicon*. Hillsdale, NJ: Lawrence Erlbaum, 115–64.

176

———————— and Moon, R. (1994). 'Lexical Substitutability', in B. T. S. Atkins and A. Zampolli (eds.), *Computational Approaches to the Lexicon*. Oxford: Clarendon Press, 153–77.

Cignoni, L., and Peters, C. (eds.) (1991). *Computational Lexicology and Lexicography; Special Issue Dedicated to Bernard Quémada. Linguistica Computazionale VII*. Pisa: Giardini.

Clayton, T. ([1965]). 'The Preparation of Literary Text for Multiple Automated Studies: Comprehensive Identification and the Provision of Discriminants', in J. B. Bessinger and S. M. Parrish (eds.), *Literary Data Processing Conference Proceedings*. White Plains: IBM, 171–99.

Clear, J. (1993). 'From Firth Principles: Computational Tools for the Study of Collocation', in M. Baker, G. Francis, and E. Tognini-Bonelli (eds.), *Text and Technology: In Honour of John Sinclair*. Amsterdam: John Benjamins, 271–92.

Collins Cobuild English Language Dictionary (1987). London: Collins.

Collins Cobuild English Dictionary (revised edn.) (1995). London: HarperCollins.

Coombs, J. H., Renear, A. H., and DeRose, S. J. (1987). 'Markup Systems and the Future of Scholarly Text Processing'. *Communications of the ACM*, 30: 933–47.

Corns, T. N. (1982). *The Development of Milton's Prose Style*. Oxford: Clarendon Press.

——(1990). *Milton's Language*. Oxford: Basil Blackwell.

Cover, R. (ed.) (1994–) 'The XML Cover Pages [Web page]. Accessed on 5 May 2000.
<http://www.oasis-open.org/cover/>

Craig, D. H. (1991). 'Plural Pronouns in Roman Plays by Shakespeare and Jonson'. *Literary and Linguistic Computing*, 6: 180–6.

Craik, E. M., and Kaferly, D. H. A. (1987). 'The Computer and Sophocles' *Trachiniae*'. *Literary and Linguistic Computing*, 2: 86–97.

Crain, C. (1998). 'The Bard's Fingerprints: Donald Foster Uses High-Powered Computer Tests to Search for Shakespeare's Hidden Hand. His Critics Challenge him on Every Move'. *Lingua Franca*, 8: 28–39.
<http://www.linguafranca.com/9807/crain.html>

Crane, G. (editor-in-chief) (n.d.). 'Perseus Project' [Web page]. Classics Department, Tufts University. Accessed on 9 November 1999.
<http://www.perseus.tufts.edu>

——(1991). 'Generating and Parsing Classical Greek'. *Literary and Linguistic Computing*, 6: 243–5.

Crowdy, S. (1993). 'Spoken Corpus Design'. *Literary and Linguistic Computing*, 8: 259–65.

——(1995). 'The BNC Spoken Corpus', in G. Leech, G. Myers, and J. Thomas (eds.), *Spoken English on Computer: Transcription, Markup and Application*. Harlow: Longman, 224–34.

de Haan, P., and Schils, E. (1994). 'The Qsum Plot Exposed', in U. Fries, G. Tottie, and P. Schneider (eds.), *Creating and Using Language Corpora: Papers from the Fourteenth International Conference on English Language Research on Computerized Corpora*. Amsterdam: Rodopi, 93–105.

References

de Jong, J. R., and Laan, N. M. (1996). 'A Grammar for Greek Verse', in S. Hockey and N. Ide (eds.), *Research in Humanities Computing 4: Selected Papers from the 1992 ALLC–ACH Conference*. Oxford: Oxford University Press, 171–84.

de Tollenaere, F. (1973). 'The Problem of the Context in Computer-Aided Lexicography', in A. J. Aitken, R. W. Bailey, and N. Hamilton-Smith (eds.), *The Computer and Literary Studies*. Edinburgh: Edinburgh University Press, 25–35.

Dilligan, R. J., and Bender, T. K. (1973). 'The Lapses of Time: A Computer-Assisted Investigation of English Prosody', in A. J. Aitken, R. W. Bailey, and N. Hamilton-Smith (eds.), *The Computer and Literary Studies*. Edinburgh: Edinburgh University Press, 239–52.

——and Lynn, K. (1972). 'Computers and the History of Prosody'. *College English*, 34: 1103–4, 1113–23.

Dixon, P., and Mannion, D. (1993). 'Goldsmith's Periodical Essays: A Statistical Analysis of Eleven Doubtful Cases'. *Literary and Linguistic Computing*, 8: 1–19.

Dunlop, D. (1995). 'Practical Considerations in the Use of TEI Headers in a Large Corpus'. *Computers and the Humanities*, 29: 85–98.

'EAGLES (Expert Advisory Group on Language Engineering Standards) Home Page' [Web page]. (n.d.). Istituto di Linguistica Computazionale, Pisa. Accessed on 10 November 1999.
<http://www.ilc.pi.cnr.it/>

Eaves, M., Essick, R. N., and Viscomi, J. (eds.) (1999). 'The William Blake Archive' [Web page]. 28 July 1999. Institute for Advanced Technology in the Humanities, University of Virginia. Accessed on 9 November 1999.
<http://www.iath.virginia.edu/blake/>

Edwards, J. A. (1992). 'Design Principles in the Transcription of Spoken Discourse', in J. Svartvik (ed.), *Directions in Corpus Linguistics: Proceedings of Nobel Symposium 82, Stockholm, 4–8 August 1991*. Berlin: Mouton de Gruyter, 129–44.

Ejerhed, E., and Church, K. (1997). 'Written Language Corpora', in R. Cole (editor-in-chief), *Survey of the State of the Art in Human Language Technology. Linguistica Computazionale XII–XIII*. Pisa: Giardini, 384–7.

Ellegård, A. (1962a). *A Statistical Method for Determining Authorship: The Junius Letters 1769–1772*. Gothenburg: Gothenburg University.

——(1962b). *Who Was Junius?* Stockholm: Almqvist & Wiksell.

——(1978). *The Syntactic Structure of English Texts: A Computer-Based Study of Four Kinds of Text in the Brown University Corpus*. Gothenburg: Gothenburg University.

'European Language Resources Association (ELRA)' [Web page]. 21 October 1999. Accessed on 24 November 1999.
<http://www.icp.grenet.fr/ELRA/home.html>

Fang, A. C. (1996a). 'Autosys: Grammatical Tagging and Cross-Tagset Mapping', in S. Greenbaum (ed.), *Comparing English Worldwide: The International Corpus*. Oxford: Clarendon Press, 110–24.

——(1996b). 'The Survey Parser: Design and Development', in S. Greenbaum (ed.), *Comparing English Worldwide: The International Corpus*. Oxford: Clarendon Press, 142–60.

Farr, G. J. (1984). 'Lexicography and the Computer in the United States: Projects Supported by the National Endowment for the Humanities ', in A. Zampolli and A. Cappelli (eds.), *The Possibilities and Limits of the Computer in Producing and Publishing Dictionaries. Linguistica Computazionale III.* Pisa: Giardini, 107–17.

Farringdon, J. (1996). *Analysing for Authorship: A Guide to the Cusum Technique.* Cardiff: University of Wales Press.

Faulhaber, C. B. (1991). 'Textual Criticism in the 21st Century'. *Romance Philology,* 45: 123–48.

Fellbaum, C. (ed.) (1998). *WordNet: An Electronic Lexical Database.* Cambridge, Mass.: MIT Press.

Fillmore, C. J., and Atkins, B. T. S. (1994). 'Starting Where the Dictionaries Stop: The Challenge of Corpus Lexicography', in B. T. S. Atkins and A. Zampolli (eds.), *Computational Approaches to the Lexicon.* Oxford: Clarendon Press, 349–93.

Finneran, R. J. (ed.) (1996). *The Literary Text in the Digital Age.* Ann Arbor: University of Michigan Press.

Fischer, A. (1997). 'The *Oxford English Dictionary* on CD-ROM as a Historical Corpus: *To Wed* and *to Marry* Revisited', in U. Fries, V. Müller, and P. Schneider (eds.), *From Aelfric to the New York Times; Studies in English Corpus Linguistics.* Amsterdam: Rodopi, 161–72.

Fish, S. (1980). *Is There a Text in This Class? The Authority of Interpretive Communities.* Cambridge, Mass.: Harvard University Press.

Flanders, J. (1997). 'Trusting the Electronic Edition'. *Computers and the Humanities,* 31: 301–10.

Fligelstone, S., Pacey, M., and Rayson, P. (1997). 'How to Generalize the Task of Annotation', in R. Garside, G. Leech, and A. McEnery (eds.), *Corpus Annotation: Linguistic Information from Text Corpora.* Harlow: Addison Wesley Longman, 122–36.

Fogel, E. G. (1962). 'Electronic Computers and Elizabethan Texts'. *Studies in Bibliography,* 15: 15–31.

Fortier, P. A. (1989). 'Analysis of Twentieth-Century French Prose Fiction', in R. G. Potter (ed.), *Literary Computing and Literary Criticism: Theoretical and Practical Essays on Theme and Rhetoric.* Philadelphia: University of Pennsylvania Press, 77–95.

—— (1996). 'Categories, Theory, and Words in Literary Texts', in G. Perissinotto (ed.), *Research in Humanities Computing 5: Papers from the 1995 ACH–ALLC Conference.* Oxford: Oxford University Press, 91–109.

—— and McConnell, J. C. (1973). 'Computer-Aided Thematic Analysis of French Prose Fiction', in A. J. Aitken, R. W. Bailey, and N. Hamilton-Smith (eds.), *The Computer and Literary Studies.* Edinburgh: Edinburgh University Press, 167–81.

Fox, G. (1987). 'The Case for Examples', in J. M. Sinclair (ed.), *Looking Up: An Account of the COBUILD Project in Lexical Computing.* London: Collins, 137–49.

Francis, G. (1993). 'A Corpus-Driven Approach to Grammar', in M. Baker, G. Francis, and E. Tognini-Bonelli (eds.), *Text and Technology: In Honour of John Sinclair.* Amsterdam: John Benjamins, 137–56.

179

References

Francis, I. S. (1966). 'An Exposition of a Statistical Approach to the *Federalist* Dispute', in J. Leed (ed.), *The Computer and Literary Style*. Kent, Oh.: Kent State University Press, 38–78.

Francis, W. N. (1980). 'A Tagged Corpus: Problems and Prospects', in S. Greenbaum, G. Leech, and J. Svartvik (eds.), *Studies in English Linguistics for Randolph Quirk*. London: Longman, 192–209.

—— (1992). 'Language Corpora BC', in J. Svartvik (ed.), *Directions in Corpus Linguistics: Proceedings of Nobel Symposium 82, Stockholm, 4–8 August 1991*. Berlin: Mouton de Gruyter, 17–32.

—— and Kučera, H. (1964). *Manual of Information to Accompany a Standard Corpus of Present-Day Edited American English, for Use with Digital Computers*. Providence: Brown University. Accessed on 1 December 1999. <http://khnt.hit.uib.no/icame/manuals/brown/INDEX.HTM>

Frank, R., and Cameron, A. (eds.) (1973). *A Plan for the Dictionary of Old English*. Toronto: University of Toronto Press.

Friedl, J. E. F. (1997). *Mastering Regular Expressions*. Sebastopol, Calif.: O'Reilly.

Frischer, B., Guthrie, D., Tse, E., and Tweedie, F. J. (1996). ' "Sentence" Length and Word-Type at "Sentence" Beginning and End: Reliable Authorship Discriminators for Latin Prose? New Studies on the Authorship of the *Historia Augusta*', in G. Perissinotto (ed.), *Research in Humanities Computing 5: Papers from the 1995 ACH–ALLC Conference*. Oxford: Oxford University Press, 110–42.

Gabler, H. W. (1980). 'Computer-Aided Critical Edition of *Ulysses*'. *ALLC Bulletin*, 8: 232–48.

Galloway, P. (1979). 'Manuscript Filiation and Cluster Analysis: The *Lai De L'Ombre* Case', in J. Irigoin and G. P. Zarri (eds.), *La Pratique des ordinateurs dans la critique des textes*. Paris: Centre National de la Recherche Scientifique, 87–95.

Garside, R. (1987). 'The CLAWS Word-Tagging System', in R. Garside, G. Leech, and G. Sampson (eds.), *The Computational Analysis of English: A Corpus-Based Approach*. London: Longman, 30–41.

—— (1995). 'Grammatical Tagging of the Spoken Part of the British National Corpus: A Progress Report', in G. Leech, G. Myers, and J. Thomas (eds.), *Spoken English on Computer: Transcription, Mark-Up and Application*. Harlow: Longman, 161–7.

—— (1997). 'A Hybrid Grammatical Tagger: CLAWS4', in R. Garside, G. Leech, and A. McEnery (eds.), *Corpus Annotation: Linguistic Information from Text Corpora*. Harlow: Addison Wesley Longman, 102–21.

—— Leech, G., and Sampson, G. (eds.) (1987). *The Computational Analysis of English: A Corpus-Based Approach*. London: Longman.

Gatrell, S. (1996). 'Electronic Hardy', in R. J. Finneran (ed.), *The Literary Text in the Digital Age*. Ann Arbor: University of Michigan Press, 185–92.

Gaylord, H. E. (1995). 'Character Representation'. *Computers and the Humanities*, 29: 51–73.

Getty Vocabulary Program (1999). 'About the Art and Architecture Thesaurus' [Web page]. 5 August 1999. Getty Research Institute. Accessed on 9 November 1999. <http://shiva.pub.getty.edu/aat_browser/aat_intro.html>

Gilbert, P. (1973). 'Automatic Collation: A Technique for Medieval Texts'. *Computers and the Humanities*, 7: 130–47.

—— (1979). 'The Preparation of Prose-Text Editions with the *Collate* System', in J. Irigoin and G. P. Zarri (eds), *La Pratique des ordinateurs dans la critique des textes*. Paris: Centre National de la Recherche Scientifique, 245–54.

Giordano, R. (1994). 'The Documentation of Electronic Texts Using Text Encoding Initiative Headers: An Introduction'. *Library Resources and Technical Services*, 38: 389–401.

—— (1995). 'The TEI Header and the Documentation of Electronic Texts'. *Computers and the Humanities*, 29: 75–84.

Goldfarb, C. F. (1990). *The SGML Handbook*. Oxford: Clarendon Press.

Goodman, S., and Villani, R. ([1965]). 'An Algorithm for Locating Multiple Word Co-Occurrence in Two Sets of Texts', in J. B. Bessinger and S. M. Parrish (eds.), *Literary Data Processing Conference Proceedings*. White Plains: IBM, 275–92.

Gorcy, G. (1984). 'L'Informatique et la mise en œuvre du Trésor de la Langue Française: Dictionnaire de la langue du 19e et du 20e siècle (1789–1960)', in A. Zampolli and A. Cappelli (eds.), *The Possibilities and Limits of the Computer in Producing and Publishing Dictionaries. Linguistica Computazionale III*. Pisa: Giardini, 119–44.

Granger, S. (ed.) (1997). *Learner English on Computer*. Harlow: Longman.

Graver, B., and Tetreault, R. (1998). 'Editing *Lyrical Ballads* for the Electronic Environment'. *Romanticism on the Net*, 9. Accessed on 24 October 1999. <http://users.ox.ac.uk/~scat0385/electronicLB.html>

Greenbaum, S. (ed.) (1996a). *Comparing English Worldwide: The International Corpus of English*. Oxford: Oxford University Press.

—— (1996b). 'Introducing ICE', in S. Greenbaum (ed.), *Comparing English Worldwide: the International Corpus*. Oxford: Clarendon Press, 3–12.

—— and Yibin, N. (1996). 'About the ICE Tagset', in S. Greenbaum (ed.), *Comparing English Worldwide: The International Corpus*. Oxford: Clarendon Press, 92–109.

Greenstein, D. I. (ed.) (1991). *Modelling Historical Data: Towards a Standard for Encoding and Exchanging Machine-Readable Texts*. Göttingen: Max Planck Institut für Geschichte.

Greenwood, H. H. (1992). 'St Paul Revisited: A Computational Result'. *Literary and Linguistic Computing*, 7: 211–19.

—— (1993). 'St Paul Revisited: Word Clusters in Multidimensional Space'. *Literary and Linguistic Computing*, 8: 211–19.

Griffith, J. G. (1968). 'A Taxonomic Study of the Manuscript Tradition of Juvenal'. *Museum Helveticum*, 25: 101–38.

—— (1969). 'Numerical Taxonomy and Some Primary Manuscripts of the Gospels'. *Journal of Theological Studies*, 20: 389–406.

—— (1979). 'Non-Stemmatic Classification of Manuscripts by Computer Methods', in J. Irigoin and G. P. Zarri (eds.), *La Pratique des ordinateurs dans la critique des textes*. Paris: Centre National de la Recherche Scientifique, 73–86.

References

—— (1984). 'A Three-Dimensional Model for Classifying Arrays of Manuscripts by Cluster-Analysis'. *Studia Patristica*, 15: 79–83.

Hamilton-Smith, N. (1971). 'A Versatile Concordance Program for a Textual Archive', in R. A. Wisbey (ed.), *The Computer in Literary and Linguistic Research*. Cambridge: Cambridge University Press, 235–44.

Hardcastle, R. (1993). 'Forensic Linguistics: An Assessment of the CUSUM Method for the Determination of Authorship'. *Journal of the Forensic Science Society*, 33: 95–106.

Hart, G. R. (1983). 'Problems of Writing and Phonology in Cuneiform Hittite'. *Transactions of the Philological Society*, 100–54.

Haskel, P. I. (1971). 'Collocations as a Measure of Stylistic Variety', in R. A. Wisbey (ed.), *The Computer in Literary and Linguistic Research*. Cambridge: Cambridge University Press, 159–68.

Hayward, M. (1996). 'Applications of a Connectionist Model of Poetic Meter to Problems in Generative Metrics', in S. Hockey and N. Ide (eds.), *Research in Humanities Computing 4: Selected Papers from the 1992 ALLC–ACH Conference*. Oxford: Oxford University Press, 185–92.

Healey, A. D. (1997). 'Wood-Gatherers and Cottage-Builders: Old Words and New Ways at the Dictionary of Old English', in R. Hickey, M. Kytö, I. Lancashire, and M. Rissanen (eds.), *Tracing the Trail of Time: Proceedings from the Second Diachronic Corpora Workshop*. Amsterdam: Rodopi, 33–46.

Heery, R. (1996). 'Review of Metadata Formats'. *Program*, 30: 345–73.

Heinemann, E. A. (1991). 'On the Metric Artistry of the *Chanson De Geste*'. *Olifant*, 16: 5–59.

—— (1993). 'Mapping Echoes with TACT in the Old French Epic the Charroi De Nimes'. *Literary and Linguistic Computing*, 8: 191–202.

Hilton, M. L., and Holmes, D. I. (1993). 'An Assessment of Cumulative Sum Charts for Authorship Attribution'. *Literary and Linguistic Computing*, 8: 73–80.

Hockey, S. (1980). *A Guide to Computer Applications in the Humanities*. London: Duckworth.

—— (1985). *SNOBOL Programming for the Humanities*. Oxford: Clarendon Press.

—— (1986). 'OCR: The Kurzweil Data Entry Machine'. *Literary and Linguistic Computing*, 1: 63–7.

—— (1991). 'The ACH–ACL–ALLC Text Encoding Initiative: An Overview'. Accessed on 2 December 1999. <http://www-tei.uic.edu/orgs/tei/info/teij16.html>

—— (1994). 'Evaluating Electronic Texts in the Humanities'. *Library Trends*, 42: 676–93.

—— (1996). 'Creating and Using Electronic Editions', in R. J. Finneran (ed.), *The Literary Text in the Digital Age*. Ann Arbor: University of Michigan Press, 1–21.

—— (1998). 'Textual Databases', in J. Lawler and H. Aristar Dry (eds.), *Using Computers in Linguistics: A Practical Guide*. London: Routledge, 101–33.

——— (1999). 'Making Technology Work for Scholarship: Investing in the Data', in R. Ekman and R. Quandt (eds.), *Technology and Scholarly Communication.* Berkeley: University of California Press, 17–36.

——— Freedman, J., and Cooper, J. (1991). 'The Oxford Text Searching System', in S. Hockey, N. Ide, and I. Lancashire (eds.), *Research in Humanities Computing 1: Papers from the 1989 ACH–ALLC Conference.* Oxford: Oxford University Press, 113–22.

——— and Marriott, I. (1979). 'The Oxford Concordance Project (OCP)'. *ALLC Bulletin,* 7: 35–43, 155–64, 268–75, and 8 (1980), 28–35.

Hollander, R. B., Jr (n.d.). 'Dartmouth Dante Project' [Web page]. Princeton University. Accessed on 16 November 1999. <http://www.dartmouth.edu/~library/infosys/dciswww/prod/by-name.html>

Holmes, D. (1994). 'Authorship Attribution'. *Computers and the Humanities,* 28: 87–106.

——— (1998). 'The Evolution of Stylometry in the Humanities'. *Literary and Linguistic Computing,* 13: 111–17.

——— and Forsyth, R. S. (1995). 'The *Federalist* Revisited: New Directions in Authorship Attribution'. *Literary and Linguistic Computing,* 10: 111–27.

Hoogcarspel, A. (1994a). *Guidelines for Cataloging Monographic Electronic Texts at the Center for Electronic Texts in the Humanities.* New Brunswick, NJ: Center for Electronic Texts in the Humanities.

——— (1994b). 'The Rutgers Inventory of Machine-Readable Texts in the Humanities: Cataloging and Access'. *Information Technology and Libraries,* 13: 27–34.

Hope, J. (1994). *The Authorship of Shakespeare's Plays: A Socio-Linguistic Study.* Cambridge: Cambridge University Press.

Horowitz, L. (1994). *CETH Workshop on Documenting Electronic Texts.* New Brunswick, NJ: Center for Electronic Texts in the Humanities.

Horton, T. B. (1987). *The Effectiveness of the Stylometry of Function Words in Discriminating Between Shakespeare and Fletcher.* Edinburgh: Dept of Computer Science.

Howard-Hill, T. H. (1979). *Literary Concordances: A Complete Handbook to the Preparation of Manual and Computer Concordances.* Oxford: Pergamon Press.

Howlett, D. R. (1984). 'The Use of Traditional and Computer Techniques in Compiling and Printing a Dictionary of Medieval Latin from British Sources', in A. Zampolli and A. Cappelli (eds.), *The Possibilities and Limits of the Computer in Producing and Publishing Dictionaries. Linguistica Computazionale III.* Pisa: Giardini, 153–9.

Huitfeldt, C. (1994). 'Multi-Dimensional Texts in a One-Dimensional Medium'. *Computers and the Humanities,* 28: 235–41.

ICONCLASS Research and Development Group (1999). 'The ICONCLASS Home Page' [Web page]. 16 October 1999. Universities of Utrecht and Leiden. Accessed on 9 November 1999. <http://iconclass.let.uu.nl/ >

Ide, N. (1986). 'Patterns of Imagery in William Blake's *The Four Zoas*', in *Méthodes quantitatives et informatiques dans l'étude des textes. In honour of C. Muller.* Geneva: Slatkine, 497–505.

References

——(1989). 'Meaning and Method: Computer-Assisted Analysis of Blake', in R. G. Potter (ed.), *Literary Computing and Literary Criticism: Theoretical and Practical Essays on Theme and Rhetoric.* Philadelphia: University of Pennsylvania Press, 123–41.

——Le Maitre, J., and Véronis, J. (1994). 'Outline of a Model for Lexical Databases', in A. Zampolli, N. Calzolari, and M. Palmer (eds.), *Current Issues in Computational Linguistics: In Honour of Don Walker. Linguistica Computazionale IX–X.* Pisa: Giardini, 283–320.

——and Véronis, J. (1994). 'Refining Taxonomies Extracted from Machine-Readable Dictionaries', in S. Hockey and N. Ide (eds.), *Research in Humanities Computing 2: Selected Papers from the 1990 ALLC–ACH Conference.* Oxford : Oxford University Press, 145–59.

Ilsemann, H. (1995). 'Computerized Drama Analysis'. *Literary and Linguistic Computing,* 10: 11–21.

'International Computer Archive of Medieval and Modern English (ICAME)' [Web page] (n.d.). Humanities Information Technologies at the University of Bergen. Accessed on 24 November 1999. <http://www.hit.uib.no/icame>

International Organization for Standards (1986). *Information Processing—Text and Office Systems—Standard Generalized Markup Language (SGML).* ISO 8879, Geneva: ISO.

Irizarry, E. (1991). 'One Writer, Two Authors: Resolving the Polemic of Latin America's First Published Novel'. *Literary and Linguistic Computing,* 6: 175–9.

——(1992). 'A Computer-Assisted Investigation of Gender-Related Idiolect in Octavio Paz and Rosario Castellanos'. *Computers and the Humanities,* 26: 103–17.

Jackson, M. P. (1991). 'George Wilkins and the First Two Acts of *Pericles:* New Evidence from Function Words'. *Literary and Linguistic Computing,* 6: 155–63.

Johansson, S. (1978) (in collaboration with G. N. Leech and H. Goodluck). *Manual of Information to Accompany the Lancaster-Oslo/Bergen Corpus of British English for Use with Digital Computers.* Oslo: Department of English. Accessed 1 December 1999. <http://khnt.hit.uib.no/icame/manuals/lob/INDEX.HTM>

——(1985). 'Grammatical Tagging and Total Accountability', in S. Bäckman and G. Kjellmer (eds.), *Papers on Language and Literature Presented to Alvar Ellegård and Erik Frykman.* Gothenburg: Gothenburg University, 208–19.

——(1994). 'ICAME – Quo Vadis? Reflections on the Use of Computer Corpora in Linguistics'. *Computers and the Humanities,* 28: 243–52.

——(1995). 'The Approach of the Text Encoding Initiative to the Encoding of Spoken Discourse', in G. Leech, G. Myers, and J. Thomas (eds.), *Spoken English on Computer: Transcription, Markup and Application.* Harlow: Longman, 82–98.

——and Hofland, K. (1989). *Frequency Analysis of English Vocabulary and Grammar Based on the LOB Corpus.* Oxford: Clarendon Press.

Jones, A. (1971). 'Some Oxford Projects in Oriental Languages', in R. A. Wisbey (ed.), *The Computer in Literary and Linguistic Research.* Cambridge: Cambridge University Press, 191–7.

References

Jones, S., and Sinclair, J. M. (1974). 'English Lexical Collocations: A Study in Computational Linguistics'. *Cahiers de Lexicologie*, 24: 15–61.

Källgren, G. (1996). 'Man vs. Machine: Which is the Most Reliable Annotator?', in G. Perissinotto (ed.), *Research in Humanities Computing 5: Papers from the 1995 ACH–ALLC Conference*. Oxford: Oxford University Press, 179–208.

Kennedy, G. (1998). *An Introduction to Corpus Linguistics*. London: Longman.

Kenny, A. (1977). 'The Stylometric Study of Aristotle's Ethics', in J. S. North and S. Lusignan (eds.), *Computing in the Humanities: Proceedings of the Third International Conference on Computing in the Humanities*. Waterloo: University of Waterloo Press, 11–22.

—— (1978). *The Aristotelian Ethics: A Study of the Relationship Between the Eudemian and Nicomachean Ethics of Aristotle*. Oxford: Clarendon Press.

—— (1982). *The Computation of Style*. Oxford: Pergamon.

—— (1986). *A Stylometric Study of the New Testament*. Oxford: Oxford University Press.

Kibbee, D. A. (1992). '16th-Century Bilingual Dictionaries (French–English): Organization and Access, Then and Now', in T. R. Wooldridge (ed.), *Historical Dictionary Databases*. Toronto: Centre for Computing in the Humanities, Toronto, 33–68.

Kirschenbaum, M. G. (1998). 'Documenting Digital Images: Textual Meta-Data at the Blake Archive'. *The Electronic Library*, 16: 239–41.

Klavans, J. (1994). 'Visions of the Digital Library: Views on Using Computational Linguistics and Semantic Nets in Information Retrieval', in A. Zampolli, N. Calzolari, and M. Palmer (eds.), *Current Issues in Computational Linguistics: In Honour of Don Walker. Linguistica Computazionale IX–X*. Pisa: Giardini, 227–36.

Krishnamurthy, R. (1987). 'The Process of Compilation', in J. M. Sinclair (ed.), *Looking Up: An Account of the COBUILD Project in Lexical Computing*. London: Collins, 62–85.

Kytö, M. (1996). *Manual to the Diachronic Part of the Helsinki Corpus of English Texts: Coding Conventions and Lists of Source Texts*. Helsinki: Department of English, Helsinki University. Accessed on 1 December 1999. <http://khnt.hit.uib.no/icame/manuals/HC/INDEX.HTM>

—— and Rissanen, M. (1997). 'Introduction: Language Analysis and Diachronic Corpora', in R. Hickey, M. Kytö, I. Lancashire, and M. Rissanen (eds.), *Tracing the Trail of Time: Proceedings from the Second Diachronic Corpora Workshop*. Amsterdam: Rodopi, 9–22.

Laan, N. M. (1995). 'Stylometry and Method: The Case of Euripides'. *Literary and Linguistic Computing*, 10: 271–8.

Lamel, L., and Cole, R. (1997). 'Spoken Language Corpora', in R. Cole (editor-in-chief), *Survey of the State of the Art in Human Language Technology. Linguistica Computazionale XII–XIII*. Pisa: Giardini, 388–91.

Lancashire, I. (ed.) (1991). *The Humanities Computing Yearbook 1989–90: A Comprehensive Guide to Software and Other Resources*. Oxford: Oxford University Press.

References

—— (1992). 'Bilingual Dictionaries in an English Renaissance Knowledge Base', in T. R. Wooldridge (ed.), *Historical Dictionary Databases*. Toronto: Centre for Computing in the Humanities, Toronto, 69–88.

—— (1993a). 'Chaucer's Repetends from the General Prologue of the *Canterbury Tales*', in R. A. Taylor, J. F. Burke, P. J. Eberle, I. Lancashire, and B. Merrilees (eds.), *The Centre and its Compass: Studies in Medieval Literature in Honor of Professor John Leyerle*. Kalamazoo, Mich.: Western Michigan University, 315–65.

—— (1993b). 'Computer-Assisted Critical Analysis: A Case Study of Margaret Atwood's *Handmaid's Tale*', in G. P. Landow and P. Delany (eds.), *The Digital Word: Text-Based Computing in the Humanities*. Cambridge, Mass.: MIT Press, 291–318.

—— (1993c). 'Phrasal Repetends and The Manciple's Prologue and Tale', in Ian Lancashire (ed.), *Computer-Based Chaucer Studies*. Toronto: Centre for Computing in the Humanities, Toronto, 99–122.

—— (1995). 'Computer Tools for Cognitive Stylistics', in E. Nissan and K. M. Schmidt (eds.), *From Information to Knowledge: Conceptual and Content Analysis by Computer*. Oxford: Intellect, 28–47.

—— (1996a). 'Editing English Renaissance Electronic Texts', in R. J. Finneran (ed.), *The Literary Text in the Digital Age*. Ann Arbor: University of Michigan Press, 117–43.

—— (1996b). 'Phrasal Repetends in Literary Stylistics: Shakespeare's *Hamlet* III.1', in S. Hockey and N. Ide (eds.), *Research in Humanities Computing 4: Selected Papers from the 1992 ALLC–ACH Conference*. Oxford: Oxford University Press, 34–68.

—— Bradley, J., McCarty, W., Stairs, M., and Wooldridge, T. R. (1996). *Using TACT with Electronic Texts*. New York: Modern Language Association of America.

Lavagnino, J. (1996). 'Reading, Scholarship and Hypertext Editions'. *Text*, 8: 109–24.

Ledger, G. (1995). 'An Exploration of Differences in the Pauline Epistles Using Multivariate Statistical Analysis'. *Literary and Linguistic Computing*, 10: 85–97.

Lee, A. (1989). 'Numerical Taxonomy Revisited: John Griffith, Cladistic Analysis and St Augustine's *Quaestiones in Heptateuchum*'. *Studia Patristica*, 20: 24–32.

Leech, G. (1987). 'General Introduction', in R. Garside, G. Leech, and G. Sampson (eds.), *The Computational Analysis of English: A Corpus-Based Approach*. London: Longman, 1–15.

—— (1991). 'The State of the Art in Corpus Linguistics', in K. Aijmer and B. Altenberg (eds.), *English Corpus Linguistics: Studies in Honour of Jan Svartvik*. London: Longman, 8–29.

—— (1992). 'Corpora and Theories of Linguistic Performance', in J. Svartvik (ed.), *Directions in Corpus Linguistics: Proceedings of Nobel Symposium 82, Stockholm, 4–8 August 1991*. Berlin: Mouton de Gruyter, 105–22.

—— (1993). 'Corpus Annotation Schemes'. *Literary and Linguistic Computing*, 8: 275–81.

—— (1996). 'Recommendations for the Morphosyntactic Annotation of Corpora'. EAGLES, Istituto di Linguistica Computazionale, Pisa. Accessed on 10 November 1999.
<http://www.ilc.pi.cnr.it/>

—— (1997). 'Introducing Corpus Annotation', in R. Garside, G. Leech, and A. McEnery (eds.), *Corpus Annotation: Linguistic Information from Text Corpora.* Harlow: Addison Wesley Longman, 1–18.

—— and Fligelstone, S. (1992). 'Computers and Corpus Analysis', in C. S. Butler (ed.), *Computers and Written Texts* . Oxford: Blackwell, 115–40.

—— Myers, G., and Thomas, J. (eds.) (1995). *Spoken English on Computer: Transcription, Markup and Application.* Harlow: Longman.

Leitner, G. (1991). 'The Kolhapur Corpus of Indian English: Intra-Varietal Description and/or Intervarietal Comparison', in S. Johansson and A.-B. Stenström (eds.), *English Computer Corpora: Selected Papers and Research Guide.* Berlin: Mouton de Gruyter, 215–32.

Lessard, G., and Hamm, J.-J. (1991). 'Computer-Aided Analysis of Repeated Structures: The Case of Stendhal's *Armance*'. *Literary and Linguistic Computing*, 6: 246–52.

—— —— (1996). 'Verifying Intuitions: Research and Repeated Structures in Stendhal', in S. Hockey and N. Ide (eds.), *Research in Humanities Computing 4: Selected Papers from the 1992 ALLC–ACH Conference.* Oxford: Oxford University Press, 69–80.

'Linguistic Data Consortium (LDC)' [Web page] (n.d.). University of Pennsylvania. Accessed on 24 November 1999.
<http://www.ldc.upenn.edu>

'Literature Online' [Web page] (n.d.). Chadwyck-Healey. Accessed on 24 November 1999.
<http://lion.chadwyck.com>

Liu, A., (ed.) (1999). 'The Voice of the Shuttle' [Web page]. 19 November 1999. University of California at Santa Barbara. Accessed on 30 November 1999.
<http://vos.ucsb.edu >

Louw, B. (1993). 'Irony in the Text of Insincerity in the Writer? The Diagnostic Potential of Semantic Prosodies', in M. Baker, G. Francis, and E. Tognini-Bonelli (eds.), *Text and Technology: In Honour of John Sinclair.* Amsterdam: John Benjamins, 157–76.

McCarty, W. (1991). 'Finding Implicit Patterns in Ovid's *Metamorphoses* With TACT', in T. R. Wooldridge (ed.), *A TACT Exemplar.* Toronto: Centre for Computing in the Humanities, Toronto, 37–75.

—— (1993a). 'Encoding Persons and Places in the *Metamorphoses* of Ovid:1. Engineering the Text'. *Texte*, 13/14: 121–72.

—— (1993b). 'Handmade, Computer-Assisted, and Electronic Concordances of Chaucer', in Ian Lancashire (ed.), *Computer-Based Chaucer Studies.* Toronto: Centre for Computing in the Humanities, Toronto, 49–65.

—— (1996). 'Peering through the Skylight: Towards an Electronic Edition of Ovid's *Metamorphoses*', in S. Hockey and N. Ide (eds.), *Research in Humanities*

References

Computing 4: Selected Papers from the 1992 ALLC–ACH Conference. Oxford: Oxford University Press, 240–62.

——Wright, B., and Suksi, A. (n.d.). 'Who's Who in the *Metamorphoses* of Ovid: The *Analytical Onomasticon* Project' [Web page]. King's College London. Accessed on 14 November 1999.
<http://www.kcl.ac.uk/humanities/cch/wlm/Onomasticon/>

McEnery, T., and Wilson, A. (1996). *Corpus Linguistics.* Edinburgh: Edinburgh University Press.

McGann, J. J. (1983). *A Critique of Modern Textual Criticism.* Chicago: University of Chicago Press.

——(1993). *Black Riders: The Visible Language of Modernism.* Princeton: Princeton University Press.

——(1996). 'The Rossetti Archive and Image-Based Electronic Editing', in R. J. Finneran (ed.), *The Literary Text in the Digital Age.* Ann Arbor: University of Michigan Press, 145–83.

——(ed.) (1997a). 'The Complete Writings and Pictures of Dante Gabriel Rossetti: A Hypermedia Research Archive' [Web page]. 19 March 1997. Institute for Advanced Technology in the Humanities, University of Virginia. Accessed on 9 November 1999.
<http://jefferson.village.virginia.edu/rossetti/rossetti.html>

——(1997b). 'Imagining What You Don't Know: The Theoretical Goals of the Rossetti Archive'. Accessed on 22 October 1999.
<http://www.iath.virginia.edu/~jjm2f/chum.html>

McNaught, J. (1993). 'User Needs for Textual Corpora in Natural Language Processing'. *Literary and Linguistic Computing,* 8: 227–34.

McSparran, F. (chief editor) (1999). 'Middle English Compendium' [Web page]. 25 March 1999. University of Michigan. Accessed on 9 November 1999.
<http://www.hti.umich.edu/mec/>

MacWhinney, B. (1995). *The Childes Project: Tools for Analyzing Talk.* Hillsdale, NJ: Lawrence Erlbaum.

Markman, A. (1964). 'A Computer Concordance to Middle English Texts'. *Studies in Bibliography,* 17: 55–75.

Marriott, I. (1979). 'The Authorship of the *Historia Augusta*: Two Computer Studies'. *Journal of Roman Studies,* 69: 65–77.

Marshall, I. (1987). 'Tag Selection Using Probabilistic Methods', in R. Garside, G. Leech, and G. Sampson (eds.), *The Computational Analysis of English: A Corpus-Based Approach.* London: Longman, 42–56.

Matthews, E. (1998). 'Electronic Publication' [Web page]. December 1998. Lexicon of Greek Personal Names, Oxford University. Accessed on 9 November 1999.
<http://www.lgpn.ox.ac.uk/elecpub.html>

——and Rahtz, S. (1986). 'Designing and Using a Database of Greek Personal Names', in *Méthodes quantitatives et informatiques dans l'étude des textes.* In honour of C. Muller. Geneva: Slatkine, 625–35.

Matthews, R., and Merriam, T. (1993). 'Neural Computation in Stylometry I: An Application to the Works of Shakespeare and Fletcher'. *Literary and Linguistic Computing,* 8: 203–9.

Mealand, D. L. (1992). 'On Finding Fresh Evidence in Old Texts: Reflections on Results in Computer-Assisted Biblical Research'. *Bulletin of the John Rylands University Library of Manchester*, 74: 67–87.

Meijs, W. (1992). 'Computers and Dictionaries', in C. S. Butler (ed.), *Computers and Written Texts*. Oxford: Blackwell, 141–65.

Mendenhall, T. C. (1887). 'The Characteristic Curves of Composition'. *Science*, 11: 237–49.

—— (1901). 'A Mechanical Solution of a Literary Problem'. *The Popular Science Monthly*, 60: 97–105.

Merideth, E. (1989). 'Gender Patterns in Henry James: A Stylistic Approach to Dialogue in *Daisy Miller, The Portrait of a Lady*, and *The Bostonians*', in R. G. Potter (ed.), *Literary Computing and Literary Criticism: Theoretical and Practical Essays on Theme and Rhetoric*. Philadelphia: University of Pennsylvania Press, 189–206.

Merriam, T. V. N. (1989). 'An Experiment with the *Federalist Papers*'. *Computers and the Humanities*, 23: 251–4.

—— and Matthews, R. (1994). 'Neural Computation in Stylometry II: An Application to the Works of Shakespeare and Marlowe'. *Literary and Linguistic Computing*, 9: 1–6.

Miall, D. S. (1992). 'Estimating Changes in Collocations of Key Words across a Large Text: A Case Study of Coleridge's Notebooks'. *Computers and the Humanities*, 26: 1–12.

Milic, L. T. (1967). *A Quantitative Approach to the Style of Jonathan Swift*. The Hague: Mouton.

—— (1991). 'Progress in Stylistics: Theory, Statistics, Computers'. *Computers and the Humanities*, 25: 393–401.

Miller, G. A. (principal investigator) (n.d.). 'WordNet: A Lexical Database for English' [Web page]. Cognitive Science Laboratory, Princeton University. Accessed on 3 November 1999.
<http://www.cogsci.princeton.edu/~wn/>

—— Beckwith, R., Fellbaum, C., Gross, D., and Miller, K. (n.d.). 'Introduction to WordNet: An On-Line Lexical Database'. Accessed on 2 December 1999.
<ftp://ftp.cogsci.princeton.edu/pub/wordnet/5papers.pdf>

Miller, P. (1996) 'Metadata for the Masses'. *Ariadne*. Accessed on 24 November 1999.
<http://www.ariadne.ac.uk/issue5/metadata-masses/>

—— and Greenstein, D. (eds.) (1997). 'Discovering Online Resources Across the Humanities: A Practical Implementation of the Dublin Core'. Arts and Humanities Data Service. Accessed on 24 November 1999.
<http://ahds.ac.uk/public/metadata/discovery.html>

Mindt, D. (1996). 'English Corpus Linguistics and the Foreign Language Teaching Syllabus', in J. Thomas and M. Short (eds.), *Using Corpora for Language Research: Studies in Honour of Geoffrey Leech*. London: Longman, 232–47.

Modern Language Association of America (1997). *Guidelines for Electronic Scholarly Editions*. New York: Modern Language Association of America. Accessed on 20 October 1999.

References

✓ <http://sunsite.berkeley.edu/MLA/guidelines.html>

Morton, A. Q. (1965). *The Authorship of the Pauline Epistles: A Scientific Solution.* [Saskatoon]: University of Saskatchewan.

—— (1978). *Literary Detection: How to Prove Authorship and Fraud in Literature and Documents.* New York: Charles Scribner's Sons.

—— and Levison, M. (1966). 'Some Indications of Authorship in Greek Prose', in J. Leed (ed.), *The Computer and Literary Style.* Kent, Oh.: Kent State University Press, 141–79.

—— and McLeman, J. (1966). *Paul, the Man and the Myth.* New York: Harper & Row.

—— and Winspear, A. D. (1971). *It's Greek to the Computer.* Montreal: Harvest House.

Mosteller, F., and Wallace, D. L. (1964). *Inference and Disputed Authorship: The Federalist.* Reading, Mass.: Addison-Wesley.

Muller, C. (1973). *Initiation aux méthodes de la statistique linguistique.* Paris: Hachette.

Mylonas, E., and Renear, A. (1999). 'The Text Encoding Initiative at 10: Not Just an Interchange Format Anymore – But a New Research Community'. *Computers and the Humanities,* 33: 1–9.

Nelson, G. (1996). 'The Design of the Corpus', in S. Greenbaum (ed.), *Comparing English Worldwide: The International Corpus of English.* Oxford: Oxford University Press, 27–35.

Netherlands Data Archive and Nijmegen Institute for Cognition and Information (1993). *Optical Character Recognition in the Historical Discipline: Proceedings of an International Workshop Organized by the Netherlands Historical Data Archive and Nijmegen Institute for Cognition and Information.* Göttingen: Max Planck Institut für Geschichte.

Neuman, M., Keeler, M., Kloesel, C., Ransdell, J., and Renear, A. (1992). 'The Pilot Project of the Electronic Peirce Consortium (Abstract)', in *ALLC–ACH92 Conference Abstracts and Program, Christ Church Oxford, 6–9 April 1992.* Oxford: 25–7.

Neumann, K. J. (1990). *The Authenticity of the Pauline Epistles in the Light of Stylostatistical Analysis.* Atlanta: SBL.

Nevalainen, T. (1996a). 'Gender Difference', in T. Nevalainen and H. Raumolin-Brunberg (eds.), *Sociolinguistics and Language History: Studies Based on the Corpus of Early English Correspondence.* Amsterdam: Rodopi, 77–91.

—— (1996b). 'Social Stratification', in T. Nevalainen and H. Raumolin-Brunberg (eds.) *Sociolinguistics and Language History: Studies Based on the Corpus of Early English Correspondence.* Amsterdam: Rodopi, 57–76.

—— and Raumolin-Brunberg, H. (eds.) (1996). *Sociolinguistics and Language History: Studies Based on the Corpus of Early English Correspondence.* Amsterdam: Rodopi.

Nurmi, A. (1998). *Manual for the Corpus of Early English Correspondence Sampler CEECS.* Helsinki: Department of English, University of Helsinki. Accessed on 3 December 1999.
<http://khnt.hit.uib.no/icame/manuals/ceecs/INDEX.HTM>

References

Oakes, M. P. (1998). *Statistics for Corpus Linguistics*. Edinburgh: Edinburgh University Press.

Olsen, M. (1993). 'Scanning, Keyboarding, and Data Verification: Factors in Selecting Data Collection Technologies', in Netherlands Data Archive and Nijmegen Institute for Cognition and Information, *Optical Character Recognition in the Historical Discipline: Proceedings of an International Workshop Organized by the Netherlands Historical Data Archive and Nijmegen Institute for Cognition and Information*. Göttingen: Max Planck Institut für Geschichte, 93–112.

—— and Harvey, L.-G. (1988). 'Computers in Intellectual History: Lexical Statistics and the Analysis of Political Discourse'. *Journal of Interdisciplinary History*, 18: 449–64.

Ooi, V. B. Y. (1998). *Computer Corpus Lexicography*. Edinburgh: Edinburgh University Press.

Oostdijk, N. (1988). 'A Corpus Linguistic Approach to Linguistic Variation'. *Literary and Linguistic Computing*, 3: 12–25.

Ott, W. (1973a). 'Computer Applications in Textual Criticism', in A. J. Aitken, R. W. Bailey, and N. Hamilton-Smith (eds.), *The Computer and Literary Studies*. Edinburgh: Edinburgh University Press, 199–223.

—— (1973b). 'Metrical Analysis of the Latin Hexameter: The Automation of a Philological Research Project', in A. Zampolli (ed.), *Linguistica Matematica e Calcolatori (Atti Del Convegno e Della Prima Scuola Internazionale, 1970, Pisa)*. Florence: Leo S. Olschki, 379–90.

—— (1974). *Metrische Analysen Zu Ovid, Metamorphosen Buch 1*. Tübingen: Niemeyer.

—— (1979). 'Automatic Composition for Critical Editions', in J. Irigoin and G. P. Zarri (eds.), *La Pratique des ordinateurs dans la critique des textes*. Paris: Centre National de la Recherche Scientifique, 237–40.

—— (1988). 'Software Requirements for Computer-Aided Critical Editing', in S. Butler and W. P. Stoneman (eds.), *Editing, Publishing and Computer Technology: Papers Given at the Twentieth Annual Conference on Editorial Problems*. New York: AMS Press, 81–103.

—— (1992). 'Computers and Textual Editing', in C. S. Butler (ed.), *Computers and Written Texts*. Oxford: Blackwell, 205–26.

—— (ed.) (1999) 'TuStep (Tübingen System of Text Processing Programs)' [Web page]. 5 May 1999. Accessed on 9 November 1999. <http://www.uni-tuebingen.de/zdv/tustep/tdv_eng.html>

'Oxford Text Archive' [Web page] (n.d.). Oxford University Computing Services and Arts and Humanities Data Service. Accessed on 24 November 1999. <http://ota.ahds.ac.uk/>

Oxford University Computing Service (1988). *Micro-OCP User Manual*. Oxford: Oxford University Press.

Oxford University Press (1994). *The Oxford English Dictionary Second Edition on Compact Disc*. Oxford: Oxford University Press.

Packard, D. W. (1971). 'Computer Techniques in the Study of the Minoan Linear Script A'. *Kadmos*, 10: 52–9.

References

(1974a). *Minoan Linear A*. Berkeley: University of California Press.

—— (1974b). 'Sound-Patterns in Homer'. *Transactions of the American Philological Association*, 104: 239–60.

—— (1976). 'Metrical and Grammatical Patterns in the Greek Hexameter', in A. Jones and R. F. Churchhouse (eds.), *The Computer in Literary and Linguistic Studies*. Cardiff: University of Wales Press, 85–91 .

Parrish, S. M. (1962). 'Problems in the Making of Computer Concordances'. *Studies in Bibliography*, 15: 1–14.

Partington, A. (1993). 'Corpus Evidence of Language Change', in M. Baker, G. Francis, and E. Tognini-Bonelli (eds.), *Text and Technology: In Honour of John Sinclair*. Amsterdam: John Benjamins, 177–92.

'The Penn–Helsinki Parsed Corpus of Middle English' [Web page] (n.d.). Department of Linguistics, University of Pennsylvania. Accessed on 10 November 1999.
<http://www.ling.upenn.edu/mideng/>

Peters, P. (n.d.) (with the assistance of A. Smith). *Manual of Information to Accompany the Australian Corpus of English (ACE)*. Macquarie University. Accessed on 28 October 1999.
<http://www.hit.uib.no/icame/ace/aceman.htm>

Philippides, D. M. L. (1984). *The Iambic Trimeter of Euripides: Selected Plays*. Salem, NH: Ayer.

Pierce, R. H. (1988). 'Multivariate Numerical Techniques Applied to the Study of Manuscript Tradition', in B. Fidjestøl, O. E. Haugen, and M. Rindal (eds.), *Tekstkritisk Teori Og Praksis: Nordisk Symposium i Tekstkritikk, Godøysund, 19–22. Mai 1987*. Oslo: Novus Forlag, 24–45.

Pintzuk, S., and Taylor, A. (1997). 'Annotating the Helsinki Corpus: The Brooklyn–Geneva–Amsterdam–Helsinki Corpus of Old English and the Penn–Helsinki Parsed Corpus of Middle English', in R. Hickey, M. Kytö, I. Lancashire, and M. Rissanen (eds.), *Tracing the Trail of Time: Proceedings from the Second Diachronic Corpora Workshop*. Amsterdam: Rodopi, 91–104.

Potter, R. G. (1981). 'Character Definition through Syntax: Significant Within-Play Variability in 21 English-Language Plays'. *Style*, 15: 415–34.

—— (1989). 'Changes in Shaw's Dramatic Rhetoric', in R. G. Potter (ed.), *Literary Computing and Literary Criticism: Theoretical and Practical Essays on Theme and Rhetoric*. Philadelphia: University of Pennsylvania Press, 225–58.

—— (1991). 'Statistical Analysis of Literature: A Retrospective of Computers and the Humanities'. *Computers and the Humanities*, 25: 401–29.

Proud, J. K. (1989). *The Oxford Text Archive*. Oxford: British Library Research and Development Report.

Raben, J. ([1965]). 'A Computer-Aided Study of Literary Influence: Milton to Shelley', in J. B. Bessinger and S. M. Parrish (eds.), *Literary Data Processing Conference Proceedings*. White Plains: IBM, 230–74.

Renear, A. (1997). 'Out of Praxis: Three (Meta)Theories of Textuality', in K. Sutherland (ed.), *Electronic Text: Investigations in Method and Theory*. Oxford: Clarendon Press, 107–26.

—— Durand, D., and Mylonas, E. (1996). 'Refining our Notion of What Text Really Is', in S. Hockey and N. Ide (eds.), *Research in Humanities Computing 4: Selected Papers from the 1992 ALLC/ACH Conference.* Oxford: Oxford University Press, 263–80.

Rissanen, M. (1992). 'The Diachronic Corpus as a Window to the History of English', in J. Svartvik (ed.), *Directions in Corpus Linguistics: Proceedings of Nobel Symposium 82, Stockholm, 4–8 August 1991.* Berlin: Mouton de Gruyter, 185–205.

Robey, D. (1987). 'Sound and Sense in the *Divine Comedy*'. *Literary and Linguistic Computing*, 2: 108–15.

—— (1988). 'Alliterations in Dante, Petrarch and Tasso: A Computer Analysis', in P. Hainsworth, V. Lucchesi, C. Roaf, D. Robey, and J. R. Woodhouse (eds.), *The Languages of Literature in Renaissance Italy.* Oxford: Clarendon Press, 169–89.

—— (1990). 'Rhymes in the Renaissance Epic: A Computer Analysis of Pulci, Boiardo, Ariosto and Tasso'. *Romance Studies*, 17: 97–111.

—— (1993). 'Scanning Dante's the *Divine Comedy*: A Computer-Based Approach'. *Literary and Linguistic Computing*, 8: 81–4.

—— (1999). 'Counting Syllables in the *Divine Comedy*: A Computer Analysis', in *Modern Language Review*, 94: 61–86.

Robinson, P. M. W. (1989a). 'The Collation and Textual Criticism of Icelandic Manuscripts 1: Collation'. *Literary and Linguistic Computing*, 4: 99–105.

—— (1989b). 'The Collation and Textual Criticism of Icelandic Manuscripts 2: Textual Criticism'. *Literary and Linguistic Computing*, 4: 174–81.

—— (1991). 'Textual Criticism Challenge'. July 1991. Accessed 9 November 1999. <http://lists.village.virginia.edu/lists_archive/Humanist/v05/0261.html>

—— (1994). 'Collate: A Program for Interactive Collation of Large Textual Traditions', in S. Hockey and N. Ide (eds.), *Research in Humanities Computing 3.* Oxford: Oxford University Press, 32–45.

—— (ed.) (1996). *Chaucer: The Wife of Bath's Prologue on CD-ROM.* Cambridge: Cambridge University Press.

—— (1998). 'New Methods of Editing, Exploring and Reading *The Canterbury Tales*'. Accessed on 5 May 2000. <http://www.cta.dmu.ac.uk/projects/ctp/desc2.html>

—— and O'Hara, R. J. (1996). 'Cladistic Analysis of an Old Norse Manuscript Tradition', in S. Hockey and N. Ide (eds.), *Research in Humanities Computing 4: Selected Papers from the 1992 ALLC–ACH Conference.* Oxford: Oxford University Press, 115–37.

Rommel, T. (1995). 'Aspects of Verisimilitude: Temporal and Topographical References in *Robinson Crusoe*'. *Literary and Linguistic Computing*, 10: 279–85.

Ross, D. (1973). 'Beyond the Concordance: Algorithms for Description of English Clauses and Phrases', in A. J. Aitken, R. Bailey, and N. Hamilton-Smith (eds.), *The Computer and Literary Studies.* Edinburgh: Edinburgh University Press, 85–99.

—— (1981). 'EYEBALL and the Analysis of Literary Style', in P. Patten and R. A. Holoien (eds.), *Computing in the Humanities.* Lexington, Mass.: D. C. Heath, 85–103.

References

Russell, D. B. (1967). *COCOA: A Word Count and Concordance Generator for Atlas.* Chilton: Atlas Computer Laboratory.

Sabol, C. R. (1989). 'Reliable Narration in *The Good Soldier'*, in R. G. Potter (ed.), *Literary Computing and Literary Criticism: Theoretical and Practical Essays on Theme and Rhetoric.* Philadelphia: University of Pennsylvania Press, 207–23.

Sampson, G. (1993). 'The Need for Grammatical Stocktaking'. *Literary and Linguistic Computing,* 8: 267–73.

——(1995). *English for the Computer: The SUSANNE Corpus and Analytic Scheme.* Oxford: Clarendon Press.

Sanford, A. J., Aked, J. P., Moxey, L. M., and Mullin, J. (1994). 'A Critical Examination of Assumptions Underlying the Cusum Technique of Forensic Linguistics'. *Forensic Linguistics,* 1: 151–67.

Sansone, D. (1990). 'The Computer and the *Historia Augusta*: A Note on Marriott'. *Journal of Roman Studies,* 80: 174–7.

Schmied, J., and Claridge, C. (1997). 'Classifying Text- or Genre-Variation in the Lampeter Corpus of Early Modern English Texts', in R. Hickey, M. Kytö, I. Lancashire, and M. Rissanen (eds.), *Tracing the Trail of Time: Proceedings from the Second Diachronic Corpora Workshop.* Amsterdam: Rodopi, 119–35.

Shastri, S. V. (1986) (in collaboration with C. T. Patilkulkarni and G. S. Shastri). *Manual of Information to Accompany the Kolhapur Corpus of Indian English for Use with Digital Computers* . Kolhapur: Department of English, Shivaji University. Accessed on 1 December 1999. <http://khnt.hit.uib.no/icame/,manuals/kolhapur/INDEX.HTM>

Shillingsburg, P. (1996). 'Principles for Electronic Archives, Scholarly Editions, and Tutorials', in R. J. Finneran (ed.), *The Literary Text in the Digital Age.* Ann Arbor: University of Michigan Press, 23–35.

SIL International (1999). 'LinguaLinks: Electronic Helps for Language Field Work' [Web page]. 2 August 1999. Accessed on 9 November 1999. <http://www.sil.org/lingualinks/>

Simons, G. (1998). 'The Nature of Linguistic Data and the Requirements of a Computing Environment for Linguistic Research', in J. Lawler and H. Aristar Dry (eds.), *Using Computers in Linguistics: A Practical Guide.* London: Routledge, 10–25.

——Sperberg-McQueen, C. M., and Durand, D. G. (1999). 'Rethinking TEI Markup in the Light of SGML Architectures', in *Conference Proceedings: ACH–ALLC'99 International Humanities Computing Conference June 9–14, 1999.* Charlottesville: University of Virginia, 174–81.

Sinclair, J. M. (ed.) (1987). *Looking Up: An Account of the COBUILD Project in Lexical Computing.* London: Collins ELT.

——(ed.) (1990). *Collins Cobuild English Grammar.* London: HarperCollins.

——(1991). *Corpus Concordance Collocation.* Oxford: Oxford University Press.

——(1992). 'The Automatic Analysis of Corpora', in J. Svartvik (ed.), *Directions in Corpus Linguistics: Proceedings of Nobel Symposium 82, Stockholm, 4–8 August 1991.* Berlin: Mouton de Gruyter, 379–97.

Small, I. (1991). 'The Editor as Annotator as Ideal Reader', in I. Small and M. Walsh (eds.), *The Theory and Practice of Text-Editing*. Cambridge: Cambridge University Press, 186–209.

Smith, J. B. (1973). 'Image and Imagery in Joyce's *Portrait*; A Computer-Assisted Analysis', in S. Weintraub and P. Young (eds.), *Directions in Literary Criticism: Contemporary Approaches to Literature*. University Park: Pennsylvania State University Press, 220–7.

—— (1989). 'Computer Criticism', in R. G. Potter (ed.), *Literary Computing and Literary Criticism: Theoretical and Practical Essays on Theme and Rhetoric*. Philadelphia: University of Pennsylvania Press, 13–44.

Smith, M. W. A. (1987). 'The Authorship of *Pericles*: New Evidence for Wilkins'. *Literary and Linguistic Computing*, 2: 221–30.

—— (1988). 'The Authorship of Acts I and II of *Pericles*: A New Approach Using First Words of Speeches'. *Computers and the Humanities*, 22: 23–41.

—— (1989). 'A Procedure to Determine Authorship Using Pairs of Consecutive Words: More Evidence for Wilkins's Participation in *Pericles*'. *Computers and the Humanities*, 23: 113–29.

Smith, N. (1997). 'Improving a Tagger', in R. Garside, G. Leech, and A. McEnery (eds.), *Corpus Annotation: Linguistic Information from Text Corpora*. Harlow: Addison Wesley Longman, 137–50.

Sperberg-McQueen, C. M. (1991). 'Text in the Electronic Age: Textual Study and Text Encoding with examples from Medieval Texts'. *Literary and Linguistic Computing*, 6: 34–46.

—— and Burnard, L. (eds.) (1994). *Guidelines for Electronic Text Encoding and Interchange*. Chicago and Oxford: ACH, ACL, ALLC. <http://www.uic.edu/orgs/tei/p3/doc/p3.html>

—— —— (1995). 'The Design of the TEI Encoding Scheme'. *Computers and the Humanities*, 29: 17–39.

—— and Huitfeldt, C. (1999). 'Concurrent Document Hierarchies in MECS and SGML'. *Literary and Linguistic Computing*, 14: 29–42.

Steele, K. B. (1991). '"The Whole Wealth of Thy Wit in an Instant": TACT and the Explicit Structures of Shakespeare's Plays', in T. Russon Wooldridge (ed.), *A TACT Exemplar*. Toronto: Centre for Computing in the Humanities, Toronto, 15–35.

Stevenson, B. (1989). 'Adapting Hypothesis Testing to a Literary Problem', in R. G. Potter (ed.), *Literary Computing and Literary Criticism: Theoretical and Practical Essays on Theme and Rhetoric*. Philadelphia: University of Pennsylvania Press, 61–74.

Stubbs, M. (1993). 'British Traditions in Text Analysis', in M. Baker, G. Francis, and E. Tognini-Bonelli (eds.), *Text and Technology: In Honour of John Sinclair*. Amsterdam: John Benjamins, 1–33.

—— (1996). *Text and Corpus Analysis*. Oxford: Blackwell.

Summers, D. (1996). 'Computer Lexicography: The Importance of Representativeness in Relation to Frequency (Abstract)', in J. Thomas and M. Short (eds.), *Using Corpora for Language Research: Studies in Honour of Geoffrey Leech*. London: Longman, 260–6.

References

Sutherland, K. (ed.) (1997). *Electronic Text: Investigations in Method and Theory*. Oxford: Clarendon Press.

Svartvik, J. (1968). *The Evans Statements: A Case for Forensic Linguistics*. Stockholm: Almqvist & Wiksell.

——(ed.) (1992). *Directions in Corpus Linguistics: Proceedings of Nobel Symposium 82, Stockholm, 4–8 August 1991*. Berlin: Mouton de Gruyter.

——(1996). 'Corpora are Becoming Mainstream', in J. Thomas and M. Short (eds.), *Using Corpora for Language Research: Studies in Honour of Geoffrey Leech*. London: Longman, 3–13.

——and Quirk, R. (eds.) (1980). *A Corpus of English Conversation*. Lund: CWK Gleerup.

Tetreault, R., and Graver, B., (eds.) (1998). 'Lyrical Ballads Bicentenary Project' [Web page]. 24 March 1998. Dalhousie University Electronic Text Centre. Accessed on 9 November 1999.
<http://www.dal.ca/etc/lballads/index_std.html>

Text Encoding Initiative (n.d.). 'Text Encoding Initiative Home Page' [Web page]. Accessed on 2 December 1999.
<http://www.uic.edu/orgs/tei>

Thesaurus Linguae Graecae (n.d.). 'The TLG Beta Code Manual' [Web page]. University of California at Irvine. Accessed on 16 November 1999.
<http://www.tlg.uci.edu/~tlg/>

Thomson, N. D. (1973–5). 'Literary Statistics'. Series of six articles in *ALLC Bulletin*, 1/3: 10–14; 2/1: 10–15; 2/2: 42–7; 2/3: 55–61; 3/1: 29–35; 3/2: 166–71.

——(1989). 'How to Read Articles which Depend on Statistics'. *Literary and Linguistic Computing*, 4: 6–11.

Tompa, F. W. (1992). 'An Overview of Waterloo's Database Software for the OED', in T. R. Wooldridge (ed.), *Historical Dictionary Databases*. Toronto: Centre for Computing in the Humanities, Toronto, 125–43.

——and Raymond, D. R. (1991). 'Database Design for a Dynamic Dictionary', in S. Hockey, N. Ide, and I. Lancashire (eds.), *Research in Humanities Computing 1: Papers from the 1989 ACH–ALLC Conference*. Oxford: Oxford University Press, 324–36.

Tribble, C., and Jones, G. (1990). *Concordances in the Classroom: A Resource Book for Teachers*. London: Longman.

Tweedie, F. J., Singh, S., and Holmes, D. I. (1996a). 'Neural Network Applications in Stylometry: The *Federalist Papers*'. *Computers and the Humanities*, 30: 1–10.

——(1996b). 'An Introduction to Neural Networks in Stylometry', in G. Perissinotto (ed.), *Research in Humanities Computing 5: Papers from the 1995 ACH–ALLC Conference*. Oxford: Oxford University Press, 249–63.

Uitti, K. D. (ed.) (1994). 'The Charrette Project' [Web page]. Accessed on 9 November 1999.
<http://www.princeton.edu/~lancelot>

Unicode Consortium (n.d). 'The Unicode® Standard: A Technical Introduction' [Web page]. Accessed on 16 November 1999.
<http://www.unicode.org/unicode/standard/principles.html>

van Halteren, H. (1997). *Excursions into Syntactic Databases*. Amsterdam: Rodopi.

van Herwijnen, E. (1994). *Practical SGML*. Dordrecht: Kluwer.

Venezky, R. (1987). 'Unseen Users, Unknown Systems: Computer Design for a Scholar's Dictionary', in *The Uses of Large Text Databases: Proceedings of the Third Annual Conference Waterloo November 9–10 1987*. Waterloo: UW Centre for the New OED, 113–21.

Vossen, P. (project manager) (1999). 'EuroWordNet' [Web page]. 2 August 1999. University of Amsterdam. Accessed on 9 November 1999. <http://www.hum.uva.nl/~ewn/>

——Meijs, W., and de Broeder, M. (1989). 'Meaning and Structure in Dictionary Definitions', in B. Boguraev and T. Briscoe (eds.), *Computational Lexicography for Natural Language Processing*. London: Longman, 171–92.

Wake, W. C. (1948). 'The Authenticity of the Pauline Epistles'. *Hibbert Journal*, 47/1: 50–5.

Walker, D. E., Calzolari, N., and Zampolli, A. (eds.) (1995). *Automating the Lexicon: Research and Practice in a Multilingual Environment*. Oxford: Clarendon Press.

Watt, R. J. C. (n.d.). 'The Web Concordances and Workbooks' [Web page]. Accessed on 9 November 1999. <http://www.dundee.ac.uk/english/wics/wics.htm>

——(1999). 'Concordance' [Web page]. 20 September 1999. Accessed on 9 November 1999. <http://www.rjcw.freeserve.co.uk/>

Weibel, S. (1995). 'Metadata: The Foundations of Resource Description'. *D-Lib Magazine*. Accessed on 24 November 1999. <http://www.dlib.org/dlib/July95/07weibel.html>

Weiner, E. (1985a). 'Computerizing the *Oxford English Dictionary*'. *Scholarly Publishing*, 16: 239–53.

——(1985b). 'The *New Oxford English Dictionary*'. *Journal of English Linguistics*, 18/1: 1–13.

——(1994). 'The Lexicographical Workstation and the Scholarly Dictionary', in B. T. S. Atkins and A. Zampolli (eds.), *Computational Approaches to the Lexicon*. Oxford: Clarendon Press, 413–38.

Wells, S., and Taylor, G. (1987). *William Shakespeare: A Textual Companion*. Oxford: Oxford University Press.

——————(eds.) (1991). *William Shakespeare: The Complete Works Electronic Edition*. Oxford: Oxford University Press.

Wichmann, A., Fligelstone, S., McEnery, T., and Knowles, G. (eds.) (1997). *Teaching and Language Corpora*. London: Addison Wesley Longman.

Wilks, Y., Fass, D., Guo, C.-M., McDonald, J., Plate, T., and Slator, B. (1989). 'A Tractable Machine Dictionary as a Resource for Computational Semantics', in B. Boguraev and T. Briscoe (eds.), *Computational Lexicography for Natural Language Processing*. London: Longman, 193–228.

Wilks, Y. A., Slator, B. M., and Guthrie, L. M. (1996). *Electric Words, Dictionaries, Computers and Meanings*. Cambridge, Mass: MIT Press.

References

Willett, P. (ed.) (1999). 'The Victorian Women Writers Project' [Web page]. 9 July 1999. Indiana University. Accessed on 16 November 1999. <http://www.indiana.edu/~letrs/vwwp/index.html >

Williams, C. B. (1970). *Style and Vocabulary: Numerical Studies.* London: Griffin.

Wisbey, R. (1962). 'Concordance Making by Electronic Computer: Some Experiences with the *Wiener Genesis*'. *Modern Language Review*, 57: 161–72.

——(1971). 'Publications from an Archive of Computer-Readable Literary Texts', in R. A. Wisbey (ed.), *The Computer in Literary and Linguistic Research.* Cambridge: Cambridge University Press, 19–34.

'Women Writers Project' [Web page] (n.d.). Brown University. Accessed on 5 May 2000. <http://www.wwp.brown.edu/>

Wooldridge, T. R. (1991). 'A CALL Application in Vocabulary and Grammar', in T. R. Wooldridge (ed.), *A TACT Exemplar.* Toronto: Centre for Computing in the Humanities, Toronto, 77–86.

World Wide Web Consortium (1999). 'HyperText Markup Language Home Page' [Web page]. 14 September 1999. Accessed on 16 November 1999. <http://www.w3.org/MarkUp/>

Zampolli, A. (1984). 'Lexicological and Lexicographic Activities at the Istituto Linguistica Computazionale', in A. Zampolli and A. Cappelli (eds.), *The Possibilities and Limits of the Computer in Producing and Publishing Dictionaries. Linguistica Computazionale III.* Pisa: Giardini, 237–78.

——(1987). 'Perspectives for an Italian Multifunctional Lexical Database'. *Studies in Honour of Roberto Busa S.J. Linguistica Computazionale IV–V.* Pisa: Giardini, 301–41.

——and Cappelli, A. (eds.) (1984). *The Possibilities and Limits of the Computer in Producing and Publishing Dictionaries. Linguistica Computazionale III.* Pisa: Giardini.

Zweig, R. W. (1998). 'Lessons from the *Palestine Post* Project'. *Literary and Linguistic Computing*, 13: 89–97.

Index

AAT, *see* Art and Architecture Thesaurus
accented characters:
  encoding 31
  treatment of in a concordance 54
access:
  using Internet for 3
ACH, *see* Association for Computers and
  the Humanities
ACL, *see* Association for Computational
  Linguistics
Acts 116
additional tag sets:
  in TEI 37
addresses:
  and word class tagging 99
adverbs:
  in Greek 111
Aeneid 27
Alberta, University of 153
ALLC, *see* Association for Literary and
  Linguistic Computing
Allén, S. 21
alliteration:
  in English 63, 81
  in Italian 79
allusions 68
alphabetization 55
Alt, M. 116
ambiguity:
  in corpus annotation 102
American Documentary Heritage 144
American English 16, 88, 92, 158
American Publishing House for the
  Blind 148
American Research on the Treasury of the
  French Language 23, 147
American, The 112
ampersand:
  sorting of 55
analysis:
  cladistic 129

cluster 116, 118, 130
  image 135
  morphological 101
  phylogenetic 129
  statistical 103, 115–17, 163
  syntactic 100
analytic bibliography:
  and TEI 45
annotation 99–100, 144
  of corpora 94
  in documentary editions 137
  in electronic editions 132
  in Internet editions 134
  morphosyntactic 101
  see also word class tagging
anthology:
  example in SGML encoding 35
Anthony, Susan B. 137
Antirealism 47
AP Newswire 92, 95
apostrophe:
  treatment of 53–4
Aquinas, St Thomas 5
Arabic 31
architectural forms 38
archive:
  as edition 132, 135–6
Ariosto 82
Aristotle 111–12
Art and Architecture Thesaurus 142
ARTFL, *see* American Research on the
  Treasury of the French
  Language
article:
  in language learning 87, 88
  in stylometry 111
Arts and Humanities Data Service 13, 14
ASCII 6
  lower 30
Association for Computational
  Linguistics 36

Index

Association for Computers and the
   Humanities 36
Association for Literary and Linguistic
   Computing 36
assonance 81
Aston, G. 19
Atkins, B. T. 148, 158
Atkins, S. 20
Attic Greek 102
attribute:
   in SGML 34
Atwood, M. 69
audience:
   for electronic editions 144
audio 143
Augustine, St 129
Austen, J. 69–71, 84, 112–13
Australian Corpus of English 17
AUTOSYS 99
Awkward Age, The 70

Bailey, R. W. 123
Ball, C. N. 103
Ballester, A. 32
Bank of English 21, 86, 87, 149
Barnbrook, G. 157
batch concordance 49
   advantages of 65
Bauman, S. 45
Bédier, J. 130
Belmore, N. 99
Benbow, T. 151
Bender, T. K. 81, 82
Bennet, Elizabeth 70
Bergen, University of 46
Berkowitz, L. 14
Berry-Rogghe, G. L. M. 90–1
Bertram, Lady 70
Besser, H. 142
Best, M. 134
beta code 31–2
Biber, D. 20, 85, 92–4, 95, 103, 114–15, 116
Bible 15, 68
biblical imagery:
   in Milton 74
bibliographic description:
   in TEI header 38
bibliographical codes 141
bibliography:
   of Middle English 155
Biggs, M. 47
Binongo, J. 110
Blackwell, S. 97

Blake, N. 140
Blake, W. 73, 99, 141, 143
   Blake Archive 141, 142
BNC, *see* British National Corpus
BNC sampler 19, 86
Boguraev, B. 157
Bolton. W. 15–16
book:
   electronic 166
   role of in the future 166
Booth, Catherine Mumford 39
Bornstein, G. 132
Bostonians, The 71
Bozzi, A. 101
Bradley, J. 168
Bratley, P. 149, 154
Briscoe, T. 157
British English 16, 88, 92, 158
British Library 18
British National Corpus 18–19, 95, 149
   headers in 39
   spoken part 32
   word class tagging of 97–8
Brown, S. 48
Brown Corpus 85
   collocations in 92
   composition of 16
   format of references in 27
   tag set 98, 99
   use in tagging 96
   word class tagging of 94
Brown University 15, 16
Brunner, T. F. 14
Bucher-Gillmayr, S. 68
Burnard, L. 14, 19, 35
Burr, E. 21
Burrows, J. F. 69–71, 84, 112–13, 120
Burton, D. M. 49
Busa, R., S.J. 5
Busta, Christine 68
Buzzetti, D. 47
Byrd, R. 157

California, University of at Irvine, 14
Calzolari, N. 159–60, 161
Canadian French 91
Canterbury Tales 138–41
canto 26
capitalization:
   in a concordance 53
Cappelli, A. 147
Cappelli, G. 101
catalogue:

200

as a means of finding electronic
texts 12–13
Catapano, T. 45
CD-ROM:
creation of 8–9
with packaged texts 6
Céline, L.-F. 73
CELLAR 162
Chadwyck-Healey 15
CHAINPROBS 96–7
Chambers 18
change log:
in TEI header 38
character sets 30–2
in dictionaries 149
characters:
in drama 83
encoding accented 31
use of in sorting words 53–5
Charrette Project 133
CHAT, *see* Codes for the Human Analysis
of Transcripts
Chaucer, G. 69, 81, 127, 138–41
Chesnutt, D. 136–8
chi-square 116
Child Language Data Exchange
(CHILDES) 32
Chisholm, D. 79–80
Chomsky, N. 85
Church, K. 92, 95
Cignoni, L. 147
citations:
in a concordance 52, 58–62
for a dictionary 147
in encoding 27
cladistic analysis 129
cladogram 140
Claridge, C. 18
classroom concordances 87–8
clauses:
problems in identifying 103
CLAWS 95–9
Clayton, T. 24
Clear, J. 20, 91–2
clear text 137
client 8
cluster analysis 116, 118, 130
Cobuild 20, 21, 86, 87, 95, 148
COCOA:
encoding format 18, 27–30, 89,
127
program 27
Code Declaration Table 46

codes:
bibliographical 141
linguistic 141
Codes for the Human Analysis of
Transcripts 32
Cognitive Science Laboratory,
Princeton 163
cognitive stylistics 69
Coleridge, S. T. 75, 99, 133–4
collaboration:
in editing 144
in electronic projects 170
Collate 126–8
collation 124–8
history of computer-aided 125
interactive 125
practicalities of 125
of verse text 125
*Collins Cobuild English Language
Dictionary* 148–9
collocations 63–4, 90–2, 147, 163
in Coleridge 75
in Greek 155
use of in word class tagging 102
collocative clash 86
Committee on Scholarly Editions:
of MLA 134
common words 69–71
in dictionaries 161
in English 112–13
in Greek 111
omission of 7, 65
in Shakespeare 120
in stylometry 110–13
competence:
in linguistics 85
complexity:
of humanities texts 3
composite text:
encoding of in TEI 39
computational linguistics 160
computer science 166
and dictionaries 150
conceptual indexes 136
concordances 52–3
in classroom 87–8
for a dictionary 147, 148
left-sorted 62
reverse 82
right-sorted 62, 86
use of for separating homographs 112
use of in preparing edition 131
Web 62–3

Index

concordances (*cont.*)
  see also Concordance; MonoConc;
    Oxford Concordance Program;
    WordSmith Tools
Concordance (program) 27, 62, 167
CONCUR 46
Congress, First Federal 138
connectionist model:
  of verse 83
Conrad, J. 99
Constitution, Ratification of 138
contamination:
  in manuscript traditions 129
context:
  in a concordance 58–62
  for a dictionary 147
  sorting 62
contracted forms:
  in word class tagging 95
cooccurrences 63–4, 90–2, 147
Coombs, J. H. 33, 47
core tags:
  in TEI 37
Corns, T. N. 73–5
corpus 16–20
  and computational dictionaries 161, 163
  diachronic 18
  encoding in TEI 39
  monitor 20–1
  of Old English 147
  of Swedish 100
  see also Australian Corpus of English;
    British National Corpus; Brown
    Corpus; Correspondence, Corpus of
    Early English Helsinki Corpus;
    International Computer Archive of
    Modern English; International
    Corpus of English; Kolhapur Corpus;
    Lancaster–Oslo/Bergen Corpus;
    London-Lund Corpus; Penn-Helsinki
    Parsed Corpus of Middle English;
    Wellington Corpus of Written New
    Zealand English
corpus annotation 94
corpus design 16, 19–21
corpus lexicography 147–9
corpus linguistics 85–6
correlations 116
Correspondence, Corpus of Early
  English 88–9
counts, of words 111
Craig, D. H. 69
Craik, E. M. 81

Crane, G. 101–2, 155
critical apparatus:
  encoding of 25, 37
  typesetting 131
critical edition:
  production of 124
criticism:
  of computer-aided analysis 66–7
Crowdy, S. 19, 32
culture:
  and vocabulary 89
cumulative sum 122–3
curvilinear features 115
cusum 122–3
Cyrillic 31
Czech 164

dactyl 80
Daisy Miller 71
Dante 79
Darcy 70
Dartmouth Dante Project 26
database:
  relational 128
  of variants 128
dates:
  encoding in TEI 37
  and word class tagging 99
DBT 160
de Broeder, M. 157
de Jong, J. R. 83
definitions:
  extracting information from 157
Defoe, D.:
  Robinson Crusoe 75
deformation:
  of digital images 141
demonstratives:
  in Greek 111
demographic variables 88–9
dendrogram 116
density:
  diagrams 68
  of images in Blake 73
DeRose, S. J. 33, 47
descriptive encoding 33–4
design:
  of corpora 19–21
diachronic corpora 18
diacritics:
  in a concordance 54
  in interactive retrieval 64–5
  in morphological analysis of Greek 102

diagrams, density 68
dialects, Greek 102
dialogue 69–71
  encoding of 70
Dickinson, E. 141
dictionaries:
  computational 156
  early 154
  encoding 25, 37
  historical 146, 149–54
  metrical 79–80
  printed 161, 163
  Renaissance 154
  sixteenth-century 154
Dictionary of Medieval Latin from British
  Sources 148
Dictionary of Old English 14–15, 18, 27,
  147, 154
digital images 135, 139, 141–3
digital library 65, 160, 165
  design of 166
  encoding for 47
Dilligan, R. J. 81, 82
dimensions:
  in factor analysis 93
  in multivariate analysis 116
diplomatic transcription 137
direction
  of writing 31
distinctiveness ratio 107
ditto-tag 97, 98
Divine Comedy 26, 79, 82
Dixon, P. 118
document, nature of 7, 26
document analysis 36
document management 170
document retrieval 7
  and encoding 26
document type definition 34, 35, 46
documentary editing 136–8
drama:
  encoding in COCOA format 27–30
  encoding in TEI 37
  structure of 34–5, 83–4
DTD, see document type definition
Dublin Core 13
Dunlop, D. 39
Durand, D. 47
Dutch 164
DynaText 138, 140
DynaWeb 138, 142

EAGLES 101

early printed books:
  in OCR 22
Early English Correspondence, Corpus
  of 88–9
Early Modern English 18
Early Modern Literary Studies 134
echoes 68
  finding in literature 67
Edinburgh:
  concordance projects at 27
editing:
  dictionaries 149, 153–4
  documentary 136–8
edition:
  electronic 77, 124, 132, 134
  image 141–3
  live text 138
  transition 138
editorial reconstructions:
  in a concordance 54–5
Edwards, J. A. 32
electronic edition 77
  models for 133
  overview of 124
  principles 134
  rationale for 132
  tools for 135
Electronic Pierce Consortium 144
electronic publishing:
  on World Wide Web 9
electronic Shakespeare 29
electronic text collections 65
element:
  in SGML 34
elision:
  in English verse 81
  in Greek verse 81
  in Latin verse 80
Ellegård, A. 101, 106–8, 110, 114
Elliott, Anne 71
ELRA, see European Languages Resources
  Association
Emacs 12
Emma 70–1
encoding 4
  advances in 166–7
  choosing a scheme 169–70
  in Collate 127
  to control analysis 57
  descriptive 33–4
  embedded 26
  fixed format 27
  interpretive 77

Index

encoding (*cont.*)
  need for 24
  of *Oxford English Dictionary* 151
  physical description 142
  prescriptive 33
  procedural 33
  typographic 4, 25
encoding description:
  in TEI header 38
end tag:
  in SGML 34
endangered languages 162
endings:
  removing 94
  searching for in interactive retrieval 64
  sorting on 58
English:
  American 16, 88, 92, 158
  Australian 17
  Bank of 21, 149
  British 16, 88, 92, 158
  Early Modern 18
  Indian 17
  learners of 88
  Middle 18, 154–5
  New Zealand 17
  Old 14, 18, 147
  Renaissance 49
  Stuart 89
  Tudor 89
entity:
  in SGML 35–6
epic:
  Italian Renaissance 82
Epistles, of Paul 106, 111, 118–20
errors:
  in word class tagging 98–9, 100
Estonian 164
Ethics, of Aristotle 111–12
etymologies:
  in *Oxford English Dictionary* 152
Eudemian Ethics 111–12
Euripides 80–1
European Language Resources
  Association 18
European Union 101
evaluation of computer-based work
  170–1
Evans, T. J. 123
evidence:
  from corpora 161
  in law 123
expressions, regular 56–7

Extensible Markup Language, *see* XML
EYEBALL 99

factor analysis 92–3, 116
Fang, A. C. 100
Farr, G. J. 150
Farringdon, J. 122
Faulhaber, C. B. 136
feature structures 159
Federalist Papers 108–9, 110, 122
female language 72
fiction:
  collocates in 92
file description:
  in TEI header 38
Fillmore, C. J. 148, 158
Finegan, E. 93
fingerprints, linguistic 104
Finneran, R. J. 132, 141
First Federal Congress 138
Fischer, A. 153
Fish, S. 66
fixed format encoding 27
Flanders, J. 143
Fogel, E. G. 24
font:
  for transcription of Old Norse 126
forensic linguistics 123
format:
  of concordances 58–62
Forster, E. M.
  Howards End 70
Forsyth, R. 108
Fortier, P. A. 73
Foster, D. 123
Four Zoas, The 73
Fox, G. 149
Francis, G. 87
Francis, I. S. 108
Francis, Philip 107
Francis, W. N. 16, 94
Frederica 70
French 54, 88, 147, 154, 164
  Old 68
French Canadian 91
frequency list 58
Friedl, J. E. F. 57
Frischer, B. 110, 116
function words:
  in Greek 111–12
  omission of 7
  in Shakespeare 120
  in stylometry 110–13

functional grammar 101
future tense:
in language learning 88

Gabler, H. W. 126
Galloway, P. 130
Garside, R. 95–7, 100
Gatrell, S. 144
Gaylord, H. E. 32
gender:
and language 71–2, 89
General Prologue:
to *Canterbury Tales* 140
genitives:
in word class tagging 95
genre 69, 93
German 79–80, 88, 164
early 81–2
Getty 142
Gide, A. 73
Gilbert, P. 125
Goldsmith, O. 118
Goodman, S. 67
Gospels 129
gradiency:
in word class tagging 99
grammar:
at Cobuild 87
functional 101
of Greek verse 83
logical 101
surface 101
Graver, B. 133–4
Greek 14
alphabetization 55
Attic 102
letters 31, 36
Lexicon of Greek Personal Names 150
metre 80–1, 83
morphological analysis of 101–2
Perseus Project 155
prose 113
samples 115
sentence length in 109–10
sound patterns in 78
stylometry 110, 111–12
Greene, B. 94
Greene, N. 137
Greenstein, D. I. 48
Greenwood, H. H. 119
Griffith. J. G. 129–30
Grosseto 159
Guidelines for Electronic Scholarly Editions:

from MLA 134
Guthrie, L. 156

Hamilton, A. 108
Hamm, J.-J. 69
handwriting:
in OCR 22
harshness measure 78
Hart, G. R. 77
Harvey, L.-G. 91
Haskel, P. I. 92
Hayward, M. 83
header:
in British National Corpus 39
HTML 13
TEI 13, 38–9
headwords:
in a concordance 52
Heald, Revd. W. 105
Healey, A. D. 15
Hearst, Patti 123
Heart of Darkness 99
Hebrew 36
Hebrews, Epistle to 106
Heery, R. 13
Heinemann. E. A. 68
Helsinki, University of 88
Helsinki Corpus 18, 89, 102, 153
Hengwrt manuscript 140
Henry VIII 120
hexameters 80
Heyer, G.:
Frederica 70
hiatus:
in Latin scansion 80
hidden Markov model 97
hierarchy:
of SGML document 34
semantic 160
Historia Augusta 110
historical data:
encoding 48
historical dictionaries 149–54
historical editing 136–8
Hittite 78
Hockey, S. 16, 125, 136
Hofland, K. 114
Holmes, D. 104, 108, 121, 122, 123
holonym 163–4
Homer:
sound patterns in 78
homographs:
in Italian machine dictionary 159

Hoogcarspel, A. 13
Hope, J. 120–1
Hopkins, G. 81
Horace 130
Horowitz, L. 13
Horton, T. B. 120, 121
Howard-Hill, T. H. 49
Howards End 70
Howlett, D. R. 148
HTML 8, 11–12, 32–3, 46, 134
  header 13
  use in electronic editions 133
Huitfeldt, C. 46
human annotation 99–100, 102
Humanist 128
humanities research:
  nature of 2
humanities texts:
  nature of 1–2
hyperbibliography 155
hypernym 163, 164
hypertext 132, 133, 135, 142
  encoding in TEI 37
HyperText Markup Language, *see* HTML
hyphen:
  treatment of 54
hyphenated words:
  in word class tagging 96
hyponym 161, 163
hypothesis testing 115

iambic pentameter 81, 83
iambic trimeter 80–1
IBM 151
ICAME, *see* International Computer
  Archive of Modern English
ICE, *see* International Corpus of English
ICONCLASS 142
Ide, N. 73, 158
identification:
  of variants 127
idiolect 69–72
idioms 63
  in text analysis 84
  in word class tagging 97
IDIOMTAG 97
Iliad 31–2
ill-formed text:
  word class tagging of 98
Ilsemann, H. 83
image:
  analysis 135
  digital 135, 139, 141–3

edition 137–8
imagery:
  in Blake 73
  in Milton 73–4
images:
  of pages 138
inclusiveness:
  of electronic editions 140
index:
  in a documentary edition 137
  generating for an edition 131–2
  in an interactive retrieval program
    4950
  rhyme 82
  terms 142
Index Thomisticus 5–6
indexing systems:
  hierarchical 142
Indian English 17
Indiana University 39
inflected languages 5, 58, 94
influence:
  literary 67
information retrieval 160
Iniquity of State Regulated Vice, The
    3944
initial capitals:
  in a concordance 53
INSO 138
intellectual frameworks 136
intensifiers 86
interactive retrieval 49
  merits of 64
International Computer Archive of
  Modern English 17
International Corpus of English 17, 100
  word class tagging in 99
Internet:
  for electronic editions 132
  and electronic texts 11, 12
  future of 165
  use for access 3
Internet Explorer 32
Internet Shakespeare Editions 134
interpretation:
  and encoding 45, 48
  historical 45
  literary 45
investment:
  in data 47
Irizarry, E. 71–2, 117
irony 86
Isabel (in *Portrait of a Lady*) 71

Index

Istituto di Linguistica Computazionale 159
Italian 21, 79, 161, 164
Italian Machine Dictionary 159

Jackson, M. P. 120
James, H. 70, 71, 112–13
Jay, J. 108
Joaquin, N. 110
Johansson, S. 16, 17, 32, 98–9, 99, 103,
 114
John, Gospel of 116
Jones, A. 21
Jones, G. 87–8
Jones, S. 90
Jonson, B. 69
Joyce, J. 73, 126
Junius Letters 106–8, 110
Juvenal 129

Kaferly, D. H. A. 81
Källgren, G. 99–100
Keats, J. 99
Kenny, A. 111–12, 114, 115, 116
keyboarding:
 advantages of 23
keyword in context 52, 62
keywords:
 in a concordance 52
Kibbee, D. A. 154
Klavans, J. 160
Knightley, Mr. 71
knowledge:
 machine acquisition of 160
knowledge base:
 linguistic 161
Kolhapur Corpus 17
Krishnamurthy, R. 148
Kučera, H. 94
Kurzweil Data Entry Machine 23
KWIC, *see* keyword in context
Kytö, M. 18

L'Immoraliste 73
Laan, N. M. 81, 83
Lai de l'ombre 130
Lancashire, I. 30, 57, 69, 142, 154
Lancaster, University of 18
Lancaster-Oslo/Bergen Corpus 103
 composition of 16–17
 format of references in 27
 sampling procedures for 114
 use in study of variation 92
 word class tagging of 95, 97

language:
 of females 72
 learning 87
 of males 72
language engineering:
 standards for 101
languages:
 endangered 162
 undeciphered 77
Larkin, P. 86
Latin:
 collation of medieval 125
 dictionary 155
 encoding 30
 Index Thomisticus 5–6
 medieval 148
 metre 80
 morphological analysis of 101
 Ovid 76–7
 Packard Humanities Institute
  CD-ROM 14
 prose 116
 word length 106
Laurens, Papers of Henry 136
Lavagnino, J. 133, 143
law, courts of 123
LDC, *see* Linguistic Data Consortium
LDOCE, *see* Longman Dictionary of
  Contemporary English
Le Maitre, J. 158
learners:
 of English 149
 of French 88
Ledger, G. 119
Lee, A. 129
Leech, G. 32, 85, 86, 98, 100
left-sorted concordance 62
legacy data 6
Leiden, University of 142
Leitner, G. 17
lemmatization 5, 67, 76–7, 94
length:
 of sentences 74–5, 108, 109
 of words 106, 109
Lessard, G. 69
letter:
 distributions in New Testament 119
 initial and final in Greek 119
Levin, B. 158
Lewis and Short 155
lexical database 72, 162
 design of 158–60
 for Latin 101

Index

lexical memory 163
lexical patterning 90
lexicon:
    computational 156
    Greek 155
Lexicon of Greek Personal Names 150
lexis 74
librarians 166
library, digital 47, 65, 160, 165
library catalogue:
    as a means of finding electronic
        texts 12–13
Liddell and Scott 155
Lillo, G. 83
line breaks:
    in concordance entries 62
line numbers:
    encoding in COCOA 28
    in typesetting 131
Linear A 77
Linear B 77
lineation:
    in COCOA encoding 28
LinguaLinks 162
linguistic codes 141
linguistic data:
    characteristics of 162
    repository of 159
Linguistic Data Consortium 18
linguistic knowledge base 161
linguistics, forensic 123
links:
    in electronic edition 133, 135
Linnaean taxonomy 99
Lion, *see* Literature Online
literary and linguistic computing 160
Literature Online 15
live text editions 138
LOB Corpus, *see* Lancaster–Oslo/Bergen
    Corpus
logical grammar 101
London Merchant, The 83
London-Lund Corpus 19, 92, 114
Longman 18, 149
*Longman Dictionary of Contemporary
    English* 156–8
Louw, B. 86
lower case letters:
    in a concordance 55
Luke, Gospel of 116
Lusignan, S. 154
Lynn, K. 81
Lyrical Ballads 133–4

McCarty, W. 76–7
McEnery, A. 86
McEnery, T. 21
McGann, J. J. 132, 141
machine annotation 99–100
machine dictionary:
    of Italian 159
Macintosh 126, 128
McLeman, J. 111, 119
McNaught, J. 20
Madison, J. 108
Maigret 88
male language 72
Malraux, A. 73
management:
    of electronic projects 168–9
Manly J. M. 138
Mannion, D. 118
Mansfield Park 70, 112
maps:
    in documentary editions 137
marker words:
    in *Federalist Papers* 108
Markman, A. 24
Markov model:
    hidden 97
markup, *see* encoding
markup theory 47–8
Marlowe, C. 106, 121
Marriott, I. 110
Marshall, I. 96
master text:
    in collation 126–7
Matthews, E. 150
Matthews, R. 121–2
Mealand, D. 119
MEC, *see* Middle English Compendium
MECS, *see* Multi-Element Encoding
    Scheme
Medea 81
Medieval Latin 148
Meijs, W. 146, 157
Mendenhall, T. C. 106
MEP, *see* Model Editions Partnership
Merideth, E. 71
meronym 164
Merriam, T. V. N. 121–2
metadata 13
    encoding for corpus 39
    as TEI header 38–9
Metamorphoses 76–7
metaphor:
    in text analysis 84

metre 78–83
 formal properties of 83
Mexican Spanish 71–2
Miall, D. S. 75
Michigan, University of 154
Middle English 18
 Parsed Corpus of 102
Middle English Compendium 154–5
milestone tags:
 in TEI 45
Milic, L. T. 66, 99
Mill, J. S. 106
Miller, G. A. 163
Milton, J. 67, 73–5
Mindt, D. 88
minus words 107, 117
Misfortunes of Alonso Ramírez 117
missing occurrences 88, 103, 120–1
MLA, *see* Modern Language Association
 of America
modals 88
model:
 connectionist 83
 for electronic dictionaries 158
Model Editions Partnership 45, 136–8,
 143, 145, 168
 prospectus 137
Modern Language Association of
 America 134
modernized spelling:
 encoding for 30
monitor corpus 20–1
MonoConc 167
Morgan, Augustus de 105–6
Morland, Catherine 71
morphing 141
morphological analysis 101
morphosyntactic annotation 101
Morris, W. 141
Morton, A. Q. 109–10, 110–11, 111, 113,
 114, 115, 119, 122
Mosteller, F. 108, 110
Muller, C. 115
Multi-Element Encoding Scheme 46
multi-layer perceptron 121
multimedia 155
 in electronic editions 135, 143
 and TEI 45
multiple hierarchies:
 in encoding references 28
 and SGML 45–6
multivariate analysis 92–3, 116–17, 118, 130
mutual information 91, 163

Myers, G. 32
Mylonas, E. 47

names:
 encoding of 37, 76
narrative 70–1, 93
National Historical Publications and
 Records Commission 136
natural language processing 101
navigation:
 of electronic editions 132–3
negatives:
 in text analysis 84
neologisms:
 in Milton's verse 74
Netherlands Data Archive 23
Netscape 32
network:
 use of for collaborative editing 144
networks, neural 121–2
Neumann, K. J. 119
neural networks 121–2
Nevalainen, T. 88–9
New Collins Thesaurus 157
New Testament 68, 116, 119, 129
 variants in 128
New Zealand 17
newspapers 21
 collocates in 92
 and TEI 45
Nicomachean Ethics 111–12
Nijmegen 99
 Institute for Cognition and
 Information 23
Nobel Symposium:
 on corpus linguistics 86
node:
 in collocations 64, 90
non-roman alphabet 31
non-sorting characters 55
 in interactive retrieval 64–5
non-standard characters 30–2
 as SGML entities 35–6
Norse, Old 126
notebooks:
 of Coleridge 75
notes:
 encoding in TEI 45
null occurrences 88, 103, 120–1
numbering:
 of lines in COCOA encoding 28
numbers:
 and word class tagging 99

Index

numerals:
in a concordance 55
roman 51
sorting of 55
numerical studies:
of text 105–6

O'Hara, R. 129
Oakes, M. P. 92, 115
object-oriented:
environment for linguistic research 162
OCP, *see* Oxford Concordance Program
OCR, *see* optical character recognition
OHCO, *see* ordered hierarchy of content objects
Old English 14, 18, 147
Old French 68
Old Norse 126
Olsen, M. 23, 91
on-line searching 65
Onomasticon 76–7
Ooi, V. B. Y. 160
Oostdijk, N. 93
Open Text 151
optical character recognition 21–3
ordered hierarchy of content objects 47
Orestes 81
Orlando Furioso 82
Orlando Project 170
Ostler, N. 20
Ott, W. 80, 124, 126, 128, 132
overlap:
in encoding 29
in references 28
and SGML 45–6
Ovid 76–7
Oxford Concordance Program 18, 27, 69, 79, 167
Oxford English Dictionary 74, 150–4
on CD-ROM 152
on Internet 153
Oxford Text Archive 14
Oxford Text Searching System 26
Oxford University 18
Oxford University Press 18

Packard Humanities Institute 14
Packard, D. W. 77, 78, 80, 102
padding letters 55
page images 138
page make up 131
Paradise Lost 74
Parrish, S. M. 24

parser:
in SGML 35
parser generator:
in metrics 83
parsing 100
part of speech tagging 74, 92, 94–100
participants:
in spoken text 38
participles:
finding 57
particles:
in Greek 111
in phrasal verbs 87
Partington, A. 86
Partridge, S. 140
Pat 151
patronyms 76
pattern recognition:
in neural networks 121
patterns:
in finding words 57
sound 78–83
Pauline epistles 106, 111, 118–20
PAUP 129, 140–1
Penn-Helsinki Parsed Corpus of Middle English 102
pentameters, iambic 81, 83
percentages:
in word frequencies 111
perceptron, multi-layer 121
performance:
in linguistics 85
Pericles 120
Perseus Project 101–2, 155
personification 76
persons:
references to, 76
Peters, C. 147
Petrarch 79
PHI, *see* Packard Humanities Institute
Philippides, D. M. L. 80–1
Philippine 110
philosophy:
and encoding 47
phonological transcription 79, 81
phrasal repetends 69
phrasal verbs 86–7, 91
phrases:
searching for 63
in word class tagging 97
phylogenetic analysis 129
physical appearance:
encoding for 141, 142

Picchi, E. 160
Pierce, C. S. 144
Pierce, R. H. 131
pitfalls:
of corpus linguistics 103
pizza model:
of TEI DTD 37
plain text 11
Platonism 47
Pluralism 47
plurals:
in word class tagging 96
plus words 107, 117
political texts:
collocates in 91
population:
for samples 113
Portrait of a Lady, The 71, 112
Potter, R. 66, 84
Poughkeepsie Principles 36
prediction:
in statistics 115–16
prepare file:
in Collate 128
prepositions:
in Greek 111
in language learning 88
prescriptive encoding 33
Price, Fanny 70
primary sources 2
Princeton University 133
probabilities 103, 116
in word class tagging 96–7
procedural encoding 33
profile description:
in TEI header 38
programs 3–4
functionality of 8–9
and SGML 47
in SNOBOL 79
for text analysis 50, 167
see also CLAWS; Collate; Concordance;
DBT; DynaText; DynaWeb; PAUP;
TACT TuStep
project design 170
project management 168–9
pronouns 69
in Jane Austen 70
in Roman plays of Shakespeare 69
proper names 76
prose:
collation of 125
concordance of 62

encoding in TEI 37
Greek 109
Latin 110
prosody 81
prospectus:
for electronic documentary editions
137
Proud, J. K. 14
psycholinguistics 163, 164
Public Advertiser, The 107
publication statement:
in TEI header 38
publishing houses 166
Publius 108
punctuation:
in a concordance 56
and word class tagging 95, 99

qsum, see cusum
Quaestiones in Heptateucheum 129
Quentin, H. 130
quotations, finding 68

Raben, J. 67
Rahtz, S. 150
Ramírez, Alonso 117
random sampling 113
Ratification of the Constitution 138
ratio, distinctiveness 107
Raumolin-Brunberg, H. 88–9
Raymond, D. R. 158
reception:
of electronic editions 143
references:
in a concordance 52
sorting in a concordance 62
register 93
regular expressions 56–7
regularized spelling 127
relational database 128
Renaissance:
dictionaries 154
English 49
Italian 82
Renaissance Electronic Texts:
encoding of 142
Renear, A. H. 33, 47
repeated strings 69
repetends, phrasal 69
repetition:
of words and phrases 69
representativeness:
in corpus design 114–15

resolution:
    in Greek metre 81
responsibility:
    encoding for 170
RET, *see* Renaissance Electronic Texts
retrieval, interactive 49
reusability:
    of humanities texts 3
Revelation 116
reverse sort 58
review:
    of computer-based work 170–1
revision history:
    in TEI header 38
rhyme:
    indexes 82
    schemes 58, 81–2
Rickert, E. 138
right-sorted concordance 62, 86, 148
right-to-left writing 31
Rissanen, M. 18
Robey, D. 79, 82
Robinson Crusoe 75
Robinson, P. M. W. 126–9, 138–41
Roget's II: The New Thesaurus 157
roman numerals:
    sorting of 51
Roman plays:
    of Shakespeare 69
Rommel, T. 75
Ross, D. 99
Rossetti Archive 141
Rubin, G. 94

Sabol, C. R. 120
samples 113–15
    in corpus linguistics 20, 114–15
    random 113
    rationale for in TEI header 38
    size of 114
    stratified 113–14
Sampson, G. 99, 100–1
Sanditon 70
Sanger, Papers of Margaret 137–8, 143
Sansone, D. 110
Santamaria, C. 32
scaling:
    for cusums 122
scanners 22
scansion 78
    of English 81
    of German 79–80
    of Greek 80–1

interactive 82
    of Italian 82
    of Latin 80
Schmied, J. 18
scripts, undeciphered 77
search, sequential 7
search engine 8
searchability:
    of image editions 143
    lack of in Web editions 134
semantic field:
    with collocates 90–1
semantic frames:
    representation of 163
semantic search 161
sentence:
    definition of 110
sentence length 109
    in English 110
    in *Federalist Papers* 108
    in Latin 110
    in Pauline epistles 119
    in Spanish 117
sentence structure:
    in Milton 74–5
sentences:
    identification of 109
separators:
    word 54
SGML, *see* Standard Generalized Markup
    Language
Shakespeare, W. 15–16, 83, 106, 121, 134
    authorship of 120
    electronic 29
    encoding 27–30
    Internet Shakespeare Editions 134
    in *Oxford English Dictionary* 152
    pronouns in 69
    sociolinguistic study of 120–1
shallowness:
    of electronic editions 143
Shelley, P. B. 67
Shillingsburg, P. 135
significance:
    of collocates 90
Sigüenza y Góngora, Carlos de 117
SIL, *see* Summer Institute for
    Linguistics 162
Simons, G. 162
Sinclair, J. M. 20, 85, 86–7, 87, 90, 102, 149
Singh, S. 121, 122
Slator, B. 156
slips, electronic 146–7

Small, I. 144
Smith, J. B. 73
Smith, M. W. A. 115, 120
Smith, N. 97
SNOBOL 79, 80
sociolinguistic:
  study of Shakespeare 120–1
  variables 88–9
software:
  needs for electronic texts 167
  reviewing 170–1
Solopova, E. 140
Sophocles 81
sorting:
  contexts 62
  on endings 58
  words 55
sound:
  in German 79–80
  in Greek 78
  in Italian 79
source description:
  in TEI header 38
span:
  with collocates 90
Spanish 32, 72, 164
  alphabetization of 55
  Mexican 71–2
speech input 166
speeches:
  encoding for in drama 29
spelling:
  encoding for modernized 30
  regularization of 127
Sperberg-McQueen, C. M. 35, 46, 48
SPITBOL 79, 82
spoken texts 92
  in British National Corpus 19
  encoding 32, 37
  word class tagging of 98
spondee 80
stage directions:
  encoding 29, 30
Standard Generalized Markup
    Language 33–6, 144, 167, 169
  advantages of 47
  in British National Corpus 97
  in *Canterbury Tales* 139
  with CELLAR 162
  in *Internet Shakespeare Editions* 134
  in *Middle English Compendium* 155
  in Model Editions Partnership 136,
    138

in *Oxford English Dictionary* 151
  in Oxford Text Archive 14
  in Rossetti Archive 141
  and software 47, 57
  with text analysis program 57
standards:
  for language engineering 101
Stanton-Anthony Papers 138
start tag:
  in SGML 34
statements:
  given to police 123
statistical analysis 103, 115–17
  of corpora 163
Steele, K. B. 83
stemmata 129
Stendhal 69
Stevenson, B. 115
stratified sampling 113–14
stress 81
structural encoding 25
structure:
  of lexical database 159–60
  of sentences in Milton 74–5
Stuart English 89
Stubbs, M. 85, 89
stylistics:
  cognitive 69
  literary 66
stylometry:
  criticism of 104
  and metre 81
suffixes:
  in Latin 101
  removing 94
  in word class tagging 96
Summer Institute for Linguistics 162
surface grammar 101
survey:
  for *Oxford English Dictionary* 151
Survey of English Usage 19
SUSANNE 100–1
Svartvik, J. 86, 123
Swedish 21, 100
Swift, J. 99
syllables:
  in Italian 82
  length of 80
  per word in Milton 74–5
synonyms 164
  in *Federalist Papers* 108
  in *Junius Letters* 107
syntactic analysis 100

Index

t-score 91–2
TACT 27, 68, 69, 76, 77, 83, 88, 90, 167
  encoding for 30
tag:
  in SGML 34
tag set:
  in British National Corpus 98
  in Brown Corpus 94
  design of 98
  in International Corpus of English 99
  size of 98
tagging, *see* encoding; word class
    tagging
TAGGIT 94, 96
Tasso 79
taxonomy:
  of language 99
Taylor, G. 120
teaching:
  electronic text technology 171
  language, use of corpora in 88
TEI 36–9, 136, 142, 167
  DTD 37–8
  Guidelines, 36–8
  header 13, 38–9, 134
TEILite 38
television 143
templates:
  in word class tagging 98
temporal references:
  in *Robinson Crusoe* 75
tense:
  in language learning 88
terminological data:
  encoding in TEI 37
terzina 26
Tetreault, R. 133–4
text analysis:
  programs 50
Text Encoding Initiative, *see* TEI
text retrieval programs:
  and encoding 26
text searching 7
TextPad 12
Textual Analysis Computing Tools, *see*
    TACT
textual database 160
textual essay:
  in electronic edition 134
themes 72
theory:
  of electronic text 124
  and encoding 47–8

thesaurus 77, 160
  for works of art 142
Thesaurus Linguae Graecae 14, 23, 31,
  102
Thomas, J. 32
Thomson, N. D. 115
thorn:
  encoding of 31
Thorpe, Isabella 71
Tilney, Henry 71
title statement:
  in TEI header 38
TLF, *see* Trésor de la Langue Française
TLG, *see* Thesaurus Linguae Graecae
tokens 89
Tompa, F. W. 151, 158
tool development 167
topographical references:
  in *Robinson Crusoe* 75
TOSCA 99, 100
training:
  of neural networks 121
transcription:
  phonological 79, 81
  in TEI 37
transition editions 138
Trant, J. 142
tree banks 100
tree structure 129
Trésor de la Langue Française 147
Tribble, C. 87–8
trimeter, iambic 80–1
troponym 164
Tübingen 126
Tudor English 89
Turkish 21
TuStep 126, 131–2, 167
Tweedie, F. J. 121, 122
Two Noble Kinsmen, The 120
type/token ratio 89–90, 117, 119
typesetting 124
  from a database 150
  of editions 131
  tapes 23
typographic encoding 4, 25
typographic representation:
  from OCR 22

Ulysses 126
Unabomber 123
undeciphered languages 77
Unicode 32, 162
Unix 56

upper case letters:
in a concordance 55
user interface:
for electronic editions 140
Utrecht, University of 142

van Halteren, H. 100
variants:
identification of 127
in historical editions 137
nature of 125
scribal 127
variation:
in language 92–4
Venezky, R. 154
Verena (in *The Bostonians*) 71
verbs, phrasal 86–7
Véronis, J. 158
verse 58
analysis of sound patterns in 78–83
in a concordance 62
encoding in TEI 37
in OCR 22
Victorian Women Writers Project 15, 39
video 143
Villani, R. 67
Virgil 27
Virginia, University of 141
vocabulary spread 89
Voice of the Shuttle 11
Vossen, P. 157, 164
vowels:
initial in Sophocles 81
Voyage au bout de la nuit 73

Wake, W. C. 109, 119
Walker, D. E. 159
Wall Street Journal 20
Wallace, D. L. 108, 110
Waterloo, University of 151
Watt, R. J. C. 27, 62
Waves, The 70
Web, *see* World Wide Web
Web concordance 62–3
Webster's Seventh New Collegiate Dictionary 158
weighting:
of variants 130
Weiner, E. 151, 153
Wellington Corpus of Written New Zealand English 17
Wells, S. 120

Wentworth, Captain 71
Wife of Bath's Prologue 127, 138–41
wild card characters 56
Wilks, Y. 156, 157
Willett, P. 39
Williams, C. B. 105–6
Wilson, A. 21, 86
wireless 165
Wisbey, R. 49, 81–2
witnesses:
in New Testament 128
in Wife of Bath's Prologue 139
Wittgenstein Archives 46
Woman Rebel, The 137
Women Writers Project:
at Brown University 15
Victorian 15, 39
Wooldridge, T. R. 88
Woolf, V.:
The Waves 70
word, definition of 53
word accent:
in Italian 82
in Latin scansion 80
word class tagging 92, 94–100
word frequencies:
in stylometry 110
word frequency list, *see* word list
word index 51
word length 106, 109
word list 50–1
word order:
in language learning 88
word processor:
and encoding 26
and SGML/XML 167
weaknesses of 12
word separators 53, 54
WordNet 163–4
European 164
WordPerfect 167
WordSmith Tools 167
Wordsworth, W. 133–4
WORDTAG 95
workstation:
for lexicography 151, 153–4
World Wide Web 9, 62
documents on 4, 46
for electronic editions 133
in future systems 168
searching on 162
weaknesses of 9
World Wide Web Consortium 32

Index

written sources:
  in British National Corpus 18

XML 46–7, 57, 138, 167, 169

XSL 46, 167

z-score 90
Zampolli, A. 147, 159, 160, 161